Modern Technology for Transportation Management

Steve Blough
Howard Troxler
MercuryGate International Inc.

MercuryGate
TMS that delivers.

www.mercurygate.com

MercuryGate International Inc.

Modern Technology for Transportation Management

MercuryGate International Inc.
Cary, North Carolina
www.mercurygate.com

First Edition
ISBN: 978-0-9965508-0-2
Library of Congress Control Number: 2015910473

Cover design by Stephen Bentley

Table of Contents

Chapter 1: Introduction

This book is about applying robust Transportation Management System (TMS) solutions to the modern challenges of the supply chain and logistics services provider industries.

If transportation planners from a half-century ago could see what is possible today they might conclude that we live in a Golden Age of logistics. We take for granted daily aspects of our business, such as instantaneous visibility across networks, which to our forebears would have seemed like magic.

According to the U.S. Department of Commerce, spending in the freight and transportation industries exceeded $1.33 trillion in 2012, the last year for which statistics were available. That figure represented 8.5 percent of the gross domestic product of the United States.[1] The North American supply chain is an increasingly integrated and interdependent network with many key players:

- Shippers.
- Consignees.
- Carriers – truck, rail, barge, air, vessel, last-mile delivery vehicles, and many more.
- Distribution entities such as warehouses and ports.
- Freight forwarders and customs brokers.
- Transportation brokers.
- Third and fourth-party logistics operators.
- Many, many others.

Yet whether these participants in the supply chain are mega-shippers, with billions in annual freight spend and tens of thousands of truckloads a month, or whether they are small brokers or 3PLs, all

---

[1] U.S. Department of Commerce, "The Logistics and Transportation Industry in the United States," http://selectusa.commerce.gov/industry-snapshots/logistics-and-transportation-industry-united-states.html.

of them depend in some way on transportation management systems – which brings us back to the point of this book.

We'll talk about using a TMS as a tool for contract and carrier management, for rates and rating, for capacity search, for consolidation and optimization, for tendering, booking and tracking, and for freight bill audit and invoice management – among other things.

But beyond that, we'll talk about the modern TMS as a tool for management of designed workflows, a tool for automation, a tool for flexible response to real-time exceptions, and a tool for providing control-tower visibility of our entire system.

TMS Client Categories

In discussing TMS clients we'll refer to general categories again and again: broker, shipper, 3PL, freight forwarder. All of them need to get things moved, but there are differences between them:

- o A broker is a matchmaker between customers who need something moved, and carriers who can move it. Brokers operate in an on-demand environment, often on a spot basis, relying on their relationships and contracts with carriers. Agents and sales commissions can play a big role in the broker's business.

- o The term 3PL is an abbreviation for "third-party logistics" providers. Like brokers, 3PLs work on behalf of customers, but more typically they do it on an ongoing, contract basis.

- o A shipper uses the TMS to arrange the movement of goods on its own behalf.

Shippers can be retail chains, manufacturers or large bulk suppliers. While brokers and 3PLs are acting as middlemen, the shipper's concern is getting its own supplies and materials where they need to be. Shippers might also be managing <u>inbound</u> freight from their suppliers.

o A <u>freight forwarder</u> operates on behalf of customers like a broker or 3PL, but takes on the extra responsibilities and dimensions of being the shipment's legal owner and representative - typically the case with international moves, involving all the intricacies of import/export requirements.

As a practical matter, these precisely worded distinctions tend to blend into each other in the real world. Some carriers also operate their own transportation brokerages. A 3PL might also act as a broker. A shipper who is operating internationally deals with the same issues as a freight forwarder.

About this Book

The book uses as its example the TMS and related software tools of MercuryGate International Inc., a technology company headquartered in Cary, North Carolina. You'll find more about MercuryGate and its history at the back of the book.

The chapter after this one, "The Story So Far," gives us some background on the history of our industry and the evolution of TMS systems. After that we'll get an overview of the logistics cycle and our first look at some software.

But the main theme of this book is how to think about and address modern logistics challenges with TMS solutions. The ensuing chapters are problem-oriented and delve more deeply into subjects such as:

- Knowledge of market rates
- Finding carrier capacity
- Multi-pick, multi-leg and complex loads
- Managing by workflow
- Visibility of loads in transit
- Managing & disputing invoices
- Rewarding your best carriers
- Optimization
- Managing inbound freight
- Private fleet vs. common carrier
- Mobile solutions
- Analyzing future costs

Some chapters end with suggested discussion topics. At the end of the book there is a glossary and two appendixes, one dealing with basic usage of the TMS, and the other with information about configuring and supporting the functions described in the earlier chapters.

Chapter 2: The Story So Far

In the beginning, our business was entirely manual like everybody else's.

So how did our predecessors decide what to put on which truck? They did it by experience, by the seat of the pants, by conventional wisdom, and – often – by arbitrary rules and fixed constraints.

For example, the selection of <u>mode</u> or shipping method often was based on a chart tacked up on a bulletin board that looked something like this:

< 150 lbs.	FedEx
150-5,000 lbs.	Less than truckload (LTL) ODFL, SEFL, ABFS
5,000 lbs. to 45,000 lbs.	Truckload (TL) SCNN, SWFT
> 45,000 lbs.	Intermodal NS, UP, CSX, SCNI

Certainly, such a chart made decisions simple. But as for whether the decreed mode was always the best solution, there was no time to worry about it. Changes not only required distributing new wall art, but also meant that somebody had to hang the new instructions. It was all too common to visit a shipping dock and see a routing guide several years old showing carriers that were no longer in business. Carrier selection was often a static decision tree based on arbitrary data that, even if meaningful, often left out key decision points.

The manual era of logistics was based on paper records, carbon copies, and typewritten labels and bills of lading. There was little visibility of transportation decisions across the system, and no way to know what decisions had been made along the way – until somebody at the end of the line got the bill.

Even after the dawn of the modern information age it took a long time for TMS systems to develop their potential. In many ways, they are still developing today.

'First Generation' TMS

Some clumsy automation - not much decision support.

Anybody old enough to remember early computers from, say, the 1960s or 1970s will tell you they were not necessarily easier to use – in fact, it's fair to say they often were harder to use.

Users spent a lot of time trying to satisfy the requirements of the system, instead of the system serving the needs of users. Imagine having to procure a physical floppy disk from every LTL carrier to obtain rates and flipping from one carrier's disk to another to compare costs.

So much of the logistics process was still based on static routing guides and mechanical considerations. Early systems lacked systematic tools for determining mode. Overall, we just weren't there yet in terms of using computing power to arrive at improved solutions. Rather, we primarily used computers to maintain (or even duplicate) records of transactions.

'Second Generation' TMS

Still working in isolation - but with the beginning of better mode determination and optimization.

Look at a movie from, say, the early 1980s, and the computers on desktops were bulky, huge and showed only glowing green characters on black screens. They were often local, dedicated systems, too -- there was no cloud, no Internet, and limited access to the outside world.

So we're still not going to find, in these "second generation" TMS systems, much coordination with the rest of the world. Still not much possibility for management of <u>inbound</u> freight, nor complex handling of shipments across networks or multiple locations. It also means our planning was still not tightly tied to actual execution and scheduling – we knew in general that we wanted to send it to location X, but we didn't have fine-tuned control over when it was going to get there, and certainly not much visibility along the way.

Nonetheless, these second-generation TMS installations were beginning to show improvement and promise. We could handle all modes in one place – parcel, LTL, truckload, air, rail, intermodal, and ocean. We had early optimization tools that at least helped us build better loads and get better rates out of <u>our own</u> location. We had better support for decisions about mode and route selection.

'Third Generation' TMS

Network delivery, cross-location planning, and better communication – but still not a total tool for strategy & decision-making.

.

The ability to use a TMS to manage transportation across locations is the hallmark of the next generation of systems in the 1990s, thanks to the advent of true network communication. At least a TMS user could route shipments that dynamically spanned the locations across which it needed to travel.

Better communication also meant more coordination across locations, and more opportunity to respond to real-time events. This also facilitated better cross-company, cross-functional transportation management.

And yet (we can say with the benefit of modern hindsight), there was yet another level that a modern TMS needed to achieve – the ability to drive a robust, process-driven workflow that also would respond flexibly to conditions as needed.

'Fourth Generation' TMS

A powerful tool for decision-making and development of strategy.

Today's TMS systems are tools for developing solutions and driving designed workflows, with total mastery of routing and rating. We have control of routes across all locations, tightly tied to actual execution. We can respond dynamically to changing capacity conditions. We're fully integrated with the rest of the world.

We've come a long way from just record-keeping.

Not only does a good TMS walk us through a "sunny day" workflow, when everything goes as planned, but it should anticipate the handling of "exceptions" when things go unexpectedly – the canceled stop or load, the reconsignment, the truck ordered but not used. We also should be able to develop and implement role-specific workflows to facilitate specialization and efficiency.

The modern TMS knows what should happen, has the ability to act on that knowledge, and has the power to notify users when things should have happened.

In sum, the TMS has become a full partner in getting our job done.

Closing the Skills Gaps

Another way of putting it is that a modern TMS has to be more than simply a dumb data-entry tool. It should be our partner in developing logistics approaches, and in helping human beings to bridge the skills gaps they need to perform their jobs.

- "How do I find someone to pick this up?" We'll talk about skills for procuring committed capacity from carriers through bids, bid boards, accessing truck boards and broadcasting loads, and the role of the transportation broker.

- "What's the best way to cover this load?" We'll talk about skills to combine rates (including accessorial charges), historical service levels/scorecards, and customers' stated service needs.

- "I don't have time to contact carriers on all these loads." Who does? We'll talk about skills around using route guides and sequential tendering, EDI accepts/rejects to become more efficient.

- "I need to know how to negotiate rates." We'll talk about skills to understand what rates are based upon (product characteristics, market demand), and how to model the carrier and customer sides in the TMS.

- "I don't know how to make sure I'm paying the carriers correctly." We'll talk about skills for performing freight audit and handling exceptions/dispute resolution.

Before we dig into these solutions, in the next chapter let's take our first look at some logistics concepts and how TMS solutions address them.

Chapter 3:   Managing the Logistics Life Cycle with a TMS

The job of a logistics broker, 3PL or freight forwarder is to arrange the movement of goods on behalf of a customer. The task of a shipper is to arrange the movement of its own goods, whether inbound supplies or outbound products.

The usual life cycle of a load moves from creation to booking to transit to delivery and invoicing. Here are some key steps in this process.

CREATE SHIPMENT: The first thing we must do is create the record of the thing to be moved. We might be getting orders electronically from an external order management system, or a warehouse management system (WMS). We might be getting records by email. Users might be creating records manually by entering the information directly into the system.

BUILD LOAD: We may have to go through some process of building loads for which we will hire a carrier to move. Often we'll be looking to consolidate our shipments into fewer carrier loads to realize savings. Consolidations may be manual or automated through optimization.

DETERMINE CARRIER: Mode and carrier selection is one of the most challenging areas of the transportation process. Determining which carrier to use for each move requires a knowledge of the following:

1. Identifying the origin and destination locations.
2. Understanding the information about the goods being moved such as weight, dimensions, cube, compatibility, etc.
3. Determining the rate for the different candidate carriers whether contracted carriers or spot rate carrier.

4. Detailing the performance metrics of each carrier.

TENDER LOAD: A tender is the formal offer of a load to a carrier at the proposed rate, either by email, electronic message, or a manual process. Carriers can (and do) decline tenders – in fact, knowing your carrier's accept/reject ratio is a key part of carrier management strategy, as we'll see in the carriers chapter.

TRACK LOAD: Once a carrier has agreed to move a load, we might need to create appointment information based on location constraints, obtain dispatch data such as contact information for the driver, and track the load's progress by an automatic process (EDI, GPS, driver cell phone) or by user manual entry.

DELIVER LOAD: Once we get a "delivered" tracking message, the process usually involves requiring a Proof of Delivery (POD), which can be an image of a signed document, a link to a document, an electronic signature, or some other content. (Note that a proof of pickup message may be required as well.)

SETTLE INVOICE: The invoicing process involves receiving or creating records of the carrier invoice (that is, the money we owe the carrier we hired), as well as the customer invoice (our bill to the client who hired us to move something). Shippers often are their own "customer" and deal with only the carrier invoice side, although some shippers will utilize a "Prepay and Add" approach to charge their customers for the cost of transportation.

HANDLE EXCEPTIONS: The term "exception" refers to departures from a typical, "sunny day" workflow. These include (to name a few) loads canceled, loads not ready, unexpected in-transit expenses, schedule changes, breakdowns, weather delays and invoicing mistakes. A robust system should deal with all circumstances. Exceptions have evolved into not just "triggered" exceptions but also exceptions through omission, for example, messages missing that should have been received by now.

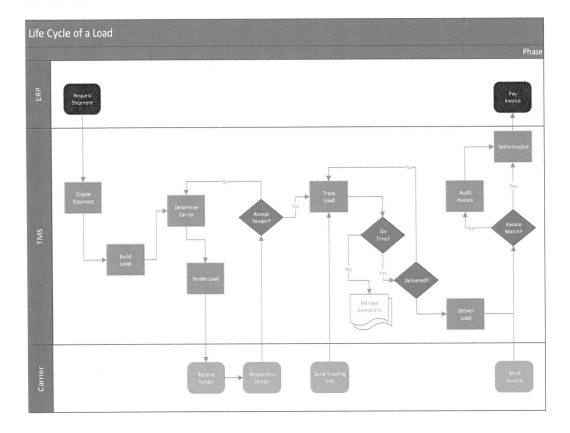

Fig. 3- 1: Typical steps in a load's life cycle.

TMS Basics

The MercuryGate TMS that is used as an example throughout this book is a web-based, cloud solution known as a "Software as a Service" (SAAS) product. Users use a browser (Firefox, Internet Explorer, etc.) and an assigned URL to launch the application.

The TMS is a tool not only for easily managing all of the basic life cycle steps described above, but also doing it with a designed, automated and dynamic workflow that responds to user actions, to changing conditions and to exceptions.

Users operate from a home-screen "dashboard" (Fig. 3-2) that presents them with a view and workflow designed for their role. Records of freight movements and invoices are presented in onscreen portlets that are more than passive lists – the system recognizes which loads and invoices are due for which user actions, and portlet displays are filtered and chosen accordingly.

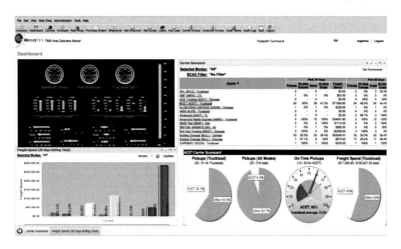

Fig. 3- 2: TMS user 'dashboard'. The display is configurable by user and role. A user representing a carrier or supplier would see an entirely different screen.

The precise arrangement of menus, toolbar options and portlets that each user sees depends on role permissions and user settings. Each TMS client has the ability to assign user logins to outside users representing carriers or vendors. These users interact with their own records in the system, for example by updating the statuses of their own loads or creating their own quote requests.

For more of an introduction and walkthrough of the TMS interface, see the appendix.

TMS Hallmarks – Hierarchy, Workflow, Reusability

Some major aspects of this TMS architecture include:

(1) A <u>hierarchy</u> of company records that starts at the top with an owning "parent" enterprise representing the TMS client. In turn, the parent enterprise owns the records of "sub-companies" that represent its customers, operating divisions, subsidiaries or any other internal organization that meets business needs.

The hierarchy is a powerful concept that works on the basis of "inheritance." The configurations and settings of the TMS flow downward from the parent enterprise and can be used to set organization-wide policies, which then can be fine-tuned or overridden at individual sub-company levels as needed.

(2) Dynamic <u>workflows</u> that guide TMS users through the logistics life cycle stages as described above. The TMS knows where each record is in the life cycle and displays information to users accordingly. What's more, multiple workflows can exist according to role and function – an operations workflow and a financial workflow, for example. Workflows for a TMS client can be designed to be as specialized or generalized as needed.

The most familiar hallmark of the MercuryGate TMS workflow is a user interface named "ezClick," which features "blue button" actions displayed to users as to-do tasks (Figs. 3-3, 3-4). Users literally see the next "button to click," and when they click it they are directed to screens for performing the necessary action. Behind the scenes, dynamic rules are responding to user actions and managing the creation of the next necessary blue button in the workflow, whether a sunny day or exception step.

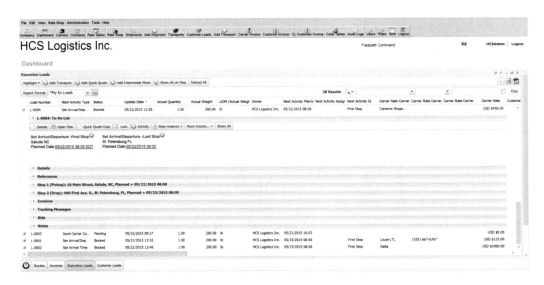

Fig. 3-3: Expanded view of a load in a TMS load list ('load board'). The expanded view shows this load's pending 'blue button actions,' each representing a step in the designed workflow.

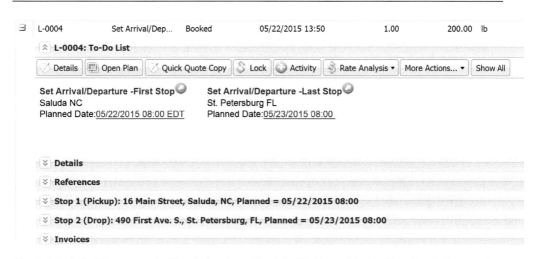

Fig. 3-4: Detail of the expanded load view from Fig. 3-3. Clicking a blue button directs the user to a screen to fulfill the next workflow step. The top row of buttons give users access to other detailed information and actions that can be performed on this load.

(3) <u>Re-usability</u> and sharing of data for companies, clients, carriers, cargo and shipping lanes that make the TMS a powerful tool for quick record creation and faster progression to execution with literally just a few mouse clicks. The TMS relies on pre-defined records for each client that relate to the kinds of information used most frequently.

Some of those key data objects, which we'll see demonstrated throughout this text, include:

- <u>Enterprises</u> and the TMS <u>hierarchy</u> discussed above.
- The record of and settings for each TMS <u>user</u>.
- Defined <u>roles</u> with names such as "Finance" or "Operations" that are assigned to those users. Each role is a defined set of permissions to perform TMS functions.
- Stored lists of "master" <u>locations</u>, <u>items</u>, <u>ship units</u> and <u>lanes</u> that are easily retrieved for record creation. Additions to these lists can be created "on the fly" as needed. Default values can be specified for quick creation of new records.
- The records of <u>carriers</u> and <u>contracts</u> available to the enterprise. Multiple contracts can exist for the same carrier by mode and service, and large TMS clients

maintain records for tens of thousands of carriers. Still the TMS is able to retrieve system rates quickly either for a given load, or in an informational rate-shop.

TMS Records of Freight Movements

We'll use these terms throughout the text:

ROUTE: A "route" in the TMS is the master record of all carrier and customer loads that are related to the same movement. To be clear, that means a TMS "route" is not a line on a map – it is a master record that owns all of the loads that are related to getting something moved.

Each route object in the TMS has a unique ID, and lists of routes are viewed in a TMS portlet known as a route board or route portlet. Users can "drill down" or "expand" the visual record of a route in a portlet to view and work with its individual loads.

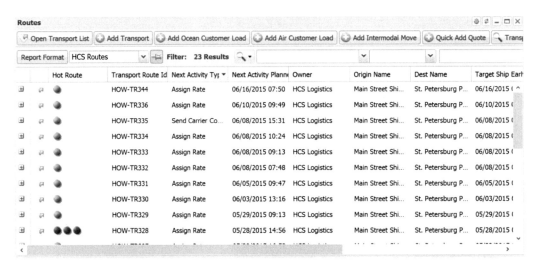

Fig. 3-5: Route records listed in a TMS route portlet. Each entry can be expanded by its left-hand plus sign to display detailed information about that route's related loads.

EXECUTION LOAD: An execution load in the TMS is the record of an individual load for which we have hired a carrier to move. An execution load is related to one or more customer loads, which are the corresponding records of what our customers have hired us to move.

In other words, we might put multiple customer loads on the same truck in the same execution load. Or a single customer load might move across multiple execution loads – for example, truck-rail-truck for a multi-leg intermodal movement.

Execution loads contain planned events, equipment requirements and all other information related to actual carrier execution. Execution loads are the owners of carrier rates and invoices. Execution loads either can be viewed from within their owning route, or individually in a TMS portlet called a load board or load list portlet.

CUSTOMER LOAD: A customer load is a load record that shows the "customer-eye" record of what the customer has hired the TMS client to move. Customers of TMS clients might even have their own logins to the TMS so they can view or update the status of "their" loads in the system.

Customer loads also can display information about execution and plan events, but typically they exist only for the customer's information. Customer loads also are the vehicle for customer rates and invoices.

Customer loads and execution loads are known as related loads when they relate to the same movement. Related loads are owned by the same route object as discussed above, and can be managed from the level of the owning route.

SHIPMENTS: A "shipment" in the TMS is an earlier version of a customer load. In fact, a customer load might be considered as the outer wrapping of a basic shipment record, which at a minimum includes information about:

- The shipment's owner
- Origin, destination and bill-to locations
- Requested pickup and delivery time windows

- Items/ship units
- Special instructions, required equipment or services
- A variety of <u>references</u> or tags of data related to the shipment

Other Essential TMS Tools

We need to know about some basic tools that we'll use constantly. They are the "report format," the "mass update", and "quick find." There is more about each tool in the appendix topics.

(1) REPORT FORMAT: Every list and portlet that a user sees in the TMS is being controlled by a "report format" of what kind of records to display.

For example, we might be looking at a list of all loads that have an "Assign Carrier Rate" blue button. Or we might be looking at all loads that have a status of "In Transit."

The TMS gives us total power over the information on the screen. This function is known as "reporting" because it determines the "report" of records that we're currently viewing. Reporting is discussed in detail in the appendix.

Be aware that any portlet or list in the TMS includes a report format option (Fig. 3-6) to choose another existing report format – or to choose the columns and filter conditions needed to create a new one of your own.

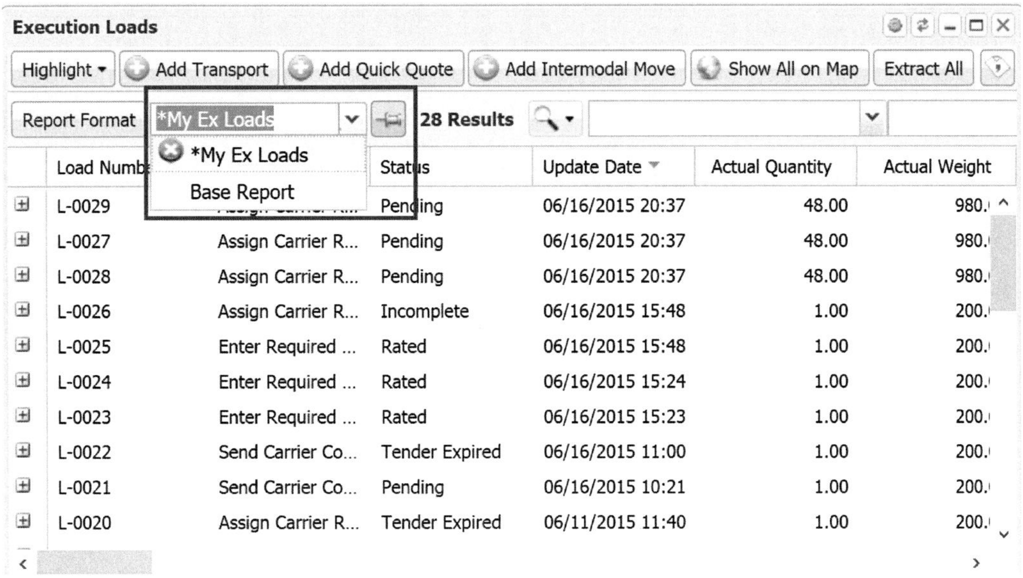

Fig. 3-6: Choosing a 'report format' for what to display in a portlet.

(2) MASS UPDATE: Another important and frequently used feature of the TMS is called the mass update command – the ability to select multiple records in a list and perform the same action on all of them (Fig. 3-7).

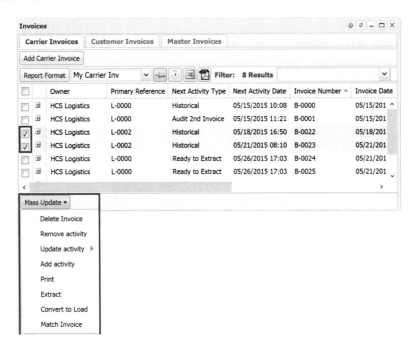

**Fig. 3-7: Choosing a command from the 'Mass Update' menu
will perform the action on all the items selected by their checkbox.**

(3) QUICK FIND: One more useful tool is the "Quick Find" feature on many list screens and portlets (Fig. 3-8). You can apply an instant filter to your list to find, for example, all records that belong to a particular owner, all loads bound for Birmingham, all shipments created in the past week – any criteria you need.

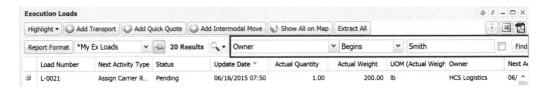

Fig. 3-8: The 'Quick Find' feature near the top right of many portlets allows a quick screening of the portlet contents based on a single field, such as a customer name. Filter options include requiring an exact match, "starts with," "greater than," and several other operators.

The filter "operator" is chosen from a dropdown menu. It is a value such as equals, more than, begins with, etc. A full list of filter operators and their usage is in the appendix.

The TMS and the Logistics Life Cycle

We began this chapter by talking about the life cycle of a logistics movement. Now let's look at how that life cycle is managed in a TMS designed workflow.

(1) CREATE SHIPMENT: Creation occurs by receipt of electronic message, warehouse or ERP integration, or manual user action. Users have the option to create these kinds of records:

- Simple point-to-point movements ("Add Shipment," "Add Transport").
- Multi-leg and intermodal movements ("Add Intermodal Move").
- Complex international multi-leg movements with air, ocean or rail legs.

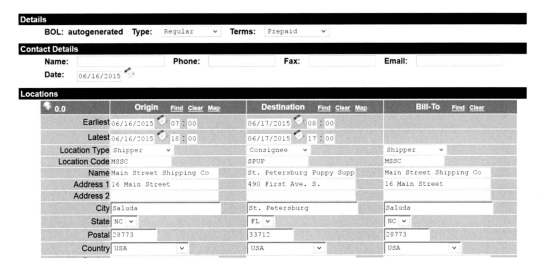

Fig. 3-9: Top of add-shipment screen with selection of origin, destination and bill-to selection and target date ranges. The rest of the screen deals with items and ship units and options such as equipment and services.

(2) BUILD LOAD: Creation of customer loads can be configured to create an associated execution load automatically, and vice-versa. Or TMS users might be tasked with associating the enterprise's pending customer loads with execution loads and routes.

Therefore loads can be created:

- Automatically, by system settings when a related load is created.
- Manually, by users working in a "Load Builder" window to consolidate customer movements onto execution loads for increased efficiency and savings.
- By automated optimization tools. See the chapter on optimization.

(3) DETERMINE CARRIER: Obtaining a carrier rate and assigning customer rates are major steps in the TMS load life cycle. Users can obtain a contract rating against existing contracts in the TMS, or can create rates manually based on known information.

Otherwise on the carrier side, users employ the TMS to go to the outside world to search for capacity by a variety of methods. They can ask carriers to submit quotes directly, or search integrated external load posting services for available equipment. For more on these methods, see the chapter titled "Finding Capacity."

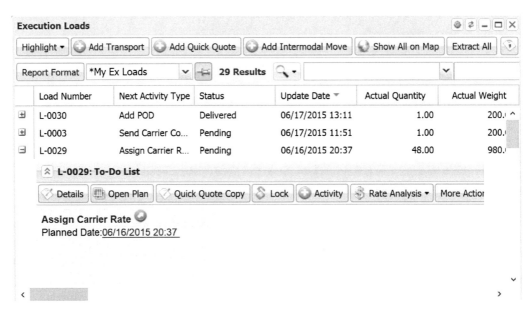

Fig. 3-10: The "Assign Carrier Rate" blue button launches a rating process and often is the first blue button that operations users see in the execution load workflow.

(4) TENDER LOAD: Once a carrier rate is selected the load is tendered (offered) to the selected carrier via email or electronic message (the carrier's method has been set up in the system). This blue button is labeled "Tender" or "Send Carrier Confirmation."

The carrier can accept the tender or decline it, in which case the user must re-rate the load and try again. A carrier can be configured to auto-accept tenders. If a tender is accepted, the carrier might require additional information such as an appointment window. Once a carrier accepts, the user might enter dispatch information obtained from the carrier regarding driver name, phone number, point of origin, and other tracking information.

(5) TRACK LOAD: A booked load might be scheduled for appointment windows either by user blue-button action ("Set Appointment Time" blue button), or by receipt of electronic message. Actual arrivals, pickups and deliveries are recorded as status messages in the system, either by user blue-button entry ("Set Arrival/Departure" blue button, Fig. 3-11) or electronic message. Carriers also can receive or create call checks to indicate progress. See the chapters on loads in transit and TMS mobile applications.

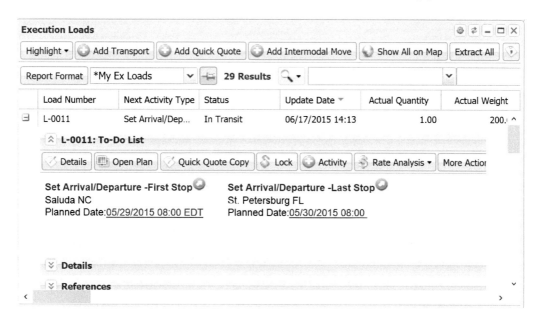

Fig. 3-11: Event-related blue buttons to enter arrival and departure information for the load, if not automatically added via carrier electronic message.

Event statuses can be viewed in a "load plan" window that is opened from the load board (Figs. 3-12, 3-13), as well as in the event-related details of an expanded load display (Fig. 3-14).

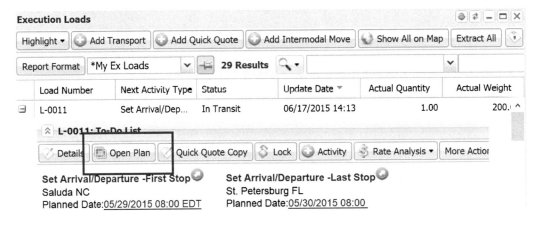

Fig. 3-12: An expanded load display in a load board features an "Open Plan" button that opens a window with event-related details.

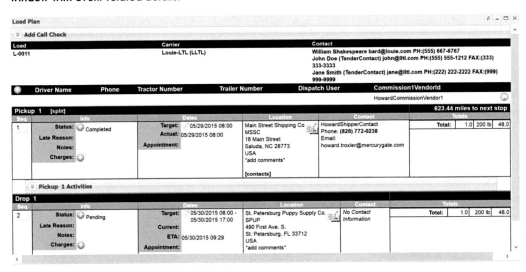

Fig. 3-13: The plan window for this load shows that the pickup event has been completed and the drop is pending, with target date range and current ETA.

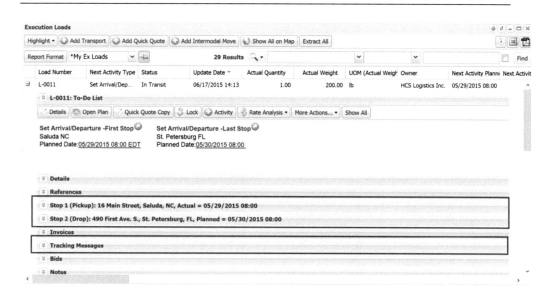

Fig. 3-14: Event appointment and status information also is available in expandable sections of a load displayed on a load board, as well as the load's tracking messages received to date.

(6) DELIVER LOAD: Upon delivery, the driver might enter via cellphone, or the user might enter in the TMS, information related to proof of delivery (POD) such as the image of a signed document, driver signature, or a link to the information.

(7) SETTLE INVOICE: The system can be set up to auto-create a carrier invoice upon delivery, to receive carrier invoices via electronic message, or for invoices to be entered by users. Invoices are tested according to predetermined conditions and flagged for review as needed. See the invoicing chapter for details. Customer invoices, if applicable, can be generated automatically upon the approval of the carrier invoice, or created by users.

(8) HANDLE EXCEPTIONS: The system automatically flags "hot" loads in danger of being late, after recognizing unexpected delays in route. The system automates the creation of detention charges when carriers are unduly delayed at a stop. Users can add, delete and modify plan events as needed. The system supports full automation of a Truck Ordered Not Used (TONU) process when users indicate a load must be canceled or rescheduled. See the "Workflow" chapter for managing these processes.

Behind the Scenes

The highly configurable TMS allows extensive fine-tuning of the logistics life cycle. Behind the scenes, the system depends on these concepts that we will mention frequently:

- System-wide settings called <u>configurations.</u> "Sysconfigs" are displayed on a series of screens available only to administrators, grouped by general functional area such as invoicing, rating, operations, etc.

- Lists of settings and options stored in a text file called the <u>code table</u>. Using text-editable code tables allows admins to make many changes in the interface without requiring a programming task. Examples would be the list of options that appear in a dropdown user menu.

- <u>Dynamic rulesets</u> carry out designated actions upon the occurrence of designated "trigger" events in the system, such as user completion of a blue button. The word "dynamic" means that the system is responding to events as they occur. Dynamic rulesets govern the flow of blue-button actions for the enterprise.

- Portlets and many blue-button displays have groups of display settings known as <u>configuration groups</u>. (This term has a different meaning from the "system" configurations discussed earlier.) Each kind of ezClick display – a route portlet, invoice portlet, or load board - is governed by its own type of config group.

These are the major tools and concepts by which our demonstration TMS tackles the problems associated with the logistics process described at the beginning of this chapter. In the following chapters we'll turn to tackling these problems in detail.

Chapter 4: Getting Market Rates

Market knowledge is everything.

Market knowledge is why you know not to pay $20 for a head of lettuce at the grocery store.

It's why you generally expect to pay something like 99 cents, or maybe $1.29, for a downloaded song.

We take market knowledge for granted in our daily lives. But we had to get that knowledge from somewhere in the first place.

We can apply the same principles to our business. Let's say you're getting ready to book your first load on an unfamiliar lane. You're using a TMS to go out into the market to find options. How do you know how much you should be paying?

If you ship from Albuquerque to Denver every day, and lately it has generally cost you $175 to $225, then you'll know that a proposed rate of $300 is high and $150 is a deal.

But what if you don't ship from Albuquerque every day – how do you get some idea of what it should cost – what it has cost lately, and which way rates are heading?

We need guidance on actual market rates and trends. There's no better yardstick than the prices others are actually paying. With this kind of market knowledge, we'll be in a better position to select the right rate, and on occasion, to be able to negotiate a better one.

Types of 'Benchmarks'

We're talking about the need for "benchmark" rates. The term 'benchmark' means a point of reference against which you can make a comparison. (It's an old term that literally comes from using the length of a workbench to measure something.)

We can speak in general of two kinds of benchmark lane data:

- Data available from external subscription sources, based on lane data fed in by clients subscribing to those services, or
- Benchmark lane analysis computed from internal historical data where appropriate.

TMS 'Rate Analysis' Window

From any load on a load board in the TMS, we can set up access to a "Rate Analysis" button that will open a window giving us detailed market information about this load's lane (Fig. 4-1).

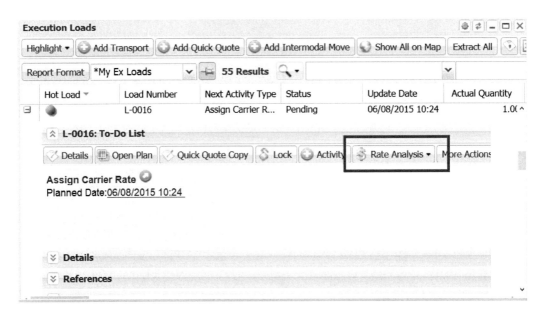

Fig. 4-1: The "Rate Analysis" button in an expanded load on a load board gives us access to subscription-based data about rates and trends on the lane.

These rates come from one of the external services with which the TMS client has an additional subscription. We can search these services for lane information that matches the current load, or modify the search. We can compare recent contract rates with the more volatile spot rate market. We can search by specific geographies and equipment type. Typically, the databases of these services are built by shared data from their members – they give data to get data.

RateFriend

RateFriend is one such service that compiles index averages based on aggregate data for more than 40 million loads per year. Users can analyze rates one at a time or benchmark dozens of lanes simultaneously.

Some features of RateFriend:

- Gives users visibility to current market rates (average rate, min/max rate) and eight-week rate trend
- Displays rate data by lane, mode (TL, LTL, Parcel, Air, Ocean, Rail, Intermodal), and equipment type
- Users can view market data for contract rates, spot rates, or both
- Logistics service providers can view market data for carriers, shippers, or both
- Market data for individual lanes can be viewed in real time
- Batch feature allows users to access rate data for multiple lanes at once
- Information from third-party rate indexing services can also be viewed within TMS

Another advantage is that shipper and carrier rate data are stored separately, allowing logistics providers to give customers market-appropriate rate quotes while maintaining acceptable margins.

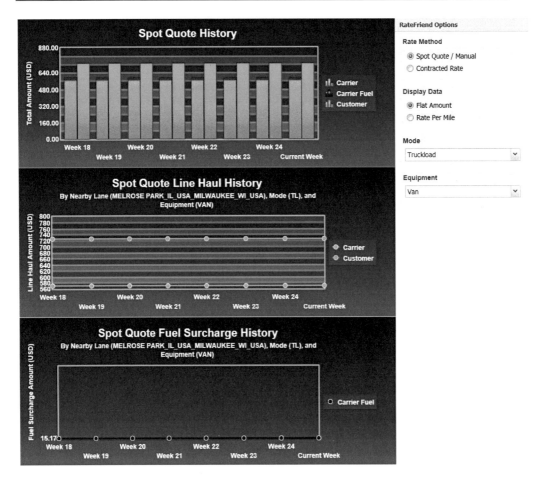

Fig. 4-2: RateFriend results screen.

Benchmarks in the 'Manage Quotes' Screen

Instead of a detailed lane-analysis window, maybe all we need is a quick benchmark, just a number representing the recent "going rate" on a lane to guide us while we're looking for rates and carrier capacity.

We'll see in the "Finding Capacity" chapter that the TMS Manage Quotes window is the user's home base for searching for carriers from multiple sources – contracts, lanes, public bid boards, posted equipment and posted capacity. We open it from the "More Actions" menu of a load expanded on a load board:

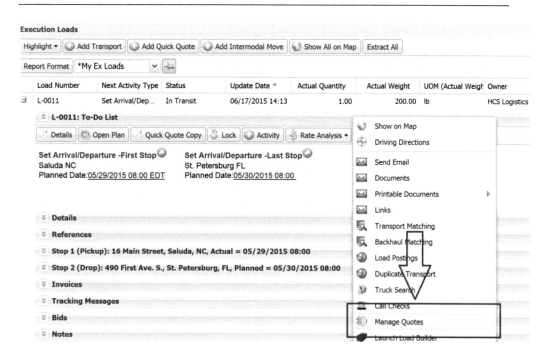

Fig. 4-3: Opening the 'Manage Quotes' window from a load on a load board.

We can set up the Manage Quotes window to display one or more benchmark rates across the top, visible as we look for carriers:

Fig. 4-4: Top of 'Manage Quotes' window showing various market averages.

These sources not only include external data services but averages from our own history for this lane. So indeed, the TMS learns from actual experience.

Take a closer look at the "Internal Rate Index" value (Fig. 4-5):

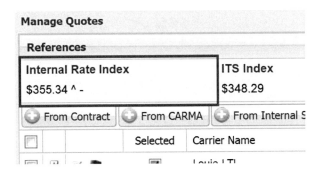

Fig. 4-5: Detail of 'Manage Quotes' screen showing Internal Rate Index calculated from TMS experience on this lane.

Notice the trailing indicators '-' and '+'. The first is a <u>trend</u> indicator for whether the latest rate has gone up or down by more than a certain amount. The second is a "coverage" indicator showing how confident we are that this rate is representative.

The possible values and meanings of the rate and coverage indicators are:

∧	Latest rate is higher than previous rate
∨	Latest rate is lower than previous rate
-	Latest rate is flat compared to previous rate
+	'Good' coverage
0	'OK' coverage
-	'Poor' coverage

Conclusion

There are two approaches to rate analysis in the TMS to guide us in our own search for rates.

Through the "Rate Analysis" window, we have detailed lane data that we can "drill down into" to see the factors at work. One example is seeing how much fuel is driving the actual rate.

Or in the Manage Quotes window, we can have one or more "value services" set up to post just a quick average in front of our eyes as we search for a carrier.

External services require additional subscription and setup. The TMS' own "historical" calculation, on the other hand, can be set up by anyone with administrative authority for the enterprise.

For information on configuration of market rate information in the TMS, see the configuration appendix of the textbook.

Chapter 5: Finding Capacity

Sometimes you will have trouble finding a truck no matter what your contracts say. Or you won't have a contract that covers your lane at the most inconvenient time.

This is the problem of finding carrier capacity, and it is one of the biggest challenges in modern logistics.

There's not an infinite number of trucks. There certainly isn't an infinite number of truck drivers, as carriers struggle to recruit and retain them. You cannot assume that capacity will always be available, or available at the rates you want to pay.

As logistics professionals we must realize that capacity is constrained not only by standing factors, but also by seasonal factors, as well as by unpredictable fluctuations that can occur at any time such as weather events.

To name just a few factors:

Seasonality. If this is apple season in Washington, the produce harvest in California or time for tomatoes or strawberries in Florida, then you'll know it when you try to find certain equipment there. "Seasonality charts" track the demand for capacity as products come to harvest or market around the country – and sometimes that demand is frustratingly and surprisingly all-consuming.

Weather. Commercial air passengers aren't the only ones who suffer when a big part of the country is shut down for weather. And, just as your flight from Florida might have been delayed by ice in Chicago, the chain reaction on freight transportation is felt throughout the system.

Regulation. Carriers operate in a regulated industry and are subject to the Federal Motor Carrier Safety Administration. As a result carrier capacity is highly sensitive to current and pending regulations pertaining to hours of service, emissions laws, and requirements for new or retrofitted equipment.

Driver shortage. This is one of the biggest issues facing today's carriers. Turnover is high, training is expensive, and modern drivers simply are less likely to tolerate the long hauls and grueling duty of their predecessors. "Home for the weekend" is a modern recruiting theme. At any given time, the single greatest constraint on a carrier's capacity is usually the number of available drivers.

Capacity Constraints Resulting From:

Seasonal/Human	Trucking Regulations	New Driver Recruiting
• Seasonality • Inclement Weather • Port and Border Closures • Poor Lead Time • Inbound Delays • Higher Accessorials • Equipment Positioning Problems	• Cost of current and pending FMCSA regulations • Hours of Service • Emissions Laws and New/Retrofitting Equipment	• Drug Free • CSA Compliant • Without Sleep Apnea • Willingness to drive fewer miles

No one is immune from these effects. It's important to note that your carrier <u>contract</u> is not a guarantee of carrier <u>capacity.</u> More than one broker has congratulated himself or herself on a dirt-cheap rate, only to be left in the same boat as everybody else.

What matters is getting a truck.

Capacity and TMS

Even in a capacity crunch there are opportunities if we have the tools to find them. A truck happens to be empty in city X on day

Y. A carrier is looking to fill a truck. A carrier sees your posted load and says, yes, I'll take it. A carrier agrees to give you a quote after all – but only if you ask.

Some of the tools we'll discuss in this chapter include:

Private Bid Boards. We'll use the TMS to create an ad-hoc, "private" bid board among carriers that we invite, offering them a specific load at an ask price.

Public Bid Boards. The TMS integrates with external, "public" boards where we post our loads to the world in general. One of these options, FreightFriend, is a sort of "social network" for carriers and brokers who "friend" each other.

Manage Quotes/Quote Mechanism. The TMS allows us to send quote requests directly to our carriers in an efficient, pre-configured process.

Posted Equipment. This is the reverse of the "bid board" approach – it's the carriers who post available equipment and locations, hoping to pick up a load, and we are using the TMS to search these postings for possible matches.

Carrier Management. This is part of our capacity strategy as well. The TMS allows us to evaluate our carriers through a scorecarding process to see where we're getting the highest success rate, and to focus on and reward those carriers. We also can use our carrier management system to leverage our knowledge of preferred and available carrier lanes.

Communication. We can use the TMS' tools to communicate market trends within our own organization.

Private Bid Board

The first tool we'll examine is the creation of a private, by-invitation bidding process inside the TMS itself.

We invite selected carriers from our company's list of carriers to bid on a specific load. Users from those carriers have their own logins to the TMS, where they can see their bids and respond to them.

Why use a private bid board? This might be done to limit exposure to a trusted set of carriers, to seek more competitive rates, or for other reasons such as the fact a lane is not included in a contract.

Users create a bid invitation for the load and set its parameters:

- Highest bid amount allowed.
- Expiration date.
- A "delta" (change) amount by which a bid must be lower than the previous bid.
- An optional "Book It Now" amount at which a carrier can accept the load immediately.

We will view our existing bids on a load either (1) from the detail screen of the load, in a section labeled "Bids", or in the "Bids" section of an ezClick load display.

(1) From a load expanded on a load board, click the button labeled "Details" (Fig 5-1). A window opens filled with details about the load (Fig. 5-2). Look for the section labeled "Bids."

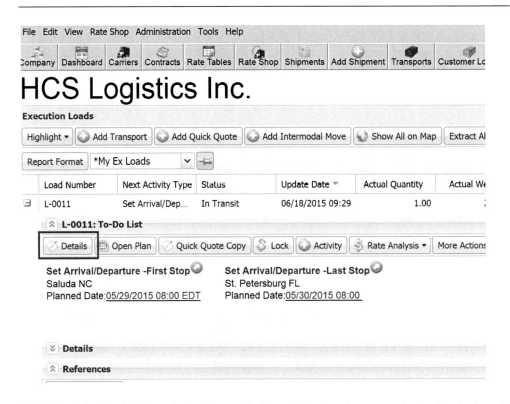

Fig. 5-1: The "Details" button of a load expanded on a load board opens a window for viewing all details about the load in one scrollable, multi-tabbed screen.

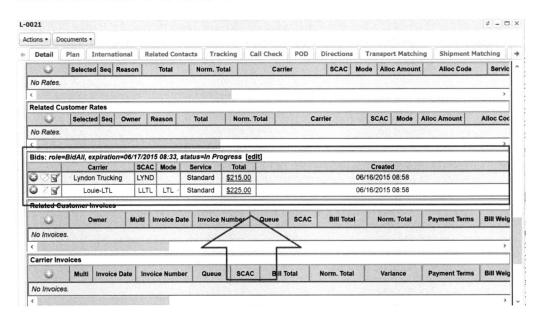

Fig. 5-2: The 'Bids' section of the scrollable details screen shows received bids for this load. Click the green checkbox to make the bid the selected carrier rate on the load. Click the 'edit' link to create a new bid or edit an existing one.

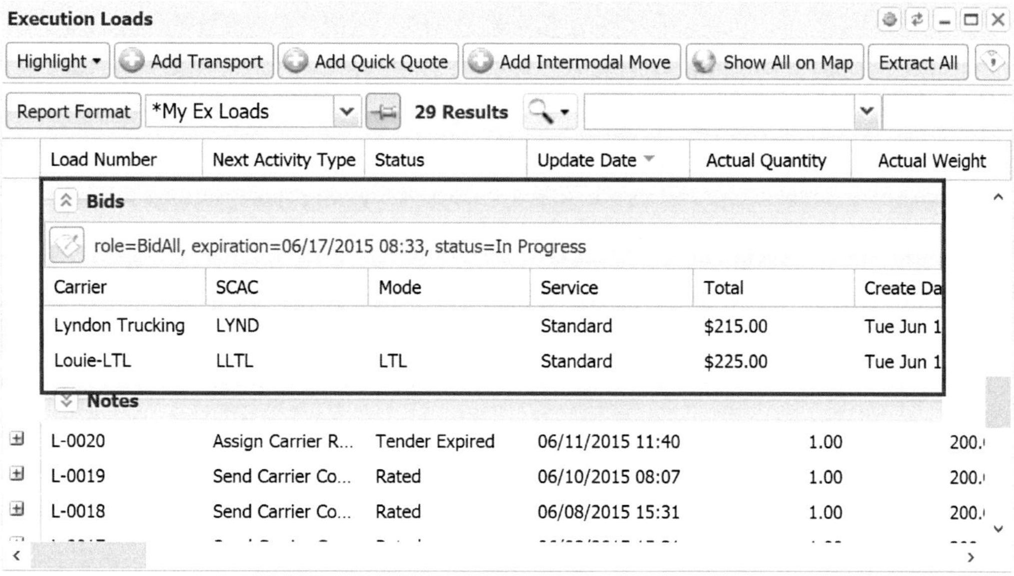

Fig. 5-3: 'Bids' also is one of the expandable horizontal sections in the record of a load shown on a load board.

In Fig. 5-2 users click the "Edit" link in the 'Bids' section to create a new bid. In the 'Bids' display show in Fig. 5-3, users click the edit icon (the piece of paper) to create a new bid. By either method a creation screen opens (Fig. 5-4):

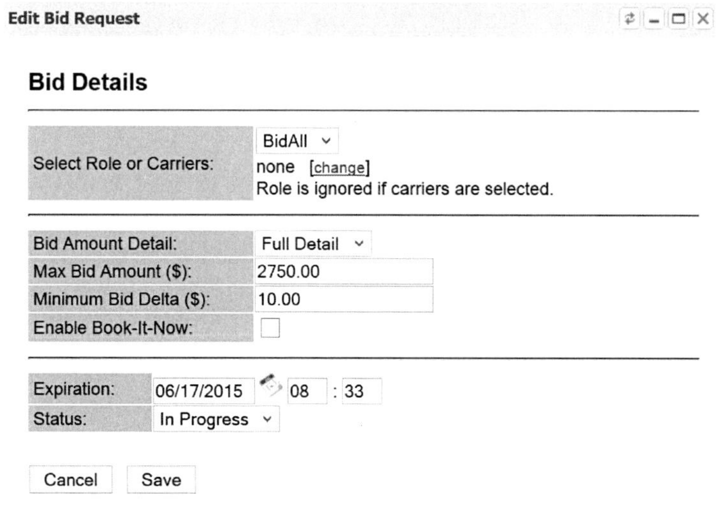

Fig. 5-4: Window for creating and editing a bid.

Each carrier-user of the TMS is assigned to one or more _bid roles_, and then TMS users issue a bid invitation to all users with that role.

The name of the role always starts with "bid" or "Bid," so that the role names will appear in the dropdown menu of options. For example, we might group northern carriers into a role named "bidNorth."

It's also a useful practice to have one role named "bidAll" to bring in all carrier-users.

Here's a discussion of the fields in the bid-creation screen:

Select Role or Carriers:	Bids are issued to any carrier-users with the selected role. Examples of role names might be "bidAll" or "bidNorth."
	After a bid is created, individual carriers can be chosen, instead of by role, as long as those carriers have contracts of type "Carrier Bid."
Bid Amount Detail:	Whether carriers will be asked to submit a single figure, or to break out their bid by charge categories.
Max Bid Amount:	Highest amount allowed for initial bid.
Minimum Bid Delta:	Min amount by which a bid must be lower than the previous bid.
Enable Book-It-Now:	Set a dollar value for a bid which, if a carrier accepts, the carrier wins the load at once.

Expiration: Set expiration date for the bid.

Status: Set this to "In Progress" to activate the bid and send emails to invited carriers.

Carrier Responses

As soon as a bid is created, emails are sent to carrier-users with the appropriate bid role.

You have been designated as one of the preferred carriers to bid on a load for HCS Logistics Inc..

Please reply by 06/22/2015 08:33 AM Eastern Time

Please click here to submit your bid. We will award the bid on price and service and we will notify the winner via email.

Bid Request:
Load: L-0021
Pickup: 06/16/2015 08:00 AM - 06/16/2015 05:00 PM
Delivery: 06/17/2015 08:00 AM - 06/17/2015 05:00 PM
Weight: 200 lb
From:
Main Street Shipping Co
16 Main Street
Saluda, NC 28773

To:
St. Petersburg Puppy Supply Co.
490 First Ave. S.
St. Petersburg, FL 33712

We appreciate you taking the time to participate in our bid process.

Fig. 5-5: Emailed bid invitation sent to carrier-user, with a link to log in to the TMS to reply.

Carrier-users log in to the TMS to submit their bids via an assigned portlet (Fig. 5-6). Incidentally this shows us a different configuration of the TMS. The carrier-user gets an interface with no menus or toolbar, and only the carrier-specific portals to which he/she has been assigned. One of these is an expandable "Bid Requests" portlet (Fig. 5-7).

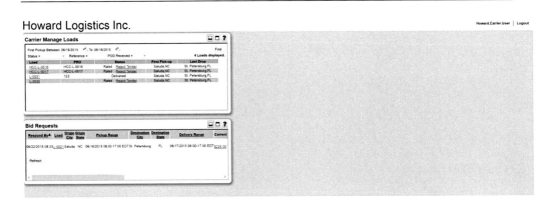

Fig. 5-6: Carrier-user's dashboard with minimal access to load status and bid information.

Fig. 5-7: Detail of expanded carrier bid portlet. The carrier-user clicks the link to enter a new bid.

Accepting Carrier Bids

Submitted carrier bids can be viewed in the "Bids" section of a load detail screen, or the expanded "Bids" section of a load on an ezClick load board, as show in Figs. 5-2 and 5-3.

Clicking the green checkmark next to a bid (Fig. 5-2) makes it the currently selected carrier rate on the load. The winning carrier receives an acceptance email, and the losing carriers receive a "regrets" email, based on their email configurations.

Public (External) Load Boards

Loads from the TMS also may be posted to external bid boards, if the TMS client has the necessary external accounts and they have been set up in the TMS. A variety of external services are available. This process is referred to as "PostLoad."

In addition, MercuryGate is the part owner of an external services called FreightFriend, which is a Facebook-style "social network" or matchmaker service between posted loads and capacity. FreightFriend appears as one of the options in the PostLoad dialog.

From a load on a load board, choose More Actions > Load Postings (Fig. 5-8):

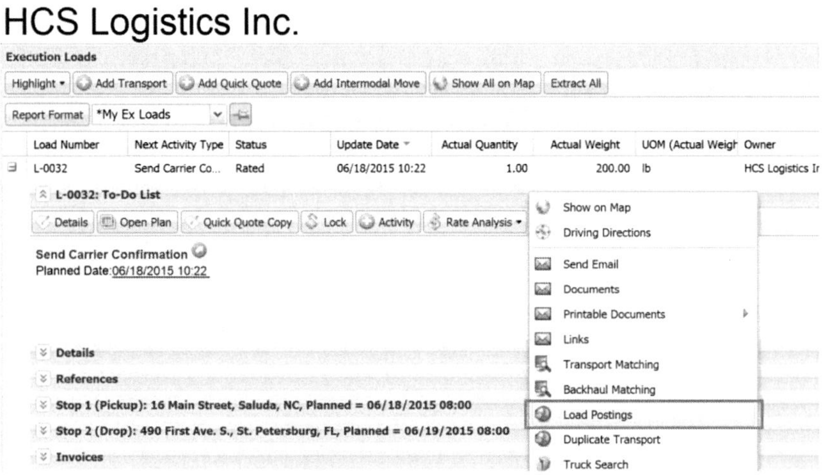

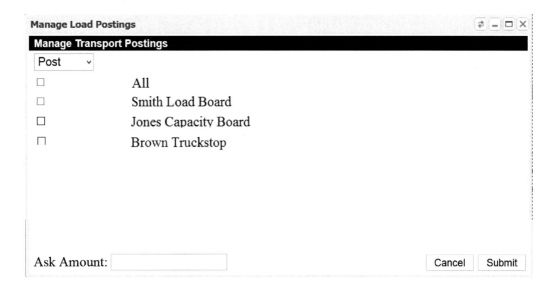

Fig. 5-8: Launching a load posting from the 'More Actions' menu of a load on a load board.

A window opens for posting the load to the selected services, in a list of the boards available to the enterprise (Fig 5-9).

Fig. 5-9: Window for posting a TMS load to an external load board.

The options in the dropdown menu are "Post," "Remove" and "Update." Select which boards to post to, a command, enter an ask amount and click "Submit." "Ask Amount' is saved on the load as a reference of type 'Target Rate" and is submitted to the posting services that support it.

Booking is not automated between the external boards and the TMS enterprise. Manual handling of carrier responses is required.

Posting a load to an external board also can be performed automatically via a dynamic ruleset. See the configurations section for setting this up.

Manage Quotes Process

The Manage Quotes window brings together the various methods of finding a carrier for a load, including carrier quotes and capacity search.

The window is opened from the "More Actions" menu of an expanded load in an ezClick load portlet (Fig.5-10):

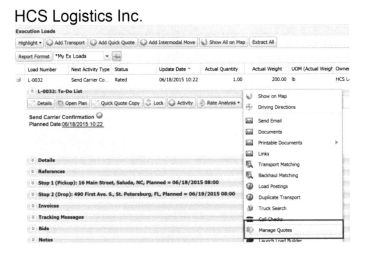

*Fig. 5-10: Opening the Manage Quotes window
from the 'More Actions' menu of a load.*

The Manage Quotes window also can be set up to appear when you click the "Assign Carrier Rate" blue button.

The exact format of the window you see will depend on system settings (Fig. 5-11):

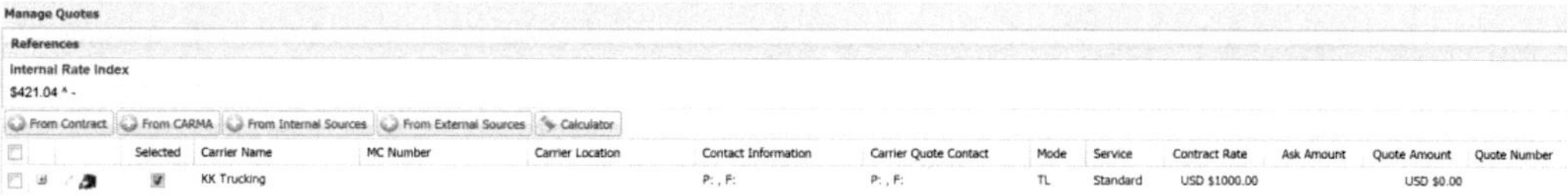

Fig. 5-11: The 'Manage Quotes' window represents 'one-stop shopping' for a carrier for this load. Tabs allow specialized searches from different sources: contract rates, carrier records, internal history, or external sources such as public load boards.

Notice that the Manage Quotes screen includes a series of buttons with labels such as "From Contract," "From Carrier" (it might say "From CARMA"), "From Internal Sources" and "From External Sources."

Each of the source buttons opens a sub-window for obtaining potential rates or carriers from that kind of source. The idea is to build a list of "possibles" in the main window from as many sources as desired.

Clicking "From Contract" opens a sub-window that displays the result of a contract rate search (Fig. 5-12). The user can select entries from the list to appear on the main screen of candidates.

HCS Logistics Inc.

Manage Quotes

Add Carrier From Contract Rates

	SCAC	Carrier Name ▲	Contract Rate	Mode	Service	Priority
	AARC	Alexis Alt Rate Carrier	USD $100.00	TL	Standard	0
	BARC	Bert's Alt Rate Carrier	USD $100.00	TL	Standard	0
	GLSC	GLS Carrier	USD $50.00	LTL	Standard	0
	PFLT	HowardCo Private Fleet	USD $1995.02	TL	Standard	0
	LLTL	Louie-LTL	USD $195.23	LTL	Standard	0
	LYND	Lyndon Trucking	USD $1091.02	TL	Standard	0
	SIMO	Simone Trucking Inc	USD $187.03	LTL	Standard	0

Fig. 5-12: Rate search from clicking 'From Contract' tab in the Manage Quotes screen.

Clicking "From Carrier" or (if configured) "From CARMA" produces a list of available carriers. You can add selected carriers from the list to the main screen for the purpose of sending quote requests.

"From Internal Sources" and "From External Sources" display fields for specifying search criteria and then a list of possible sources (Fig. 5-13). "Backhaul," "Matching" and historical choices are "internal" sources based on existing TMS data, looking for how we have covered this lane in the past. The others refer to the TMS Posted Equipment list or external load boards used in a capacity search.

Fig. 5-13: 'From Internal Sources' or 'From External Sources' option in Manage Quotes opens a search screen based on geographic and equipment information supplied by the user. The sources to search are specified by checkboxes at the bottom of the screen.

Once a list of one or more candidates has been built from the various sources back in the main Manage Quotes screen, users can select entries from the list and operate on them with a command from the window's mass-update menu.

The mass-update options include removing the selected carriers from the list, sending them a quote request, or set an "ask" amount for the load (Fig. 5-14).

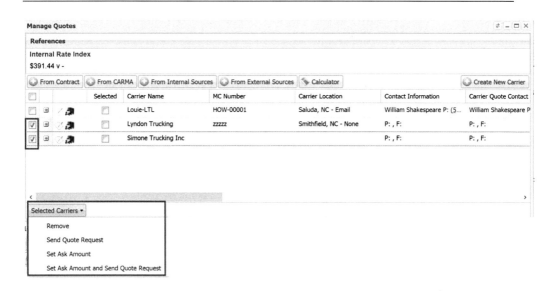

Fig. 5-14: The Mass Update menu in the Manage Quotes window performs the command for the carriers selected by their left-hand checkbox.

Finally, clicking the "Selected" checkbox of a quote makes it the selected rate on the load (Fig. 5-15). The load now can be tendered to the selected carrier. Only one rate can be the currently selected rate for the load.

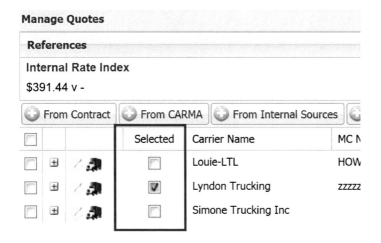

Fig. 5-15: Detail of Manage Quotes window. Clicking a carrier's 'Selected' box makes it the currently selected carrier and rate for the load.

Carrier Quote Process

A user also can directly request a quote from a carrier from the Manage Quotes screen. The carrier's record in the TMS has to include a configured quote process.

Once a list of candidate carriers has been built in the Manage Quotes window, use the mass-update command "Send Quote Request" (Fig. 5-16).

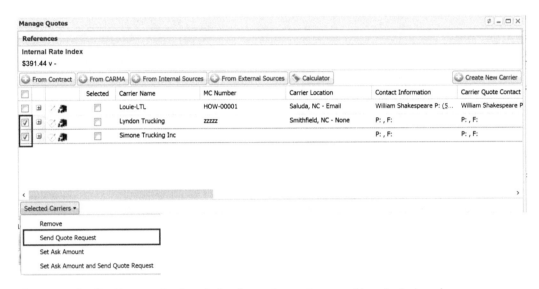

Fig. 5-16: Using the Manage Quotes window to send a quote request to selected carriers.

The recipient specified in the carrier's quote configurations will receive an email (Fig. 5-17).

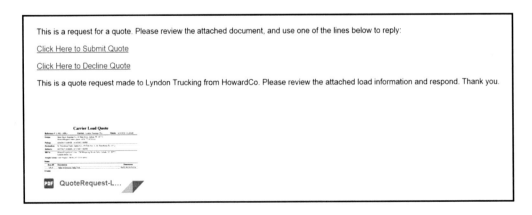

Fig. 5-17: Quote request sent to carrier representative via email.

Clicking the link to submit a quote opens a form onscreen (Fig. 5-18):

Quote Reply

Please enter quote:

Amount: $ [   ] USD

Quote Number: [   ]

Quote Expiration: [   ] ✎ [   ] : [   ]

Contact Information:

Name: [   ]

Email: [   ]

Phone: [   ]

Fax: [   ]

[Submit Quote]

Fig. 5-18: Carrier's quote response form opened by clicking email link.

Submitted quotes and their details are viewed and accessed by refreshing the Manage Quotes screen. Clicking the details icon next to the carrier opens a window with more information (Figs. 5-19, 5-20). Double-clicking a row in the "Quote Amount" column opens a field for editing the amount directly (Fig. 5-21).

Manage Quotes

References

Internal Rate Index

$391.44 v -

[⊕ From Contract] [⊕ From CARMA] [⊕ From Internal Sources] [⊕ From External S|

☐			Selected	Carrier Name	MC Number
☐	⊞	✎	☐	Louie-LTL	HOW-00001
☑	⊞	✎	☐	Lyndon Trucking	zzzzz
☑	⊞	✎	☐	Simone Trucking Inc	

Fig. 5-19: Click the carrier's editing icon to open a window for viewing/editing quote details.

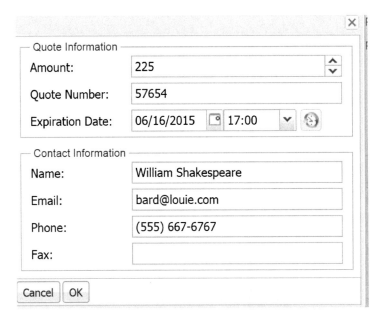

Fig. 5-20: Window for viewing and editing carrier quotes.

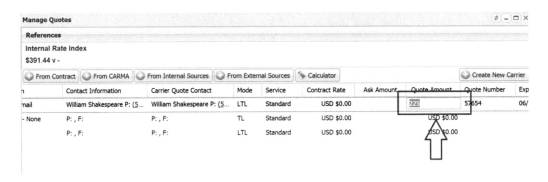

Fig. 5-21: Clicking in the field allows direct editing of the quote amount.

Selecting a Quote

As we saw in Fig. 5-15, clicking the "Selected" checkbox of a quote in the main Manage Quotes window makes it the selected rate on the load. The load now can be tendered to the selected carrier.

Posted Equipment/Capacity Search

The search for posted carrier capacity works in the opposite direction from a bid board. In the bid-board process, TMS users post their loads with the goal of getting a carrier offer to move them.

In a capacity search, carriers have posted their available equipment and routes either internally in the TMS, or to a public board. TMS users search for an available truck that meets their needs. (For public boards, user accounts must exist and have been configured in the TMS.)

Remember that the "Manage Quotes" window includes options for searching internal and external sources for possible carriers (Fig. 5-22).

Fig. 5-22: The 'From Internal Sources' button in the Manage Quotes window opens a search screen for searching TMS records, including records of equipment posted by carriers.

Fig. 5-23: Search screen that results from clicking "From Internal Sources". One of the sources to search is equipment posted by carriers in the TMS. Users can narrow their search results by specifying origin, destination, radius, mode, desired equipment and other factors.

Results are grouped by carrier SCAC at the bottom of the search screen. Expanding a carrier's entry shows one or more lines of equipment currently posted by that carrier (Fig. 5-24).

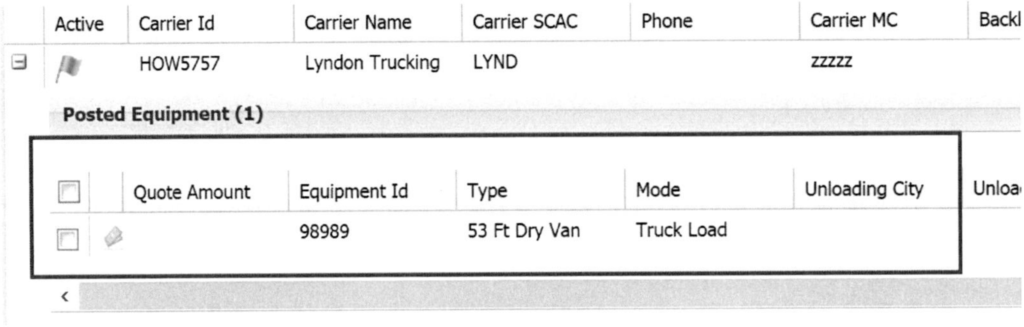

Active	Carrier Id	Carrier Name	Carrier SCAC	Phone	Carrier MC	Backl
	HOW5757	Lyndon Trucking	LYND		zzzzz	

Posted Equipment (1)

	Quote Amount	Equipment Id	Type	Mode	Unloading City	Unloa
		98989	53 Ft Dry Van	Truck Load		

Fig. 5-24: Results portion of "From Internal Sources" search screen. The carrier "Lyndon Trucking" has posted a 53-foot dry van that matches our search criteria.

The user can add any carrier's posted equipment to the list of candidates back in the main Manage Quotes screen. Choose the equipment's left-hand checkbox and then click the "Add Selected" button at the bottom right of the screen.

Carrier Posting

Carrier-users logged into the TMS post their equipment in a portlet named "Combined Capacity." The user clicks an add button to post new equipment (Fig. 5-25).

Posting information includes equipment type, available date range, desired origin and destination (as general or specific as desired), and driver contact information.

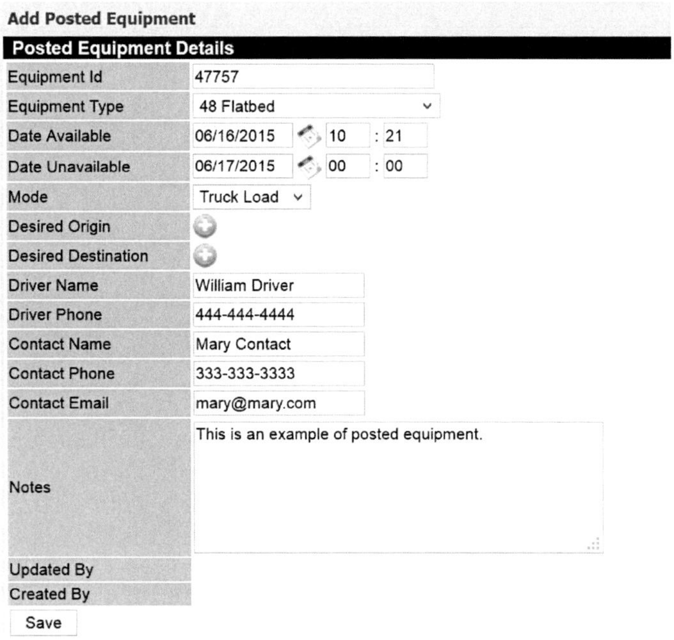

Add Posted Equipment

Posted Equipment Details	
Equipment Id	47757
Equipment Type	48 Flatbed
Date Available	06/16/2015 10 : 21
Date Unavailable	06/17/2015 00 : 00
Mode	Truck Load
Desired Origin	
Desired Destination	
Driver Name	William Driver
Driver Phone	444-444-4444
Contact Name	Mary Contact
Contact Phone	333-333-3333
Contact Email	mary@mary.com
Notes	This is an example of posted equipment.
Updated By	
Created By	

Save

Fig. 5-25: Carrier-user's screen for posting available equipment.

Identifying Possible Matches after Post

The TMS can be configured so that when a carrier internally posts a new piece of equipment, the system automatically searches existing uncovered loads for possible matching loads.

These loads are automatically assigned a new blue button labeled "Get Truck Rate," allowing the user to assign the load to the posted capacity (Fig. 5-26).

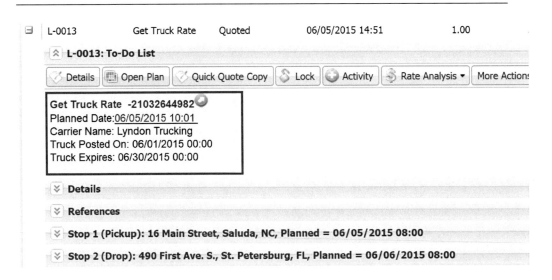

Fig. 5-26: Detail of load on a load board that has been flagged for a possible match to newly posted carrier equipment. The blue button opens a screen allowing the user to assign the capacity.

Carrier Records Management

As we'll see in more detail in the chapter on carriers, part of the job of being a logistics provider is knowing which carriers are your best bets. This requires active and aggressive management of carrier records.

After all, how useful is it to have great contract rates with a carrier who refuses every tender offer? Or what if some carriers have such a poor on-time record they're actually costing you money and future business?

Searching for capacity in a capacity crunch is no time for wasted effort. Knowing which carriers have been the most reliable in the past, and knowing which carriers more readily serve the lanes you're trying to cover, are important weapons in the hunt.

We'll talk about two tools for getting a precise handle on our carriers, instead of relying on guesswork, favoritism or seat-of-the-pants judgment. One of these is a carrier scorecard portlet in the TMS. The other is the kind of detailed records available from MercuryGate's standalone carrier management system, Carma.

The 'Carrier Scorecard' Portlet

The TMS features a "carrier scorecard" portlet that summarizes carrier performance by certain key metrics. The user chooses a time frame and a carrier from the list (Fig. 5-27):

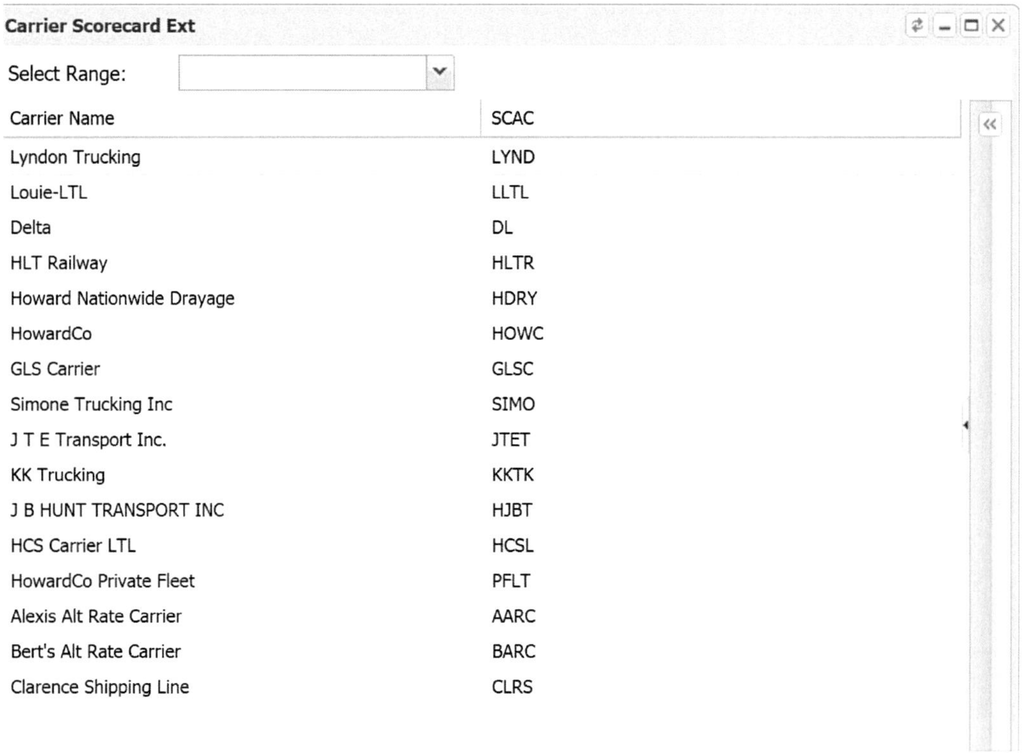

Carrier Scorecard Ext		
Select Range:		
Carrier Name	SCAC	
Lyndon Trucking	LYND	
Louie-LTL	LLTL	
Delta	DL	
HLT Railway	HLTR	
Howard Nationwide Drayage	HDRY	
HowardCo	HOWC	
GLS Carrier	GLSC	
Simone Trucking Inc	SIMO	
J T E Transport Inc.	JTET	
KK Trucking	KKTK	
J B HUNT TRANSPORT INC	HJBT	
HCS Carrier LTL	HCSL	
HowardCo Private Fleet	PFLT	
Alexis Alt Rate Carrier	AARC	
Bert's Alt Rate Carrier	BARC	
Clarence Shipping Line	CLRS	

Fig. 5-27: Initial screen of carrier scorecard portlet, presenting list of carriers available for user's view.

When the user specifies a date range and chooses a carrier, a detail window is available on the right side of the portlet that displays detailed statistics for this carrier (Fig. 5-28). Besides pickup and drop late percentage, the statistics include percentage of tenders rejected and information about status messages.

Carrier Scorecard: ███████
03/01/2015-03/31/2015

Load Count: 1
Spend: $75.00

ON TIME METRICS		
	Pickup	**Delivery**
Total	42	51
Late	31 (73.81%)	45 (88.24%)
Goal %		

TENDER EFFICEINCY			
	Accepted	**Rejected**	**Expired**
EDI	0	0	0
Email	3	0	0
Other	0	0	0
%	100.00%	0.00%	0.00%
Goal %			

FREIGHT CLAIMS		
	Open	**Closed**
Count	0	0

STATUS UPDATES - Avg Hours to Update		
	Pickup	**Delivery**
imdemo	Count: 1 Avg. Hours: 2.75	Count: 1 Avg. Hours: 0.01
Goal Hours		

Print

Fig. 5-28: Detail of carrier scorecard portlet showing statistics for selected carrier and time frame.

Carma

MercuryGate's Carma application (the name is derived from "carrier records management") is a standalone product, available by separate customer agreement that offers a robust and actively managed repository of carrier records.

For example, it's important to stay on top of a carrier's insurance status up to the very minute. Beyond insurance, however,

Carma allows us to update many other kinds of carrier information automatically from external sources. Carma features automatic rulesets that can determine a carrier's active status by multiple designed criteria. We also can use Carma to keep records of carrier equipment and the lanes that a carrier serves or prefers.

The home screen of a carrier record in Carma features a series of tabs down the left-hand side, each leading to a detailed sub-screen of data about that kind of record (Fig. 5-29).

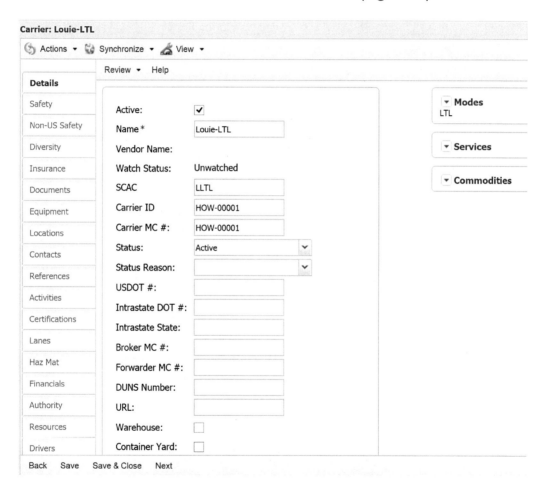

Fig. 5-29: Carma carrier detail window, with tabs leading to sub-windows.

For example, the "Analytics" tab of a Carma carrier record (Fig. 5-30) shows Carma statistics for pickup/drop, freight spend and tender rejection ratio.

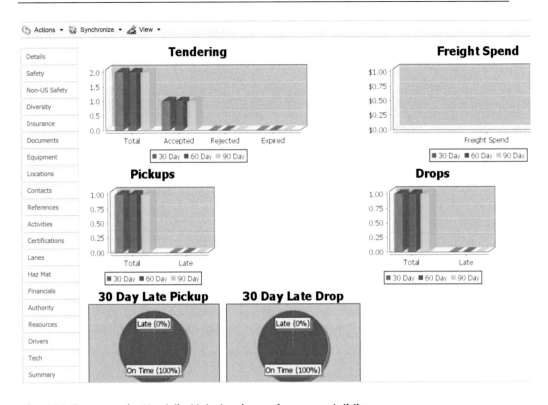

Fig. 5-30: Carma carrier 'Analytics' tab showing performance statistics.

Carma and Capacity Search

Carma carrier records become an active and useful part of our capacity search when they are integrated with the TMS.

From the "Manage Quotes" screen opened from a load, one of our search options is "From CARMA" (Fig. 5-31).

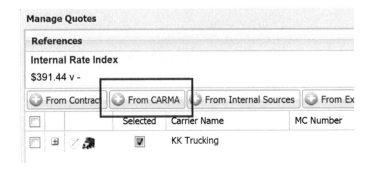

Fig. 5-31: 'From CARMA' option in Manage Quotes window.

When we choose "From CARMA" in the Manage Quotes screen, we're presented with an initial screen in which we can narrow down our choices (Fig. 5-32). Or we can just click "OK" to look at all carriers with a Carma lane definition that might be available for this load.

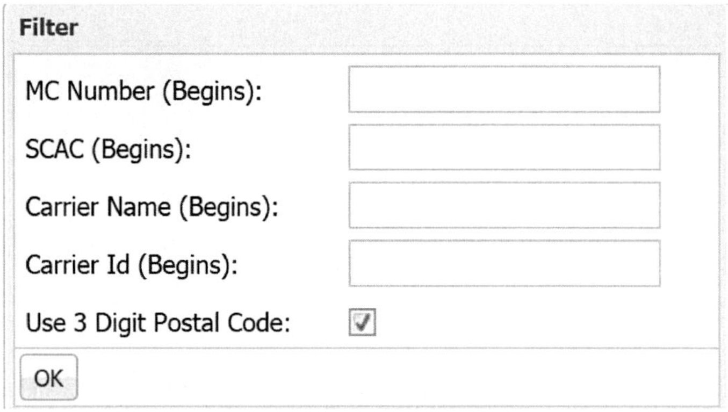

Filter

MC Number (Begins):	
SCAC (Begins):	
Carrier Name (Begins):	
Carrier Id (Begins):	
Use 3 Digit Postal Code:	☑

OK

Fig. 5-32: Screen for filtering Carma carriers in Manage Quotes screen.

A list of carriers with matching lanes in Carma is returned. We can select entries from this list and return to the main Manage Quotes screen to continue with the process of asking for carrier quotes, etc.

Communicating Market Trends

Another tool for dealing with capacity challenges is sharing trends, news and spot information throughout the organization. The TMS news portlet allows the quick posting of trending information and documents such as a seasonality chart.

Communicate Market Trends

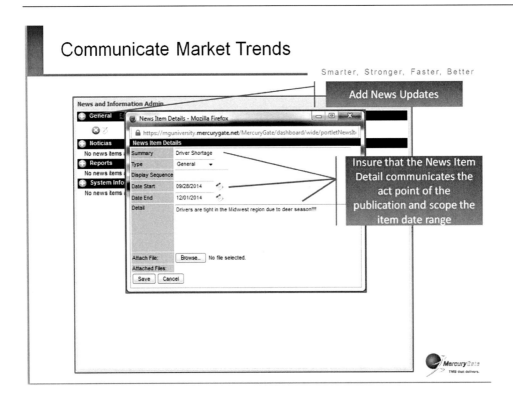

Chapter Discussion

1. Why isn't it enough to have contracts with carriers to give us the trucks we need? Why is it possible for a contract with "the lowest rates" to be no help to us?

2. Why would there be circumstances in which TMS clients would invite a subset of their carriers to a "private" bid board?

3. What is the relationship between managing data about our best carriers and being more efficient in solving capacity challenges?

Chapter 6: 'Multi-Everything' Moves

So far we've been dealing with relatively simple point-to-point moves. Although these are common in the transportation industry, more complex moves often are needed to reduce costs. Modern transportation professionals must adapt to the dominant industry trend toward smaller shipments.

Our arsenal therefore must include more complex solutions not for the sheer sake of being complex, but because they make the most sense. To be worthwhile a complex move needs to save us one or more of (1) money, (2) time, (3) trucks, (4) mileage or (5) dock and facility capacity.

For example, it might make sense to consolidate multiple pickups onto execution loads in a cross-dock or pooling scenario. On the outbound side, it might make sense to consolidate customer shipments onto multi-drop loads.

A single customer shipment might be best moved across multiple execution loads, a multi-leg scenario. The savings from an intermodal move with a middle rail or air leg can be considerable. On the other hand, we might consider an intermodal move, yet still opt for a single truckload leg to save time versus rail.

On top of this, some moves are international and by necessity include all the various considerations we just named, plus the complexity of import/export regulations.

Multi-pick, multi-leg, intermodal, international - these are categories of complex moves that a TMS solution must be able to handle. But the prospect of "simple" moves mixed with "complex" moves pose challenges to the smooth management of a logistics workflow.

After all, we have customer shipments that might move across multiple execution loads. We have execution loads carrying multiple customer shipments. We're simultaneously managing one-to-one, one-to-many, and many-to-one relationships. On top of all that, we can have international import/export regulatory considerations. How do we keep track of it all, and which loads are related to which?

A TMS Solution

In the TMS, the approach to the problem of complex moves is the organization of freight movements under a top-level, master record called a route. In this context, the word "route" does not mean a line on a map. It means a TMS record that groups all the individual loads that are related to carrying out the movement.

That means a route includes both customer loads (the customer's record of the move) and execution loads (the carrier's record of the move.) All customer and execution loads that are part of the same route are called related loads. For any route, we can view all of its related execution and customer loads simultaneously in a master display.

The key point is that individual loads are now managed as interdependent entities. We know that the timing of events for one depends on the other. We know that recording the "in-gate" activity of an execution load at the rail ramp completes the previous pickup dray leg of the intermodal movement. We know that our outbound multi-drop load is waiting for the delivery of X number of inbound loads. And we are able to allocate costs appropriately across our customer records.

Figure 6-1 shows the record of a route expanded on a route board.

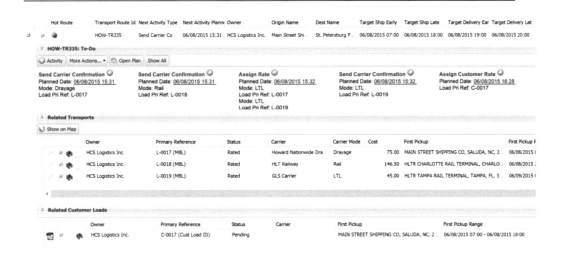

Fig. 6-1: Expanded view of a route record. The user can see the array of blue button activities pending for all the route's related loads, as well as lists of all execution and customer loads related to the move and their statuses.

Notice that at the top of the route display, we get a "to-do" list of pending blue buttons that are visible (based on the user's permissions) on all loads that are part of the route.

Next comes a "related transports" section (Fig. 6-2) that shows this route actually has three execution loads – that is, three different legs.

		Owner	Primary Reference	Status	Carrier	Carrier Mode	Cost	First Pickup
		HCS Logistics Inc.	L-0017 (MBL)	Rated	Howard Nationwide Dra...	Drayage	75.00	MAIN STREET SHIPPING CO, SALUDA, NC, 2...
		HCS Logistics Inc.	L-0018 (MBL)	Rated	HLT Railway	Rail	146.50	HLTR CHARLOTTE RAIL TERMINAL, CHARLO...
		HCS Logistics Inc.	L-0019 (MBL)	Rated	GLS Carrier	LTL	45.00	HLTR TAMPA RAIL TERMINAL, TAMPA, FL, 3...

Fig. 6-2: This route is associated with three execution loads, from pickup to rail ramp, from rail ramp to rail ramp, and from rail ramp to destination.

Meanwhile we see in the "Related Customer Loads" section (Fig. 6-3) that only one customer load is associated with this route. That single customer load is moving across all three carrier legs.

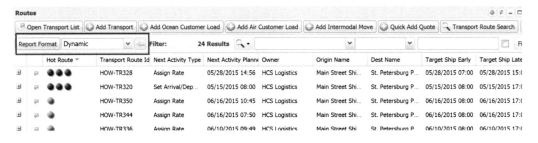

Fig. 6-3: Detail of "Related Customer Loads" list in a route display.

Route Board

Like all portlets, the TMS route board's specific columns, sort order and filtered values are controlled from the "Report Format" function (Fig. 6-4).

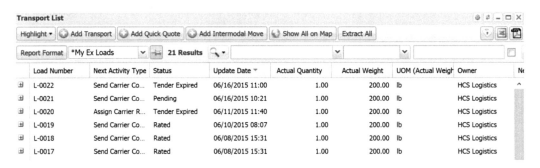

Fig. 6-4: Detail of route portlet and report format selection.

Notice the first (left-hand) button at the top of the portlet, "Open Transport List". This action opens a new <u>load board</u> that displays the execution loads that belong to the routes being displayed in the route portlet (Fig. 6-5). We can view our data from the level of the owning route, or we can view all our execution loads in a single load board if that's best for the workflow.

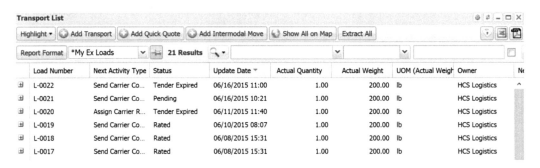

Fig. 6-5: Load board showing all execution loads related to routes in the route portlet. The list is opened from the "Open Transport List" button on the route board.

The next series of buttons relate to options for creating load and route records, if they are displayed by the user's permissions. We'll take a look at each.

Fig. 6-6: Detail from route portlet showing buttons for various load creation options.

Add Transport

"Add Transport" opens a window for the creation of an execution load (Fig. 6-7). The user chooses an owning enterprise, pickup and drop events, equipment and services, and initial rating options. The system can be set up to auto-create both a related customer load and the owning route, triggered by the creation of the execution load.

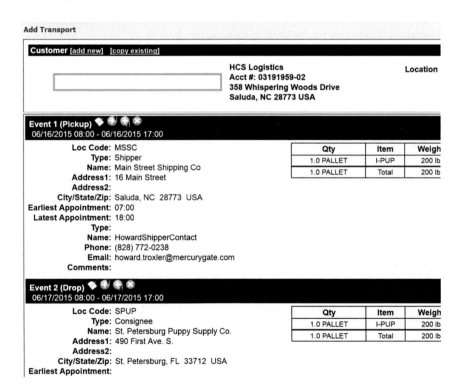

Fig. 6-7: 'Add Transport' window for creating a load, opened from route portlet. Values for owning customer, origin, destination and items start from default values but are editable by the user.

Add Ocean/Air Customer Load

These buttons might be used either by: (1) Customer-users who are logged in to create their own desired movements in the system or (2) TMS operators creating records on the customer side first, with the intention of creating corresponding execution loads.

Both the "Ocean" and "Air" buttons open a creation window with multiple specialized sections that deal with the intricacies of international and complex movements. These fields are entirely customizable, both by subsection (we can omit or include entire subsections as desired) and individual field (required, read-only, editable, or hidden).

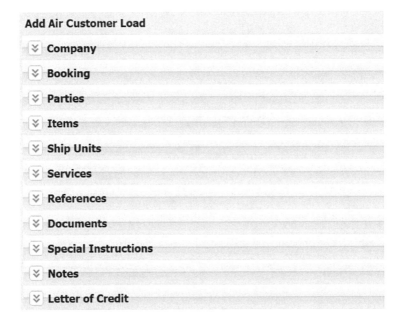

Fig. 6-8: Detail of the creation window opened by an "add customer load" button on the route portlet. Data about the load is organized by sub-sections, which are expanded by clicking their entry in the list.

About the sections:

Company:	Owning enterprise name, notes if needed
Booking:	Designation as import/export, time frame inco terms, power of attorney, insurance
Parties:	Entry of required parties such as beneficial owner, notify party, consignee, etc.
Items: Ship Units:	Contents of load.
Services:	Specified as needed.
References:	Additional tags of information such as serial numbers, etc. as needed.
Documents:	List of existing documents associated with load, ability to add/upload new ones.
Special Instructions:	As needed.
Notes:	As needed.
Letter of Credit:	Letter of credit number, issue & expire dates, document.

Add Intermodal Move

With this button users create a customer shipment but design the move across multiple execution legs. (Depending on the company's settings, this button might also be labeled "Add Shipment," but it does the same thing.)

In the creation screen (Fig. 6-9) the user chooses an owner for the shipment, sets info for origin, destination and bill-to addresses, and sets date windows and item information. The user selects a shipment <u>type</u> that corresponds to an intermodal move:

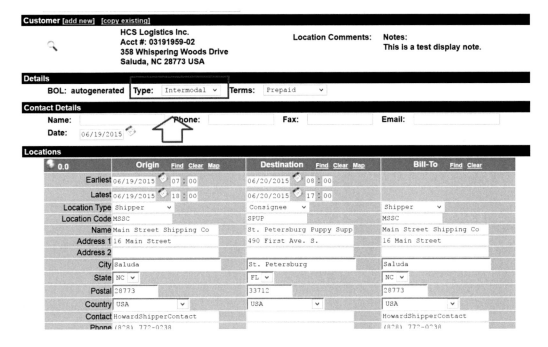

Fig. 6-9: Top of creation screen opened by 'Add Intermodal Move.' User chooses owner, shipment type, date windows, etc.

At the bottom of the screen (Fig. 6-10) there are options for how to save the new load, right above the "Save" button. One of them is "Multi-Leg" – the user checks it and clicks Save.

References

Value	Type
	⌄
	⌄
	⌄

Rating Values

Linear Feet: [   ]   Rating Coun

Save Options

Manual Rate	☐	Customer ⌄
System Rate	☐	Customer ⌄
Copy Rate	☐	
Multi-Leg	☑	
Multi-Stop	☐	
Add Another	☐	

[SAVE]

Fig. 6-10: Bottom of creation screen opened by 'Add Intermodal Move' with option to specify multi-leg movement.

The user is taken to the next screen for multi-leg creation (Fig. 6-11). The first and last entries in this screen deal with any special equipment that is being brought in for this move, but for right now let's just focus on the origin and destination entries.

Fig. 6-11: Detail of multi-leg creation screen opened as a consequence of 'Add Intermodal Move'.

We know the original pickup and the final destination. But we are building an intermodal move. Let's add a drayage leg from pickup in Western North Carolina to a rail ramp in Charlotte. Then we'll put our shipment on a train to Tampa, and then create a final dray leg from Tampa to St. Petersburg.

In the dropdown menu for the destination of the first leg, select "Enter New" and choose the location (Fig. 6-12):

Fig. 6-12: Detail of multi-leg creation screen. We're inserting a new stop to create a dray leg from the original pickup to our first rail ramp.

We'll add a stop in Charlotte. (In this example our locations have previously been created and are available from the master location list for the enterprise.) Notice Charlotte also becomes the origin of the second (middle) leg (Fig. 6-13). We'll again "Enter New" for the destination of our middle leg and select our Tampa rail ramp as its destination.

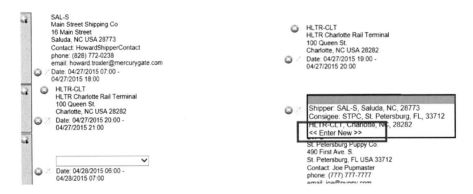

Fig. 6-13: The Charlotte rail ramp is the destination for our first dray leg and automatically becomes the origin of our middle rail leg. Now we'll choose the rail destination, which in turn becomes the origin of the delivery rail leg.

Fig. 6-14: The final dray leg takes the Tampa rail ramp as the origin and goes to the final delivery point.

For each leg, on the right-hand side of the window, icons exist to search any rate schedules in the system for rail, air or ocean rates, and for adding a contract or manual carrier rate to this leg. So we either can add carriers and rates in this screen, or undergo a rating process once the loads are created.

Once we click "Save" in the multi-leg creation window, the system creates <u>three</u> execution loads to move our single shipment, one for each carrier and leg. We can see our three newly created loads as part of the same route in the route portlet, or as three loads waiting to be processed in the load portlet (Fig. 6-15).

Load Pri Ref: L-0024

Related Transports

Show on Map

	Owner	Primary Reference	Status	Carrier	Carrier Mode	Cost	First Pickup
	HCS Logistics	L-0023 (MBL)	Pending			0.00	MAIN STREET SHIPPING CO, SALUDA, NC, 2...
	HCS Logistics	L-0024 (MBL)	Pending			0.00	HLTR CHARLOTTE RAIL TERMINAL, CHARLO...
	HCS Logistics	L-0025 (MBL)	Pending			0.00	HLTR TAMPA RAIL TERMINAL, TAMPA, FL, 3...

Execution Loads

Highlight ▾ Add Transport Add Quick Quote Add Intermodal Move Show All on Map Extract All

Report Format *My Ex Loads ▾ 24 Results

	Load Number	Next Activity Type	Status	Update Date	Actual Quantity	Actual Weight
⊞	L-0023	Assign Carrier R...	Pending	06/16/2015 15:17	1.00	200.
⊞	L-0024	Assign Carrier R...	Pending	06/16/2015 15:17	1.00	200.
⊞	L-0025	Assign Carrier R...	Pending	06/16/2015 15:17	1.00	200.
⊞	L-0022	Send Carrier Co...	Tender Expired	06/16/2015 11:00	1.00	200.
⊞	L-0021	Send Carrier Co...	Pending	06/16/2015 10:21	1.00	200.

Fig. 6-15: The three execution legs we just created are visible in the "Related Loads" display of their owning route, or as three entries in a load board.

Quick Add Quote

"Quick Add Quote," a button which also exists on a load board, allows the creation of a quoted rate for customers. The process searches across available customer contract rates in the system, and also allows for a manual quote to the customer. The quote is based on simple origin, dest and freight information, without full details of the intended movement.

The typical next step is an "Accept Quote" blue button action, performed by customer-users with their own login to the system, or by TMS users in response to customer acceptance by other means.

Other Route Board Features

The route board has several other features intended to improve accessibility to information, search functions and execution. Notice there are icons beside each entry in the execution and customer loads section (Fig. 6-16):

Related Transports

Show on Map

	Owner	Primary Reference	Status
	HCS Logistics	L-0023 (MBL)	Pendin
	HCS Logistics	L-0024 (MBL)	Pendin
	HCS Logistics	L-0025 (MBL)	Pendin

Fig. 6-16: Detail of a route display shows its related execution loads. Each entry can be opened in a detail window or opened in a load board. The binoculars icon opens a 'More Actions' menu as from a load expanded on a load board.

The "piece of paper" icon opens a detail window for this load. The green-arrow icon opens this load in a load list window.

The "binoculars" icon opens a More Actions menu, like that in a load board, for actions that can be performed on this load (Fig. 6-17):

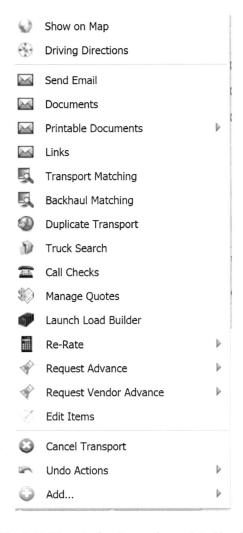

Fig. 6-17: 'More Actions' menu for a related load.

ASSIGN RATE: A blue button unique to the route portlet, usually labeled "Assign Rate," is configured to bring <u>all</u> rating activities and blue buttons on the route's loads into the same master window for convenience and workflow management (Fig. 6-18).

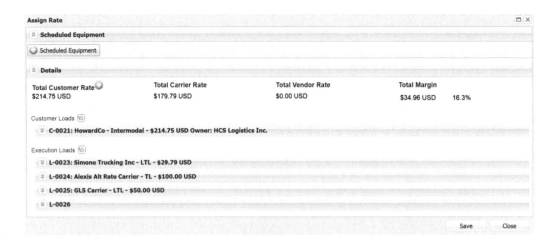

Fig. 6-18: Window opened by 'Assign Rate' blue button action on route portlet. Users see overall financial information about the route, based on known rates and invoices. The record of each customer and execution load associated with the route can be expanded to display blue-button actions related to rating.

Notice the array of route financials across the top of the window showing current total customer rates (revenue) and carrier/vendor rates (expenses) across all loads for this route, and a margin calculation (Fig. 6-19):

Fig. 6-19: Detail of 'Assign Rate' window showing financials and margin calculation.

SUPER SEARCH: The route portlet has a "super search" feature, more sophisticated than ordinary filters, which allows users to filter on a variety of factors (Fig. 6-20):

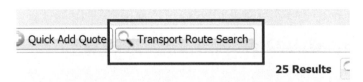

Transport Route Search						_ □ ×
≈ **Events**						^

Event 1

Type:	Pickup ⌄
Early:	▭
Late:	▭
Appointment:	▭
Actual:	▭
Location Code:	▭
City:	▭
State:	▭
Postal Code:	▭
Country:	⌄

Event 2

Type:	Drop ⌄
Early:	▭
Late:	▭
Appointment:	▭
Actual:	▭
Location Code:	▭
City:	▭
State:	▭
Postal Code:	▭
Country:	⌄

≈ **Execution Loads**

Activities

Activity Type:	⌄
Status:	⌄
Planned Date:	▭
Completed Date:	▭

References

Reference Type		Value
⌄	
⌄	
⌄	

Status

Carrier Rate

Fig. 6-20: The route board's 'super search' feature allows detailed filtering at the level of individual fields in a route record.

We also can use super-search criteria in report formats for the portlet (Fig. 6-21):

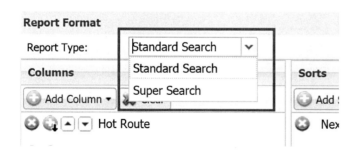

Report Format

Report Type:	Standard Search ⌄	
Columns	Standard Search	**Sorts**
⊙ Add Column ▾	Super Search	⊙ Add
⊗ ⊙ [▲] [▼] Hot Route		⊗ Nex

Fig. 6-21: Choosing 'Super Search' for a report format opens a "tree" of fields that can be selected and specified in a sophisticated filter.

DATA BUCKETS: Besides all the usual fields that can be used in reports (such as route id, next activity, origin and destination fields, etc.), a route object has 24 customizable fields called "data buckets" (Fig. 6-22). These fields can hold any string value, number or date as set up for the enterprise. Their values are updated behind the scenes by dynamic rulesets.

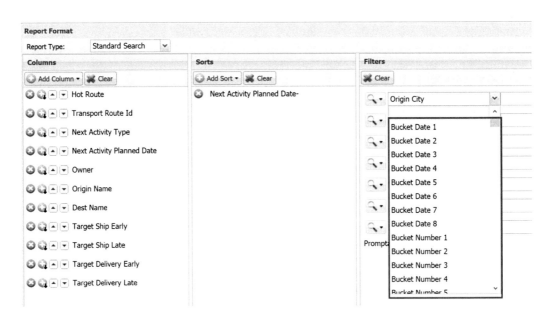

Fig. 6-22: 'Data buckets' are entirely customizable fields available in reports. The 'bucket' fields are renamed according to the business practice, and their values are updated by dynamic rulesets.

ROUTE PLAN: The route portlet can be configured to show an "Open Plan" button for the route which opens a window listing all events on the route's related loads, which can be edited if system settings allow (Fig. 6-23).

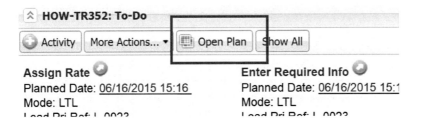

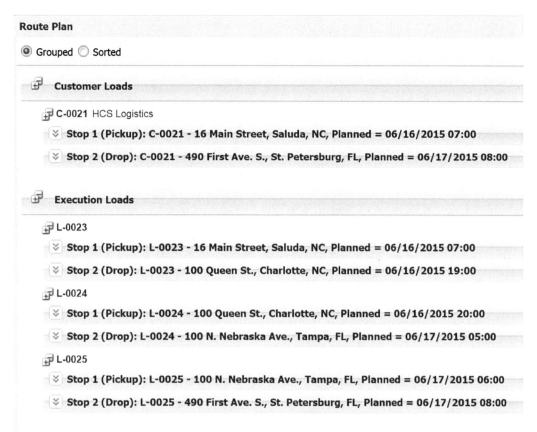

Fig. 6-23: 'Open Plan' button in a route display and the resulting plan window.

'HOT ROUTE' INDICATOR: The system can be set up to flag routes with loads that either are late, or in danger of being late (Fig. 6-24). 'Hot Route' is a field that can be chosen in the report format. For more on hot routes see the chapters on workflows.

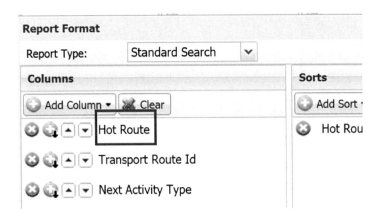

Fig. 6-24: 'Hot' routes displayed on a route board (above). Report format that uses 'hot' status as the first column in the route board (bottom).

COLOR-CODED LOAD STATUS: Clicking the "Show on Map" button for a route's execution or customer loads displays the related loads in color-coded status: gray for pending, magenta for in transit, red for completed (Fig. 6-25).

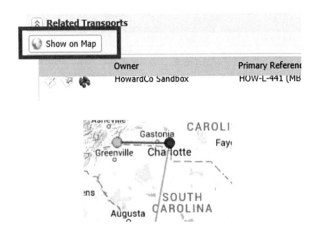

Fig. 6-25: Map display of route legs color-coded by status.

International Loads

Crossing international borders introduces a new layer of complexity. Imports and exports require several new fields of information. Additional blue-button actions are available to facilitate the submission of import-export filings to government authorities.

There are many available fields; not all are used in every circumstance. Some of the categories include:

Move Information	Type, surety number, AMS #
Conveyance	Vessel/Airline Name, number, Lloyd's code, etc.
Letter of Credit	Number, issue date, expire date
Immediate Fields	Immediate transportation number, date
Blanket Period	Begin/end date
Exporter	License number, date, etc.
Destination Control St.	Required in some cases
Export Details	Identifying numbers by cargo type
ISF	Import Security Filing information
AES	Automated Export Service filing info
Point of Origin	Location code, name, address
Container Stuffing Loc	Who/where container was stuffed
Final Dest Port	For remaining entries, location info
Port of Export	
Port of Entry	
Port of Unloading	
Final Destination	

During the life cycle of a load, several blue button actions (typically created by dynamic ruleset as part of the designed workflow) are related to international movements:

- Enter Export Details
- Submit to AES
- Import Security Filing
- Verify DPS (denied party screening – parties forbidden under US law)
- Verify Legs (confirm legs of movement)
- Verify Parties (confirm parties, make sure required parties are present)
- Enter Import Details
- Verify Carrier Info
- Verify Export
- Verify Import

- Verify Shipment Info

The route portlet has the most fully integrated functionality for creating international loads. Buttons for creating air and ocean international moves reside on the route (Fig. 6-26) and take the user through a series of creation steps.

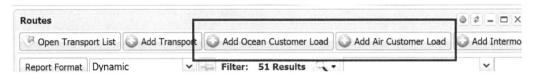

Fig. 6-26: Creation of ocean, air customer load records via the route board.

We'll do an international air movement. Clicking "Add Air Customer Load" opens a creation window with several expandable sections as we saw earlier.

The window consists of expandable subsections for choosing the load's owner from the hierarchy (Fig. 6-27):

Fig. 6-27: Customer detail of customer load creation screen.

For supplying basic desired booking information (Fig. 6-28):

Fig. 6-28: Booking detail of customer load creation screen.

For identifying required parties (regulations often require the identification of parties such as the U.S. "principal party in interest," the intermediate and ultimate consignees, etc. (Fig. 6-29) :

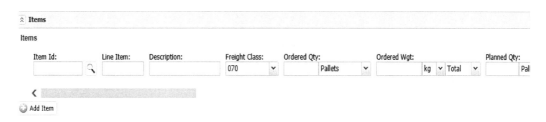

Fig. 6-29: Identifying related parties for the international move. The types of parties required or available are configurable.

For specifying the actual items/ship units of the load (Fig. 6-30):

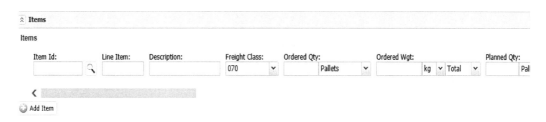

Fig. 6-30: Freight-related detail of the load creation screen.

For specifying required services, if any (Fig. 6-31):

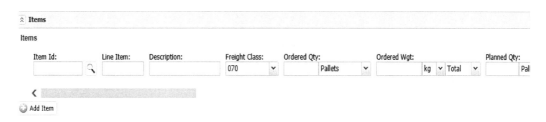

Fig. 6-31: Specifying required/requested services in the load creation screen.

For attaching references, required documents, and special instructions to the load, an additional all-purpose "Notes" field, and finally, information about the load's "letter of credit," another international requirement.

Each of the steps described above is fully configurable – whether it needs to be included in the workflow, and if so, which of its individual fields should be required, editable, read only or hidden.

Chapter Discussion

1. What are the considerations that drive us toward, or away from, complex (multi-pick, multi-drop, multi-leg) solutions for a freight movement? What are the potential advantages versus disadvantages?

2. What are the advantages of using a master-level route object to organize all loads related to a movement, including both customer-facing and carrier-facing records? Are there any disadvantages? What do we gain from the use of routes beyond simply seeing all our blue buttons in one place?

Chapter 7: Workflows, Exceptions & Control Reports

In the chapter titled "The Story So Far" we set expectations for modern TMS systems. We want them to be a tool for designing and managing process-driven workflows that also can respond flexibly to exceptions.

What do we mean by "process-driven workflow"? We mean that a modern TMS must:

(1) Allow us to create processes that are as specialized or as general as our business requires.

(2) Automate the progression of user steps in those designed workflows, responding dynamically and directing users to the next step as actions are completed.

(3) Respond flexibly as exception conditions arise that take our workflow off the optimal "sunny-day" path, making sure that records and unfinished tasks never hang uselessly and unnoticed.

(4) Provide us a control-tower view with which we can tell at once what is working across our operation and what is not.

It is the capacity to design, create and drive active workflows that transforms a TMS from a passive collection of records to an active tool for driving our logistics process to a successful conclusion, time after time.

TMS Workflows – The Basics

Let's return to the MercuryGate TMS to see how the workflow concept is designed and carried out.

Every record that users see on the dashboard is visible because it is part a designed workflow. Every route, every load and invoice seen in a portlet is communicating to the user: "Here is what needs to happen to me next."

	Load Number	Next Activity Type	Status	Update Date ▼	Actual Quantity	Actual
⊞	L-0026	Assign Carrier Rate	Pending	06/19/2015 11:08	1.00	
⊞	L-0023	Enter Required Info	Rated	06/19/2015 11:06	1.00	
⊞	L-0024	Enter Required Info	Rated	06/19/2015 11:06	1.00	
⊞	L-0025	Enter Required Info	Rated	06/19/2015 11:06	1.00	
⊞	L-0017	Send Carrier Confirmation	Rated	06/19/2015 11:03	1.00	
⊞	L-0018	Send Carrier Confirmation	Rated	06/19/2015 11:03	1.00	
⊞	L-0019	Send Carrier Confirmation	Rated	06/19/2015 11:03	1.00	
⊞	L-0034-11	Enter Required Info	Delivered	06/19/2015 11:02	1.00	
⊞	L-0034-4	Dispatch	Delivered	06/18/2015 21:41	1.00	
⊞	L-0034-5	Dispatch	Delivered	06/18/2015 21:40	1.00	

Fig. 7-1: Load board showing the next blue-button activity pending for each load.

The hallmark of the TMS workflow is the <u>blue button</u>. Each blue button represents a pending task on its owning object (route, load or invoice). When the user clicks the button, the action is performed, or a new window opens for additional input.

Assign Carrier Rate ⬤
Planned Date:<u>06/16/2015 15:48</u>

Enter Required Info ⬤
Planned Date:<u>06/16/2015 15:48</u>

Send Carrier Confirmation ⬤
Planned Date:<u>06/19/2015 09:00</u>

Fig. 7-2: Examples of common blue buttons in TMS workflows.

As blue-button tasks are completed, the system automatically hides them and displays new ones, until the prearranged workflow is finished, and the route, load or invoice drops off the list of records that need to be worked.

Important points:

(1) Different workflows can be designed by role. That means we can have separate workflows operating simultaneously for users trying to get loads covered, versus users working loads in transit, versus financial users, versus supervisors who need to see everything.

Each user sees his or her role's particular sequence of blue buttons, pertaining to tasks that role performs. (Of course, if you want everyone in the same flow, you can have that too.)

(2) Workflows respond dynamically to real-time events. Behind the scenes, dynamic rulesets are set up so that once Button X is finished, Button Y is posted next, unless Button Z has already been pushed, and so forth.

(3) A well-designed workflow is equipped to deal with exceptions to the "sunny day" workflow. Examples:

- Carrier rejects a tender and we have to go back to the rating process.
- Carrier arrives at pickup, load not ready, now we have to cancel or reschedule and we might owe "Truck Ordered Not Used" charges.
- Carrier shows up, is instructed to go to location Y instead.
- Carrier shows up, must wait too long, is owed "detention" charges for the extra time.
- Carrier shows up late, will be late for the next stop too.
- Truck breaks down.
- Truck in transit is ordered to a new destination.
- Carrier needs more cash along the way to meet unexpected expense.
- Carrier delivers, but the goods are over, short or damaged.
- Carrier tries to deliver, goods are refused.
- You owe extra per-diem charges for a container return.

Much of this chapter will be showing how a workflow deals with these possibilities.

Portlets as 'To-Do Lists'

Each portlet is set up to recognize a specified subset of blue buttons. If a blue button is not on that portlet's recognized list, it doesn't get shown in that portlet.

So the routes, loads and invoices that users see all have at least one pending blue-button activity that the portlet "recognizes." In other words, we can set up portlets that handle only the activities that we need.

We can fine-tune portlets even further with report formats that display only records with specific blue buttons – for example, we might want to display only loads with a next activity of "Assigned Carrier Rate" or "Tender."

Figure 7-3 shows an invoice portlet from MercuryGate's standard brokerage model. Notice that under the "Report Format" options, we can set the portlet to display only invoices with a specific pending blue-button activity, such as "Audit Invoice". But we can switch the report being shown simply by choosing another menu option.

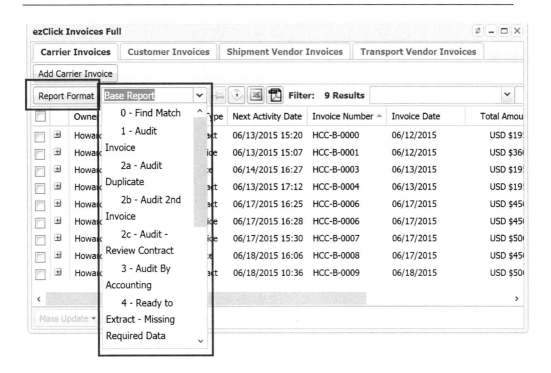

Fig. 7-3: Report options in an invoice portlet, giving users several options for displaying invoices in a particular state.

It works the same way in the load board – we can set up reports to view only loads awaiting a rating, only loads that need a tender, or only loads with blue buttons X, Y and Z.

If it makes sense in the context of your company's workflow, a user can call up a list of all records waiting only for task X and carry them out. Or maybe it makes more sense to start with the list of <u>all</u> pending blue buttons and attack the work that way. The point is, it depends on the individual client's needs.

'Master' and 'Milestone' Activities

Sometimes users will click on a button and see a new window that contains even more blue buttons.

The first blue button clicked was a <u>master activity</u> that owns all the sub-activities in the window. The master is not finished until the subs are finished. Master activities are ways for designers to group together a sub-list of tasks that are logically related. As a hypothetical example, we might group together a sequence of tasks related to finding a carrier under a single master blue button called "Find Carrier" (Fig. 7-4).

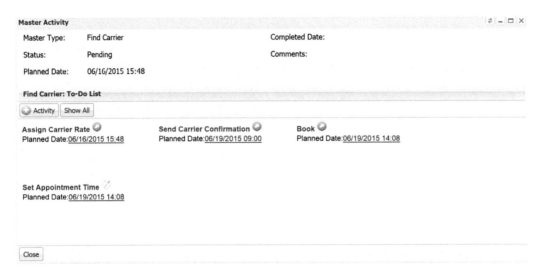

Fig. 7-4: A master activity window, containing the blue button's sub-activities. Master activities often are used to groups of thematically related tasks, in this example, obtaining a carrier for a load.

Master activities are especially useful in international moves, where several individual steps in the import/export process might be lumped into a master with a name such as "Verify Export."

A milestone activity also groups sub-activities, but the focus is on when milestones are completed. An excellent example would be a grouping of tasks that must be completed by the cutoff date for an ocean leg.

The sub-activities in a master or milestone are configurable, as we'll see in the appendix on configurations.

'Sunny Day' Workflow

Let's take one of many possible workflows from the standpoint of a broker or 3PL serving a customer.

(1) A quote for the customer is created via the user click of an "Add Quick Quote" button on the load board or route portlet.

This creates the record of a proposed load with a customer rate in the system.

(2) Triggered by the creation of a customer rate, the system puts a "Send Customer Confirmation" blue button on the load. A user clicks the blue button to send an email and documents about the quote to the customer.

Send Customer Confirmation
Planned Date:06/19/2015 00:00

(3) The completion of the "Send Customer Confirmation" button triggers the addition of a button labeled "Accept Quote." We're now waiting for the customer to say yes, either by clicking an email link or by some other method.

Accept Quote
Planned Date:06/19/2015 00:00

(4) The customer accepts at the rate we quoted. We click "Accept Quote". Now the system creates an "Assign Carrier Rate" blue button for system or manual rating. (Of course, many clients assign carrier rates first and customer rates later – it works both ways.)

Assign Carrier Rate
Planned Date:06/16/2015 15:48

(5) The selection of a carrier rate triggers the system to complete the "Assign Carrier Rate" blue button and add a new one labeled "Tender" or "Send Carrier Confirmation." (Both names are commonly used for the tender action.) When the user clicks this button, it sends an email with tender documents to the carrier.

Send Carrier Confirmation
Planned Date:06/19/2015 09:00

(6) The carrier accepts by clicking a link in the email or by some other method. The carrier also might be set up to auto-

accept a tender. Once accepted the load status moves to "Booked" and the system creates blue buttons for adding appointment, arrival and departure updates to the load.

Set Arrival/Departure -First Stop
Saluda NC
Planned Date:06/18/2015 08:00 EDT

Set Arrival/Departure -Last Stop
St. Petersburg FL
Planned Date:06/19/2015 08:00

Carriers can update and complete blue buttons automatically by electronic messages along the way, or by logging into the TMS if they are authorized. Otherwise TMS operations users can enter information manually. We'll learn more in the chapter on tracking loads in transit.

(7) When we get a message saying the load is delivered, a dynamic ruleset typically adds an "Add POD" blue button (POD = Proof of Delivery). Users complete this activity by uploading a document or a link to a document. This often is the last step for a load on a load board and the action moves to the invoice side.

Add POD
Planned Date:06/18/2015 21:11

(8) Carrier invoices can be created automatically by the system upon delivery, by receipt of an electronic carrier message, or by user entry upon receipt of an email or paper invoice. The system automatically matches new invoices to a known load, or adds a "Find Match" blue button to an unmatched invoice.

Find Match
Planned Date: 06/19/2015 09:00

(9) Triggered by the creation of an invoice, the system tests for duplicates or charges out of tolerance (within limits determined by system settings). "Well-behaved" invoices might go directly to a blue button labeled "Ready to Extract," meaning they are ready to be sent to the external accounting system.

Ready to Extract
Planned Date: 05/26/2015 17:03

(10) Invoices needing some further check are assigned a blue button by the system labeled "Audit Invoice," "Audit 2nd Invoice" or "Audit Duplicate," as the case may be. Users can query the carrier and reject or approve invoices as needed.

Audit Invoice
Planned Date: 06/19/2015 10:30

(11) Typically invoices with a pending "Ready to Extract" blue button are sent by a periodic scheduled task, or by user action. Once carrier invoices are approved, we can auto-generate or manually create and send a <u>customer</u> invoice based on the known rate. Customer invoices also are extracted to the external accounting system.

(12) This completes the workflow. We might put an activity of type "Historical" on the invoice so we can still find it later, or if it is a customer invoice, we might add a pending "Credit" or "Credit and Rebill" blue button in case those activities are needed later.

Credit Invoice
Planned Date: 06/02/2015 16:25

Credit and Rebill
Planned Date: 06/02/2015 16:25

Variance from the 'Sunny Day'

Now let's see how the system should perform for some "non-sunny-day" eventualities. Some of the ones we'll discuss:

- Carrier Rejects Tender
- Truck Ordered Not Used (TONU)
- Detention Charges
- Cash Advances
- Reconsignment

- Diverting Items
- Over, Short & Damaged (OS&D)
- Container Return
- Driver Late/"Hot" Load or Route

<u>CARRIER REJECTS TENDER</u>: When a carrier rejects a tender, the load moves to "Tender Rejected" status. One way to handle this, certainly, would be to assign users to deal with such loads manually.

However, for the purpose of our workflow, perhaps we want the load back to a "Pending" status with a new "Assign Carrier Rate" blue button so the user can start again. The mechanism for achieving this is a dynamic ruleset that looks for a load status change from "Tendered" to "Tender Rejected."

Step 1: The load is in "Tendered" status (Fig. 7-5).

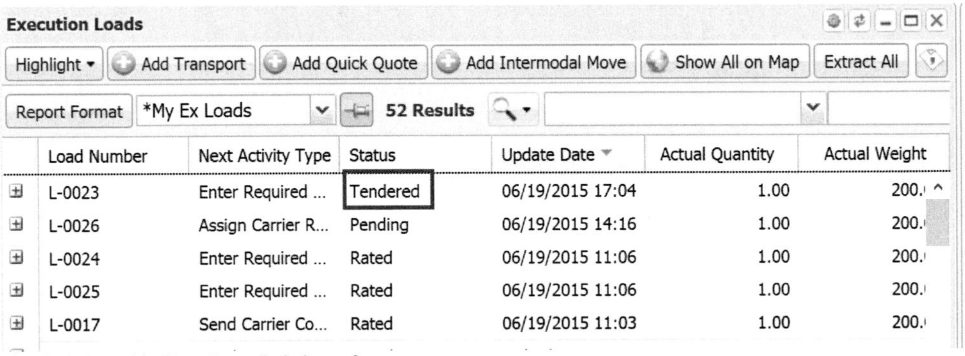
Execution Loads
Highlight
Add Transport
Add Quick Quote
Add Intermodal Move
Show All on Map
Extract All
Report Format
*My Ex Loads
52 Results
Load Number | Next Activity Type | Status | Update Date | Actual Quantity | Actual Weight
L-0023 | Enter Required ... | Tendered | 06/19/2015 17:04 | 1.00 | 200.
L-0026 | Assign Carrier R... | Pending | 06/19/2015 14:16 | 1.00 | 200.
L-0024 | Enter Required ... | Rated | 06/19/2015 11:06 | 1.00 | 200.
L-0025 | Enter Required ... | Rated | 06/19/2015 11:06 | 1.00 | 200.
L-0017 | Send Carrier Co... | Rated | 06/19/2015 11:03 | 1.00 | 200.

Fig. 7-5: Load in 'Tendered' status – for now.

Step 2: Carrier declines the tender via the email (Fig. 7-6):

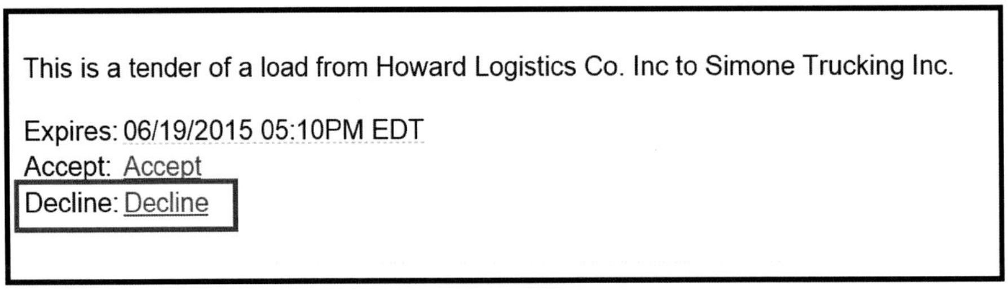
This is a tender of a load from Howard Logistics Co. Inc to Simone Trucking Inc.
Expires: 06/19/2015 05:10PM EDT
Accept: Accept
Decline: Decline

Fig. 7-6: Carrier declines tender. In the TMS, load correctly moves to 'Tender Rejected' status.

Step 3: Thanks to the dynamic ruleset operating behind the scenes, the load is returned to "Pending" status with a fresh "Assign Carrier Rate" blue button, where it can make progress instead of sitting in a "rejected" pile (Fig. 7-7).

Execution Loads					
	Load Number	Next Activity Type	Status	Update Date ▼	Actual Quantity	Actual W
⊞	L-0023	Assign Carrier Rate	Pending	06/19/2015 17:13	1.00	^
⊞	L-0026	Assign Carrier Rate	Pending	06/19/2015 14:16	1.00	
⊞	L-0024	Enter Required Info	Rated	06/19/2015 11:06	1.00	
⊞	L-0025	Enter Required Info	Rated	06/19/2015 11:06	1.00	

Fig. 7-7: Instead of sitting in a 'rejected' file waiting for manual correction, the load is returned automatically to the pool of loads ready to receive a carrier rate.

TRUCK ORDERED NOT USED (TONU): When a pickup is not ready or must be rescheduled we often owe the carrier a TONU charge. When informed by the carrier, the TMS user cancels or reschedules from the load's "More Actions" menu (Fig. 7-8):

Fig. 7-8: User can choose to cancel or reschedule pickup from the "Undo Actions" command in the More Actions menu of a load on a load board.

If we cancel right away, we can move right to a TONU step. But if we choose the "not ready" command, the system still needs to know whether we will cancel this load, or reschedule it. In this design the workflow presents both options (Fig. 7-9):

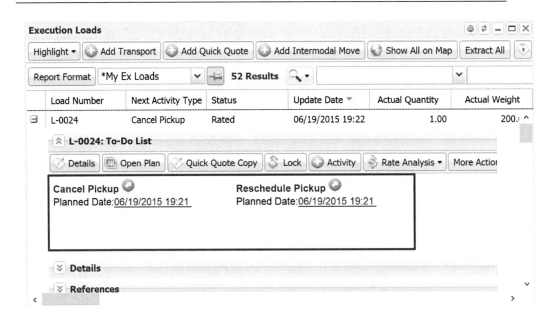

Fig. 7-9: User has chosen "Pickup Not Ready." The workflow posts two blue buttons, one giving the user the option to cancel the load, the other to reschedule the pickup. Whichever the user chooses, the system removes the other.

If the user chooses "Reschedule," the system next needs to know whether to use the same carrier, or whether to switch to a new carrier because of the reschedule. A blue button titled "Assign TONU", when clicked, opens a window asking us (Fig. 7-10):

Fig. 7-10: User clicks "Assign TONU" blue button as next step in rescheduling pickup. User chooses between keeping the existing carrier on the load, or removing to re-rate and find a new carriers.

We will enter a charge manually (based on our terms with the carrier) for the TONU charge, and decide whether this carrier keeps the load, or is removed from the load for a reschedule.

If the carrier is kept: The TONU charge is added to the existing rate and the dynamic ruleset rolls the load back to "Set

Appointment Time," "Set Arrival Time" and "Set Departure Time" for the new events.

If the carrier is removed: The "old" load now contains only the old carrier's TONU charge and moves into the invoicing process. (The old load is marked "Delivered" to trigger invoicing.). The system automatically creates a <u>new</u> load for the load that is yet to be delivered, setting it to the "Assign Carrier Rate" blue button.

<u>DETENTION CHARGES</u>: Agreements with carriers might include liability for <u>detention charges</u> if a driver is unduly delayed at a stop, as measured by the difference between arrival and departure status messages. Typically the system is set to allow a period of "free time" and a period of normal stop time before detention starts.

Once a detention charge kicks in, the system automatically creates an "Authorize Detention" blue button for the user. Clicking the button opens a window for entering a charge, typically computed on a per-hour basis:

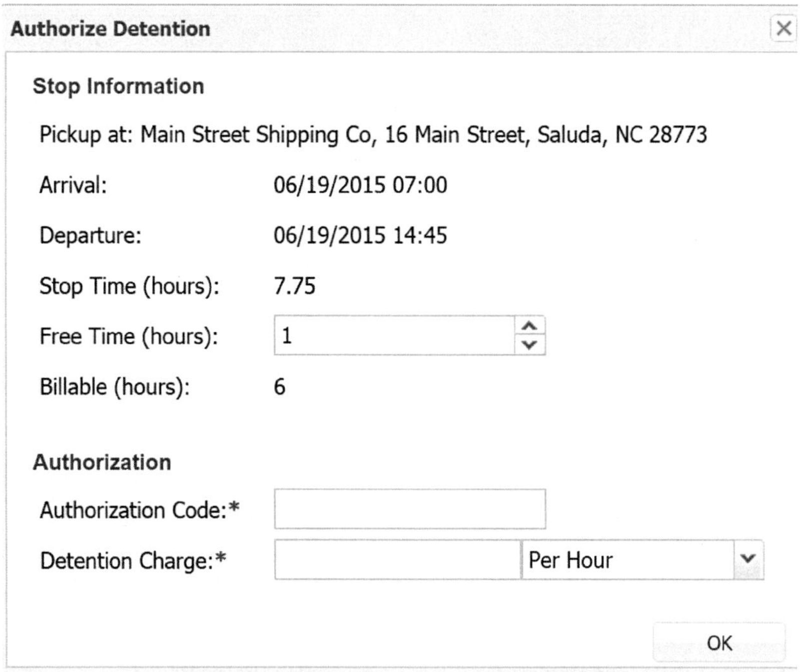

Authorize Detention ✕

Stop Information

Pickup at: Main Street Shipping Co, 16 Main Street, Saluda, NC 28773

Arrival:	06/19/2015 07:00
Departure:	06/19/2015 14:45
Stop Time (hours):	7.75
Free Time (hours):	1
Billable (hours):	6

Authorization

Authorization Code:*   [   ]

Detention Charge:*   [   ] [Per Hour ▾]

[OK]

Fig. 7-11: Window opened from 'Authorize Detention' blue button.

CASH ADVANCES: Some agreements with carriers include the practice of providing cash advances to drivers or vendors in the field to meet expenses in transit. The most common reason is fuel, but advances also can cover spot labor and other expenses along the way.

To start the process after a carrier request, a TMS user chooses "Request Advance" or "Request Vendor Advance" from the "More Actions" menu of an expanded load. A window opens for the user to enter the amount of the advance request (Fig. 7-12).

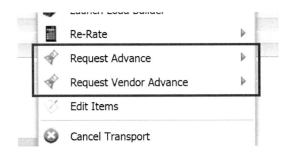

Fig. 7-12: After choosing a request-advance option from the More Actions window, a user sees a window for entering the advance amount.

System settings determine whether the amount requested is below an auto-approve threshold, or whether it requires supervisor approval. If the latter, an "Approve Advance" blue button is added to the load.

Once a carrier's advance request is approved in the TMS, the request is automatically sent to an outside, third-part processor that delivers the funds to the driver by adding funds to a prepaid card or some other method. In the TMS, the advance expense is represented by a vendor invoice on the load (to the third-party processor) and an "adjustment rate" to be deducted from the eventual carrier payment.

RECONSIGNMENT: In this scenario the carrier is directed to a different location in transit, either by the TMS user or by a contact from a stop on the route. The TMS user must adjust the load's plan to reflect the new reality. The user starts with the "Append New Drop" command from the More Actions menu of the expanded load (Fig. 7-13).

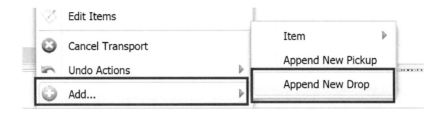

Fig. 7-13: We have learned the carrier must go to a new location, so we add a stop.

The user is taken through a series of screens for choosing a new location, the date and time of the new drop, and which items should be picked up or dropped. Once the event is added it appears in the sections of the expanded load (Fig. 7-14):

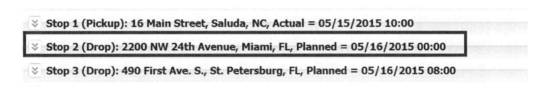

Fig. 7-14: New stop is added to the load.

It is up to your company's practices and the circumstance as to whether the old stop should be removed from the load. The carrier still might be owed a stop charge, or the distance might matter.

To remove a stop, go to the load's Plan tab, select the items to remove (removing all items removes the stop), and select "Remove Selected Shipments" from the Mass Update menu (Fig. 7-15).

			[contacts]		2 Total: |2.0| 28 lb
Drop 1 ⬆ ⬇					95.00 miles to next
Info		Dates	Location	Contact	nents
Status: ⬤ Pending		Target: 10/18/2014 08:00 - 10/18/2014 17:00	HT Logistics HTHQ	Howard Troxler Phone: (828) 772-0238	Shipment Q Weight
Late Reason: ⬤		Current:	358 Whispering Woods Dr Saluda, NC 28773	Email: howard.troxler@mercurygate.com	☑ 1. 14 lb
Notes: ⬤		Appointment: ⬤	US *add comments* [change] [search by mileage] [contacts]	5000304 [change]	1 Total: 1. 14 lb

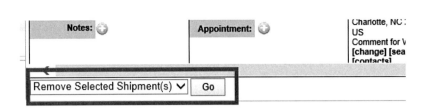

Fig. 7-15: Removing the shipments from a stop, which removes the stop from the plan.

The last question is whether the carrier rate should be adjusted according to your terms with the carrier. From the load's "Details" section you can open a window for editing the carrier rate (Fig. 7-16):

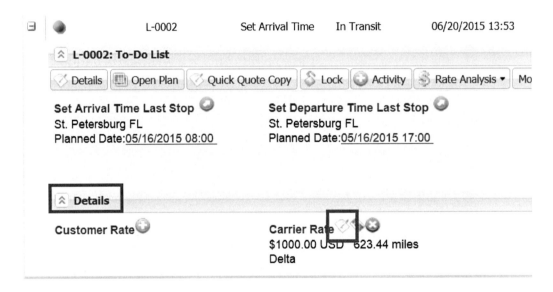

Fig. 7-16: "Details" horizontal section of an expanded load includes the carrier rate. Click the details (piece of paper) icon to edit the rate.

Click the editing icon (the one that looks like a piece of paper) next to "Carrier Rate" and a window opens for you to edit the carrier charges on the load (Fig. 7-17). Notice you can either adjust the mileage, adjust the charge to an overall flat rate, or add an accessorial charge in the items beneath the fuel surcharge.

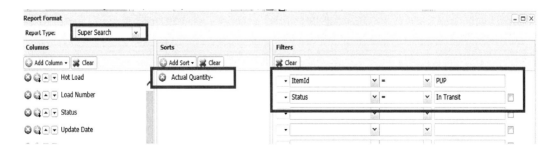

Fig. 7-17: Window for editing existing carrier rate to reflect changes due to additional stop.

DIVERTING ITEMS: In this scenario we need to take freight off a truck already in transit and get it to a different location on a timely basis. The example would be a customer with an emergency need for a quantity of item X, when you already have a shipment of item X going somewhere else that can be re-directed. If this is the nature of your business, then the freight you have in transit at any given time is in a sense a "mobile warehouse" available for redirection on demand.

The first step is to identify what's available right now, in terms of the needed item. One strategy would be to use the load board's "super search" feature to filter on (1) the requested item ID for (2) loads currently in transit (3) sorted by quantity so we can see what resources are at our disposal (Fig. 7-18).

Fig. 7-18: Route report using "super search" to identify all loads in transit with a quantity of the requested item, ranked by quantity.

Once we have our list of candidate loads....

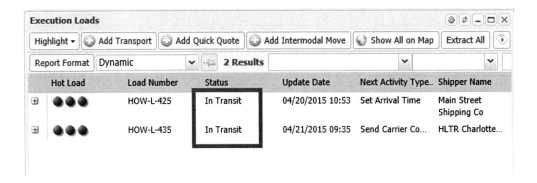

Fig. 7-18: Loads carrying the item we need. We'll click the "Show All on Map" button.

.. we can show them visually on a map to assist in planning our strategy for diversion (Fig. 7-19).

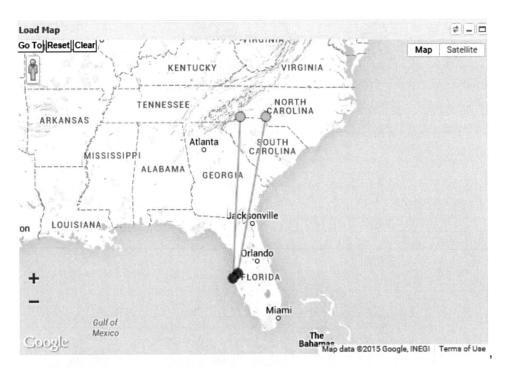

Fig. 7-19: The map view helps us decide which load to re-route.

Choose the load to be redirected and add a new stop and drop quantity as in the Reconsignment topic above. This might be the new consignee's location, or it could be an intermediate location such as a distribution center, which – now that the goods are onsite - would become the origin for a new load. The old consignee is notified of the change as needed, and the new consignee is scheduled for appointment and normal execution.

OVER, SHORT & DAMAGED (CLAIMS PROCESS): When a consignee informs the carrier of an overage, a shortage or a damaged quantity, a blue button usually labeled "Assign Overages" is added to the load. Users can add the activity with the "+Activity" button.

The blue button allows the user to specify overage, shortage and damaged quantity. For an overage or damage, the blue button gives the user the option of creating a return leg, with the previous destination as its origin, and the previous origin as its destination. A reference indicating the quantity is added to the item record.

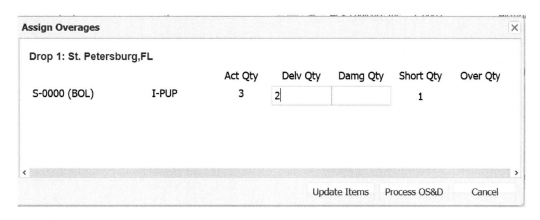

Fig. 7-20: "Assign Overages" window. Consignee reports receiving only 2 of 3 items.

The "Update Items" button updates item quantities without completing the task. The "Process OS&D" button opens a window (Fig. 7-21) to create a new load for an over/damaged quantity that will originate at the existing load's drop point and end at the original shipment's origin.

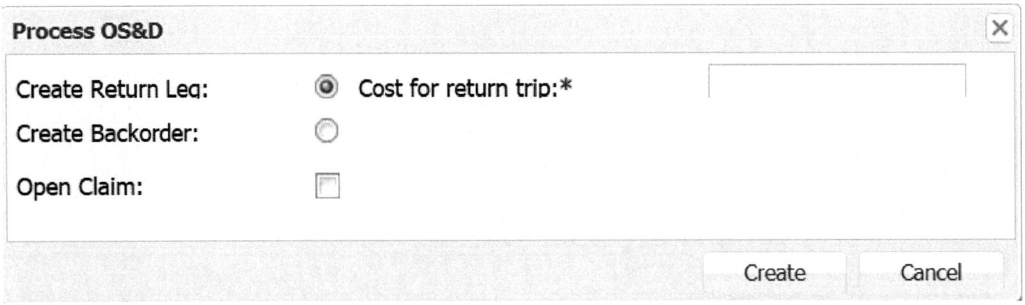

Fig. 7-21: Window opened by "Process OS&D" to create return leg for over/damaged quantity, with option to create a claim record.

The "Create Return Leg" option creates the new load. "Create Backorder" is a placeholder for future functionality. The "Open Claim" option adds a manage-claim activity to the load, represented by a blue button usually labeled "Manage Claim."

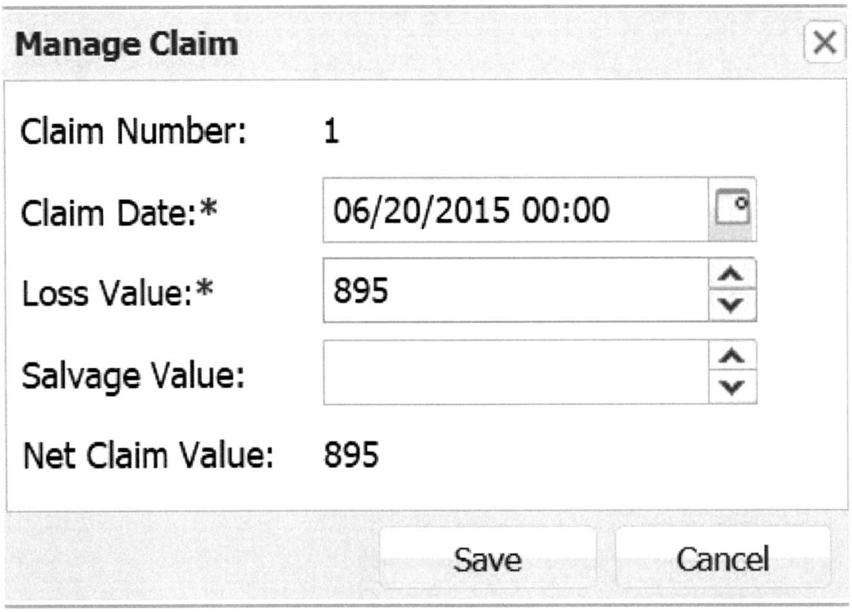

Fig. 7-22: Window opened by "Manage Claim" blue button to add claim information to the load. Use a report format to show all loads with claim actions for user processing.

The "Manage Claim" blue button simply adds references to the load indicating claim amounts for further manual processing.

The TMS also offers a more sophisticated claim-handling method to clients by integrating with an external subscription service.

CONTAINER RETURN: A rail or ocean leg might involve unloading a container at the destination rail ramp or delivery to the final destination with the responsibility for returning the container. The physical return is part of our arrangement with the destination drayage carrier. Typically we have X days to return the container before a daily charge kicks in. The system adds a "Container Return" blue button to the load when:

(1) The load in question is the middle leg of an intermodal move.
(2) The load has a reference of type "VendorID" with its value being the vendor id of the vendor in question.
(3) The load acquires an "Out-Gate" activity in "Complete" status.

The "Container Return" blue button opens a window for entering information. The vendor ID has been determined by the load reference, and the arrival date by the "Out-Gate" message. The window includes fields for how many days until the return and how much should be charged at a per-diem rate.

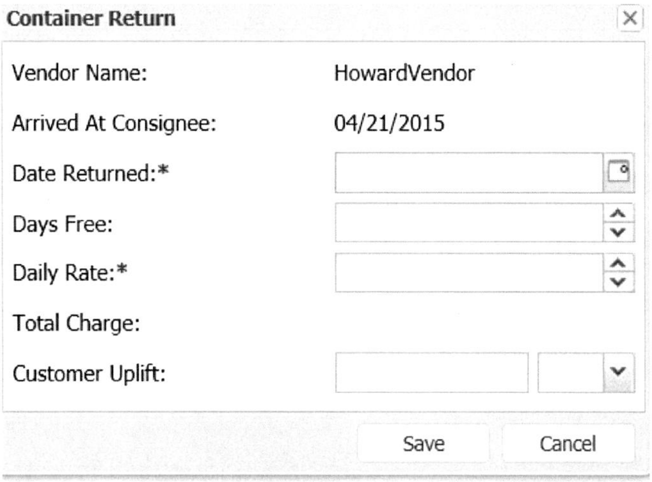

Fig. 7-23: 'Container Return' blue button window.

<u>DRIVER LATE:</u> We must respond to real-time events such as breakdowns, traffic detours, and other factors that impact subsequent events on a multi-stop load or a multi-load route.

As appointment and event information and status messages are updated in the TMS, the system can recalculate an ETA for subsequent events, and flag loads and routes with a "hot" indicator showing there is a reason for concern (Fig. 7-24):

Routes

	Hot Route ▾	Transport Route Id	Next Activity Type	Next Activity Planne	Owner	Origin Name
	●●●	HOW-TR360	Assign Rate	06/18/2015 10:19	HCS Logistics Inc.	Main Stre
	●●●	HOW-TR328	Assign Rate	05/28/2015 14:56	HCS Logistics Inc.	Main Stre
	●●●	HOW-TR320	Set Arrival/Dep..	05/15/2015 08:00	HCS Logistics Inc.	Main Stre
	●	HOW-TR383	Assign Rate	06/18/2015 21:26	HCS Logistics Inc.	Main Stre
	●	HOW-TR382	Assign Rate	06/18/2015 21:26	HCS Logistics Inc.	Main Stre
	●	HOW-TR381	Assign Rate	06/18/2015 21:26	HCS Logistics Inc.	Main Stre
	●	HOW-TR380	Assign Rate	06/18/2015 21:26	HCS Logistics Inc.	Main Stre

Execution Loads

	Hot Load ▾	Load Number	Next Activity Type	Status	Update Date	Actual Quantity
	●●●	L-0001	Set Arrival/Dep...	Booked	05/21/2015 13:53	1/
	●●●	L-0009	Dispatch	Booked	06/03/2015 10:16	1/
	●●●	L-0032	Dispatch	In Transit	06/19/2015 19:45	1.
	●	L-0000	Add POD	Delivered	05/26/2015 13:23	1/
	●	L-0002	Set Arrival Time	Booked	05/21/2015 13:45	1.
	●	L-0003	Send Carrier Co...	Pending	06/17/2015 14:11	1/
	●	L-0004	Set Arrival/Dep...	Booked	05/22/2015 13:50	1.
	●	L-0005	Send Carrier Co...	Pending	05/22/2015 16:43	1/

Fig. 7-24: 'Hot' routes and loads displayed in portlets.

The "Hot Route" and "Hot Load" columns are available in a report format, like any other – be sure to create or use a report that has the column in the place you want. You can sort your report format so that the "hottest" entries appear at the top, awaiting your action (Fig. 7-25):

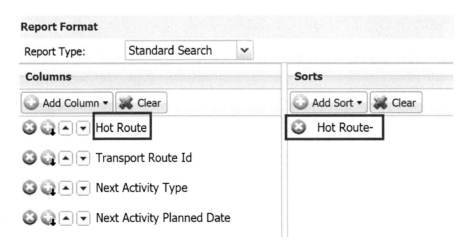

Fig. 7-25: Configuring a report format to display the 'Hot Route' column, with the 'hottest' (highest) values displayed on top.

If automatic ETA recalculation is turned on, then the "hot" status of a load and its owning route are recalculated:

(1) When a time changes in the load's plan, set in the "Plan" tab or in a variety of other windows,

(2) When the system receives a status message indicating an arrival, pickup, delivery, or other relevant information.

(3) On a call check that creates a status message on the load.

(4) When an appointment time is added or updated.

With hot routes and loads flagged at the top of the portlets, users now have the opportunity to view the plan events and respond, either by changing events (as in the "Reconsignment" process described above) or by notifying the affected parties.

Control Reports

We'll use the term "control reports" to make sure the system is under control, and that what is supposed to be happening is happening. We can use TMS reports to flag trouble spots that we need to know about.

Even in a well-designed workflow, things can fall through the cracks. Don't forget that the "sunny day" workflow depends on one step being finished and the next being added.

But what if the previous step is never finished? What if a carrier simply never shows up for a pickup? Our "Set Arrival Time" blue button just sits on the load.

What happens if a carrier is scheduled for a call check or overdue for a status message but never checks in? What if a load is delivered, but proof of delivery is never provided? The load stays stuck on the "Add POD" blue button, holding up the invoicing process.

In these cases, one weapon is to use the report format function to rank our activities by the age of their planned dates. Figure 7-26 shows a simple report format, for example, that does it for all "Next Activity" types on a load board:

Fig. 7-26: A load board report format that sorts loads by their "Next Activity" planned date, oldest to newest.

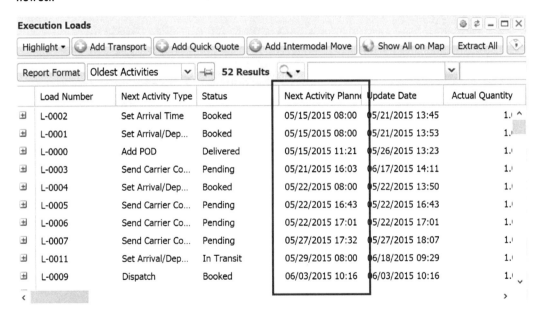

Fig. 7-27: Loads sorted by their next pending activity's planned date, oldest to newest. If this is early June already, why are there incomplete events from the middle of last month?

Example: Identifying Bottlenecks

You can use the system to generate "metadata" about what's going on in your enterprise. For example, because every activity has a planned date and a completion date (once it's finished), we can research the bottlenecks and efficiencies in our workflow.

Here's an example using a report we'll create for our activities in the TMS, then using MercuryEdge, the standalone data-analysis application provided to MercuryGate clients.

First we need an activities report in the TMS that contains our activity type, with creation and complete dates. Go to an overall list of activities for your enterprise via the menu (View > Activities), click Report Format and create the report (Fig. 7-28):

	DETAIL REPORT (Change)		
	Scheduler...	Use	Save...

COLUMNS		SORT		FILTE	
pick clear		**clear**		**clear**	
− + ▶	Primary Reference ∨	▼	∨		∨
− + ▲ ▶	Type ∨	▲ ▼	∨		∨
− + ▲ ▶	Planned Date ∨	▲ ▼	∨		∨
− + ▲ ▶	Completed Date ∨	▲ ▼	∨		∨
− + ▲ ▼	∨	▲	∨		∨

Fig. 7-28: We'll open this TMS report in MercuryEdge to calculate average time between activity creation and completion date, by activity type.

Now our report will be available to us in MercuryEdge via the "Reports" window. Choosing the report opens a spreadsheet with the same fields that would be shown in the TMS (Fig. 7-29). We would filter the report further to choose only activities that already have been completed.

My Activities Sel ×

Report Type: Activity ▾   **Data Level:** HowardCo Sandbox   **Run Date:** 04/21/2015 11:06:31AM   **Total Rows:** 51

Primary Reference	Create Date	Type	Planned Date	Completed Date
HOW-L-384	2015-03-13 14:34	Assign Carrier Rate	2015-03-13 14:34	2015-03-13 14:47
HOW L-304	2015-03-13 14:47	Tender	2015-03-13 14:55	2015-04-06 11:33
HOW-L-385	2015-03-17 11:37	Assign Carrier Rate	2015-03-17 11:37	2015-03-19 09:19
HOW-L-386	2015-03-19 09:26	Assign Carrier Rate	2015-03-19 09:26	2015-03-19 09:26
HOW-C-117	2015-03-19 09:26	Assign Customer Rate	2015-03-19 10:26	2015-03-19 09:26
HOW-L-387	2015-03-20 16:09	Assign Carrier Rate	2015-03-20 16:09	2015-03-20 17:14
HOW-I-388	2015-03-20 17:27	Assign Carrier Rate	2015-03-20 17:27	2015-04-06 11:17

Fig. 7-29: Activity report from the TMS opened in MercuryEdge.

Use MercuryEdge's "calculated column" command to add a column that subtracts creation date from the completion date for each activity. Finally we use the "Summarize" command to calculate an average value for each activity type (Fig. 7-30). This is what we set out to find – for each blue button that we use, what's the average time between its creation and user completion?

Fig. 7-30: We used MercuryEdge to calculate an average "time to completion" for activity types that we use.

These kinds of reports are creative solutions. As a TMS manager, you have access to report formats and analytical tools to create your own questions about performance of the system.

Chapter Discussion

1. What is the advantage of having a designed workflow and an arranged sequence of "blue buttons" for users of the TMS system?
2. When would it be better to use highly specialized workflows by user function, as opposed to a general workflow that all users would use?

Chapter 8: Visibility of Loads in Transit

From booking a load until the point of delivery, we have a vital interest in keeping track of the load's status and location.

Was it picked up on schedule, and if not, what do we do about it? Is it moving as expected? What is the last thing we know? Have we learned of any change, delay or situation that requires action?

Historically in our business we've progressed from having from little or no visibility in transit to a system of status messages, call checks and loads that keep us updated on appointments, pickups, events and locations. We also can track loads automatically via cell phone and GPS technology by various commercial services.

Upon arrival and delivery of a load, we'll also see how to record Proof of Delivery, an important step usually required by customers, and usually necessary for triggering the invoicing process.

Status Messages

A status message is a standard record attached to a load that represents a report about the load, such as an appointment, pickup or delivery message.

Status messages are created in the TMS different ways:

- Automatically upon receipt of a standard EDI 214 (electronic) message from a carrier.
- By a carrier-user who is logged into the TMS, updating loads on behalf of the carrier.
- By an internal TMS user, updating loads in the system based on information provided by the carrier.

Each status message has a code that relates to a list of options declared in the enterprise's code table. Here's a typical list:

A - Arrived
A1 - Departed Shipper
A3 - Shipment Returned to Shipper

A5 - Unable to Locate
A7 - Refused by Consignee
A9 - Shipment Damaged
AA - Pickup Appointment Date/Time
AB - Delivery Appointment Date/Time
AD - Delivery Appointment Scheduled
AF - Actual Pickup
AG - Estimated Delivery
AH - Attempted Delivery
AI - Shipment has been Reconsigned
AJ - Tendered for Delivery
AM - Loaded on Truck
AN - Diverted to Air Carrier
AP - Delivery Not Completed
AR - Rail Arrival at Destination Intermodal Ramp
AV - Available for Delivery
AW - Past Cut-Off Time
B - Damaged
B2 - Trap for Customer
B6 - Estimated to Arrive at Carrier Terminal
BA - Connecting Line or Cartage Pick-up
BC - Storage in Transit
BH - Insufficient Time to Complete Delivery
BI - Cartage Agent
BS - Refused by Customer
C1 - Estimated to Depart Terminal Location
CA - Shipment Cancelled
CD - Carrier Departed Delivery Location
CL - Trailer Closed Out
CP - Completed Loading at Pick-up Location
D1 - Completed Unloading at Delivery Location
E - Estimated to Arrive (En Route)
HB - Held - Refused
HC - Held - Consignee closed
HD - Held - Refused Shipment
I1 - In-Gate
J - Delivered to Connecting Line
J1 - Delivered to Connecting Line
K - Customs
K1 - Arrived at Customs
L - Loading
L1 - Loading
NS - Normal Status

OA - Out-Gate
OO - Paperwork Received
P - Departure From Location
P1 - Departed Terminal Location
PR - U.S. Customs Hold at In-Bound Location
R1 - Received from Prior Carrier
RB - Delivery Appointment Requested
RL - Rail Departure from Origin Intermodal Ramp
S1 - Trailer Spotted at Consignee
SD - Shipment Delayed
T - At Terminal; Intra-Terminal Movement
WE - Weather Prevented Movement
X1 - Arrived at Delivery Location
X2 - Estimated Date and/or Time of Arrival
      at Consignees Location
X3 - Arrived at Pick-up Location
X4 - Arrived at Terminal Location
X5 - Arrived at Delivery Location
X6 - En Route to Delivery Location
X8 - Arrived at Pick-up Location Loading Dock
X9 - Delivery Appointment Secured
XB - Shipment Acknowledged

Among the most commonly used are X3 (arrived at pick-up location), AF (pickup complete), X1 (arrived at delivery location), and D1 (delivery complete).

The receipt of an AF status message automatically changes a TMS load status from "Booked" to "In Transit," and a D1 message changes it from "In Transit" to "Delivered." (Which message codes are treated as arrival and departure messages can be overridden in the code table.)

Furthermore, the receipt of status message can be used as the basis of a dynamic ruleset in the TMS to add a new blue-button activity or perform some other desired function.

Status messages can be viewed in the "Tracking Messages" section of a load expanded on a load board (Fig. 8-1):

Tracking Messages			
Date	Type	Details	Location
05/16/2015 02:29	E	Estimated to Arrive (En Route)	St. Petersburg, FL
05/15/2015 18:30	D1	Completed Unloading at Deliver...	St. Petersburg, FL
05/15/2015 01:00	AF	Actual Pickup	Saluda, NC

Fig. 8-1: Tracking messages displayed in one of the expandable sections of a load on a load board.

… or on the "Tracking" tab of a load list screen detail window (Fig. 8-2):

Fig. 8-2: Tracking messages also are viewable on the "Tracking" tab of a load detail screen.

Status messages can be added manually from a load's plan window by clicking the "Status" hotspot (Fig. 8-3).

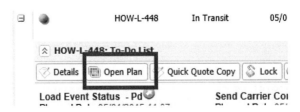

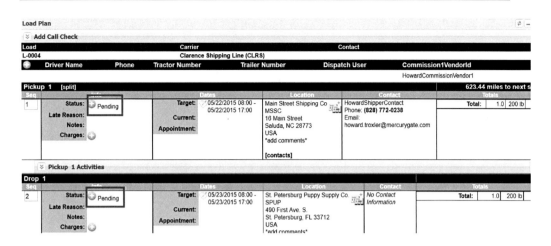

Fig. 8-3: Click the load's "Open Plan" button, then in the plan window, click the plus sign next to a stop status to add a status message about that stop.

Clicking the link opens an "Add Status Message" window. The user chooses the message code from a dropdown menu, then chooses the time of the message entry. The system can be set up to require the user to enter a reason if the message is being entered behind schedule (Fig. 8-4).

Add Status Message	
Drop	490 First Ave. S. St. Petersburg, FL
SCAC	**SIMO** (Simone Trucking Inc) **[Choose Carrier] [Enter SCAC]**
PRO	0909090909
Message	D1 - Completed Unloading at Delivery Location ⌄
Date	⌄
Additional Reference	
Reference #1	CarReqDoc ⌄
Save Options	
Add Another	☐
	SAVE CANCEL

Fig. 8-4: 'Add Status Message' window.

Status messages also can be added from the event-related sections of a load expanded on a load board:

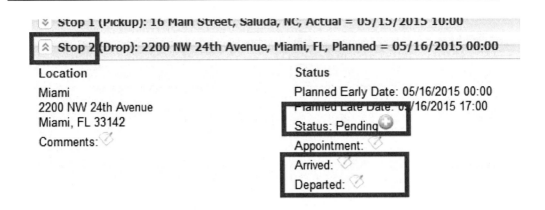

Fig. 8-5: Ability to update status from an event section in an expanded load on a load board.

A driver using the TMS Mobile application can enter a status message via smartphone (Fig. 8-6, 8-7):

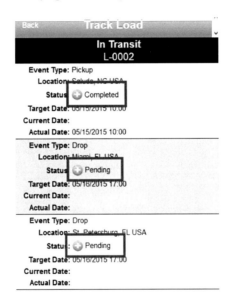

Fig. 8-6: TMS Mobile user screen with ability to enter status messages for a stop.

Fig. 8-7: TMS Mobile user screen for entering status message.

Based on arrival and departure status messages, the TMS enterprise's ETA calculator sets a "hot load" or "hot route" warning as needed. Arrival and departure messages also are used to trigger an "Authorize Detention" blue button if needed.

Call Checks

A <u>call check</u> is added to a load to show the carrier's location at a precise point in time. Either we have contacted the carrier/driver for this information and enter it manually, or the carrier or driver has sent it to the system by a manual or automatic process.

Depending on business practices, call checks might be made for a load on a regularly scheduled basis. The system can be set up to generate a "Call Check" blue button (using a scheduled report) to remind the user a check is needed.

While status messages and call checks are displayed separately, they are related in general purpose. In fact, the system can be set up to create a status message as well when a call check is created.

Creating & Viewing

Call checks can be created by users from the "Details" section of a load expanded on a load board, or from the "Plan" or "Call Check" tab of a load details window. The user enters the information into a simple screen showing time and location (Fig. 8-8):

Information	
Type:	Status Check
Date:	05/01/2015 11 : 30
City:	
State:	
Postal Code:	
Country:	USA
Geo Location:	Latitude: Longitude:

Save

Fig. 8-8: Call check entry form.

Drivers using the TMS Mobile application can enter a call check via their smartphone (Fig. 8-9):

TMS Mobile

Track Load

Call Check Load

Load Board

Reports

News and Events

Switch Company

Settings

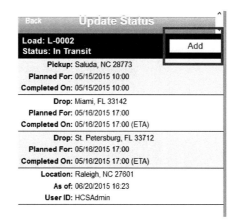

Fig. 8-9: Call check entry from mobile application.

Once created, call checks are listed in the load detail's "Call Check" tab. The latest check is displayed under the load's expanded "Details" section, with a plus-sign icon for updating (Fig. 8-10).

Fig. 8-10: Latest call check in load display, with add button.

Appointments, Arrivals, Departures

A TMS workflow can include blue buttons labeled "Set Appointment Time," "Set Arrival Time" and "Set Departure Time" for each stop on a load. These blue buttons open an Add Status Message window for the appropriate event (Fig. 8-11).

Set Arrival Time First Stop
Saluda NC
Planned Date:04/27/2015 07:00 EDT

Fig. 8-11: "Set Arrival Time" and "Set Departure Time" blue buttons open a status message window.

A different blue button used in some implementations is titled "Set Arrival/Departure." It opens a window that puts all these functions into a single interface for the user to record events for a stop (Fig. 8-12):

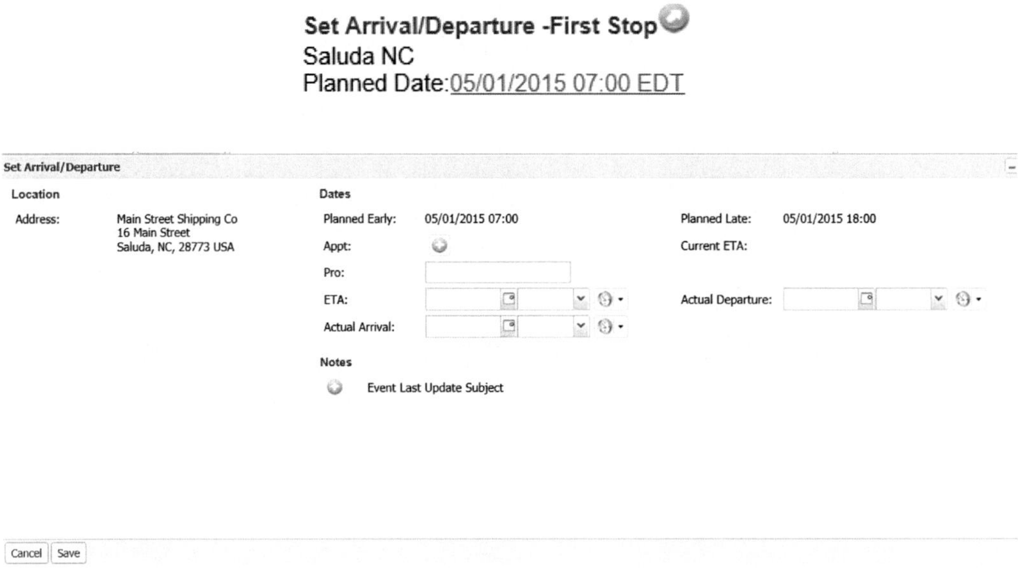

Fig. 8-12: "Set Arrival/Departure" window allows entry of all information for one stop.

The 'Set Arrival/Departure' screen allows the user to set an appointment time, an ETA, and actual arrival and departure times to the event record as needed. Status messages are added to the load.

Load Tracking Services

The TMS allows integration with various commercial load-tracking services. A separate customer agreement with the external service is required, as well as setup by MercuryGate's integration team.

With these services, drivers might enter arrival and departure messages via their smartphone, with the external service providing automatic call checks to the TMS on a regular basis.

If external load tracking is set up, TMS users can initiate it manually by clicking a button on the load's Plan tab, which takes the user to a login screen for the external service. However, the more common practice is to use a dynamic ruleset to request tracking automatically once a load has been dispatched.

The "Dispatch" blue button activity (which triggers external load tracking) is used to enter a driver's name and telephone number that will be used to track the load, along with other information (Fig. 8-13).

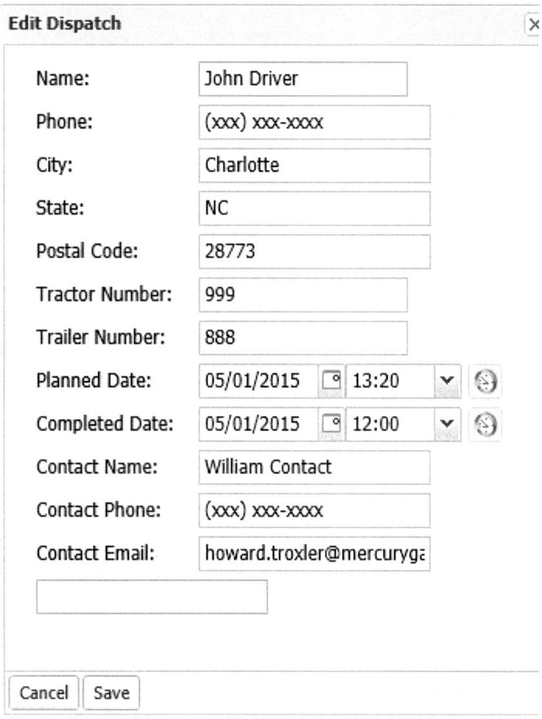

Edit Dispatch   ☒

Name:	John Driver
Phone:	(xxx) xxx-xxxx
City:	Charlotte
State:	NC
Postal Code:	28773
Tractor Number:	999
Trailer Number:	888
Planned Date:	05/01/2015 ▣ 13:20 ˅ ⊙
Completed Date:	05/01/2015 ▣ 12:00 ˅ ⊙
Contact Name:	William Contact
Contact Phone:	(xxx) xxx-xxxx
Contact Email:	howard.troxler@mercurygɑ

Cancel   Save

Fig. 8-13: Window opened by 'Dispatch' blue button.

Once load tracking is triggered, the driver receives information via text messages or smartphone app. The driver's responses via smartphone create status messages back in the TMS viewed in the "Tracking" section of an expanded load on a load board, or on the "Tracking" tab of a load detail window (Fig. 8-14).

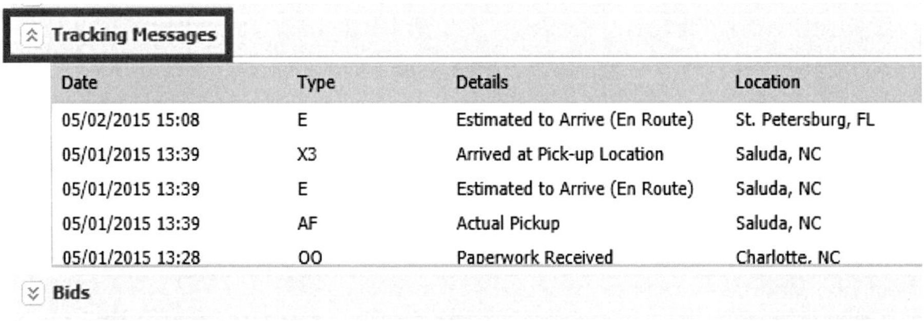

Tracking Messages

Date	Type	Details	Location
05/02/2015 15:08	E	Estimated to Arrive (En Route)	St. Petersburg, FL
05/01/2015 13:39	X3	Arrived at Pick-up Location	Saluda, NC
05/01/2015 13:39	E	Estimated to Arrive (En Route)	Saluda, NC
05/01/2015 13:39	AF	Actual Pickup	Saluda, NC
05/01/2015 13:28	OO	Paperwork Received	Charlotte, NC

Bids

Fig. 8-14: Status messages received via load tracking service.

The external service also might send automatic call checks at configured intervals, which are then visible on the "Call Check" tab of the load's details window (Fig. 8-15):

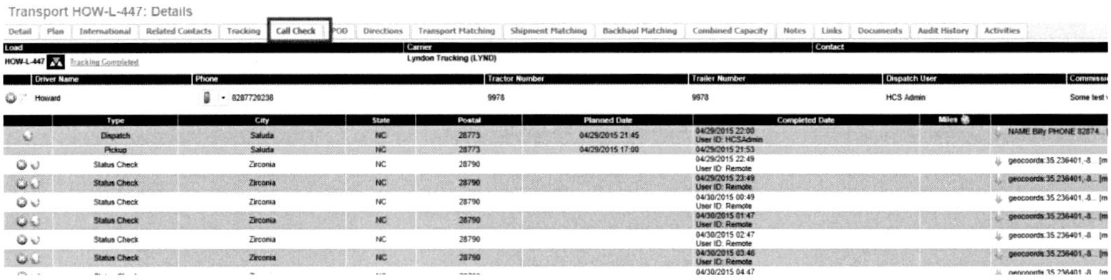

Fig. 8-15: Call checks generated by external load-tracking service.

Finally, some newer tracking technology relies on tracking devices installed directly on carrier equipment, instead of being based on driver interaction. These services detect when the load has gone in transit, automatically calculate distance and ETA, and recognize when the load has reached the delivery.

Proof of Delivery

The receipt of a delivery status message automatically moves the status of a TMS load to "Delivered." In a typical workflow, an important step remains – the addition of a Proof of Delivery, or "POD" (usually produced "pee-oh-dee," not "pod"). Quite often a customer insists on a POD as a condition of paying the bill.

A POD typically is the uploaded image of a document or signature. When a load moves to "Delivered" status, the load gets a blue button (via dynamic ruleset triggered by the status change) that is labeled "Add POD."

Clicking the button opens the load's Documents tab, with an icon (the green plus sign) for adding a document from the local system or device (Fig. 8-16):

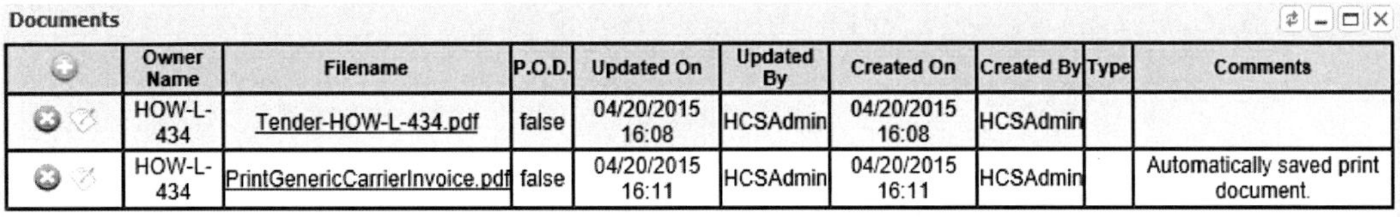

	Owner Name	Filename	P.O.D.	Updated On	Updated By	Created On	Created By	Type	Comments
⊗ ✎	HOW-L-434	Tender-HOW-L-434.pdf	false	04/20/2015 16:08	HCSAdmin	04/20/2015 16:08	HCSAdmin		
⊗ ✎	HOW-L-434	PrintGenericCarrierInvoice.pdf	false	04/20/2015 16:11	HCSAdmin	04/20/2015 16:11	HCSAdmin		Automatically saved print document.

Fig. 8-16: 'Add POD' blue button opens the load's list of existing documents, with the ability to upload an image of the proof of delivery.

Clicking the add icon (green plus sign) opens a window for selecting a file and specifying its type (Fig. 8-17):

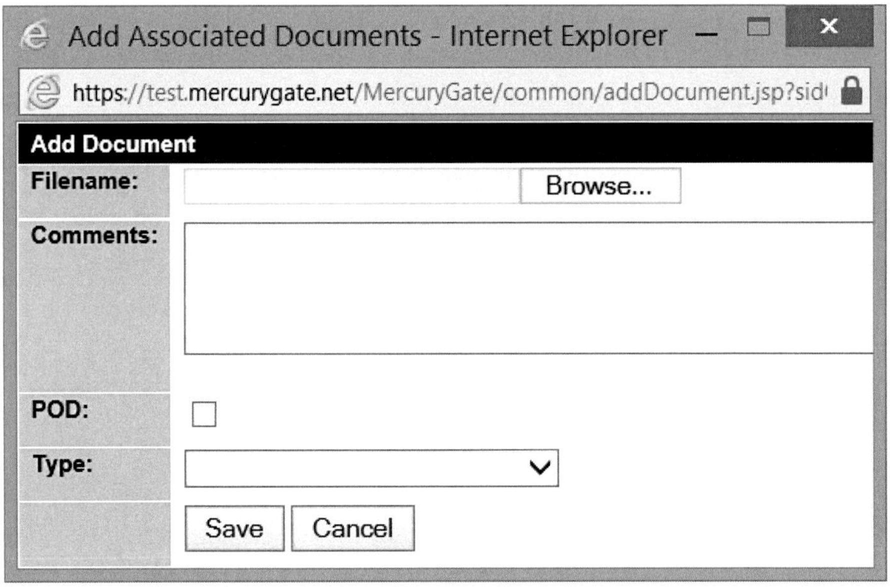

Fig. 8-17: Window for uploading a file to the load. For a proof of delivery, check the "POD" checkbox.

Use the "Browse" button to select a file from the local system, and enter optional comments to be displayed in the document list.

The "POD" checkbox tells the system this document is intended as a Proof of Delivery. When it is checked, the window also displays the option for associating this document with a specific stop (for example, if uploading multiple PODs for multiple drops – Fig. 8-18).

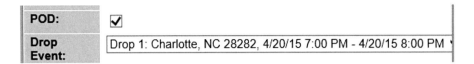

Fig. 8-18: Option to associate a POD with a specific drop.

Lastly, in the upload dialog select a document <u>type</u> from the list of types used by the enterprise. Typically there is a "POD" document type.

PODs also can be added from the TMS Mobile application. After a delivery status message has been added, the user has the opportunity to add Proof of Delivery information, such as the image of a document or a signature (Fig. 8-19):

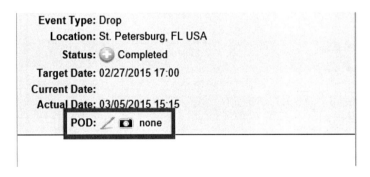

Fig. 8-19: Mobile app user records delivery, now is able to upload POD.

Clicking the "pencil" icon opens a window for adding a signature (Fig. 8-20):

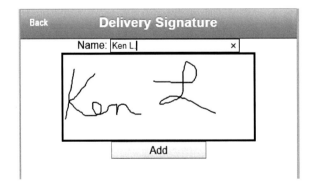

Fig. 8-20: POD signature entered directly on mobile device.

Clicking the "camera" icon allows the user to capture an image of the POD document with the smartphone, or choose an existing image file for upload.

With the addition of a POD, the workflow is finished on the execution side and the load drops off the load board. The action now moves to the invoicing side, and the invoices portlet.

Chapter 9: Managing and Disputing Invoices

It would be nice to say that after a load gets delivered, the rest is automatic. You get a bill from your carrier. You send a bill to your customer. Everybody gets paid. Everybody is happy.

That would be nice to say. But it would not be true. The truth is that you must be responsible for the active management of the invoicing process – both the invoices that you send, and the ones you expect to get.

If you are passive about managing invoices in the logistics industry, you will suffer. It's that simple. That's not necessarily because of dishonesty (although there is some here and there). It's just the world can be clumsy, complicated, manual, and filled with errors – and in your business, you are the one on the hook for it.

Whether you're dealing with just a few carriers, or with thousands, there will be times that:

- They didn't send the bill. But you were supposed to pay it anyway.
- They sent it electronically but it vanished.
- They sent it by mail and somebody threw it away.
- They sent it by email and somebody deleted it.
- They sent it but you forgot to pay it.
- They sent it but it got marked it as paid.
- They sent it, you paid it -- and then they sent it again.
- They sent it. Then they sent another one. Then they sent another one.
- They sent it. Then they sent one with entirely different charges.
- They sent it. But it's for a load you never moved.

The list goes on. And that's just the carrier, accounts-payable side. In some businesses, the customer/accounts-receivable side doesn't even kick in until the carrier invoice is approved. What happens if it never gets approved, or falls through the cracks? You might not have a true picture either of payables or receivables.

Even in our digital age, the invoicing and settlement side of the logistics industry sometimes remains surprisingly inaccurate, with the absence of strong audit and reporting.

'Freight Bill Audit'

The process of putting our carrier invoices through tests for accuracy is known as "freight bill audit." We need to know that what we're getting billed is reasonably related to what we expected to pay, based on the rates on the load.

In the MercuryGate TMS, all newly created invoices automatically go through a screening process that flags invoices for further inspection as needed. These tests include:

- Whether the invoice matches a known load.
- Whether the invoice is a duplicate or additional invoice for the same load.
- Whether the charges are within a certain tolerance range compared to expected rates.

Invoices that fail any of these tests are flagged for review. In the TMS, that means they are assigned a user blue-button activity labeled "Audit Invoice" (Fig. 9-1). A typical report in the invoices window shows all invoices with a pending "audit" activity.

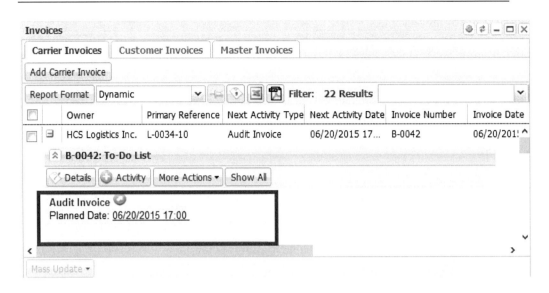

Fig. 9-1: Carrier invoice flagged by the system with an 'Audit Invoice' blue button.

Users clicking the "Audit Invoice" button open a screen to review the invoice charges and compare them against the expected rates. They can approve, reject or dispute the invoice with the carrier. We'll look at the audit screen in a bit.

We also can require, as a condition of approval, that we have received certain required documents. It's a common requirement of many businesses that they see a proof of delivery (POD) with the invoice.

Finally, once an invoice is approved, it is marked in the TMS as ready to be extracted to the client's external accounting system. (The TMS does a lot of things well, but it is not intended to be a full-scale accounting system.)

Let's take a closer look at the steps of the freight-bill audit process.

Unmatched invoices

Carrier invoices are created by a variety of methods: by electronic message, by import from an external system, or by manual user entry (as from the receipt of an email or a paper invoice).

One of the first steps is to make sure we really owe the money. It's possible – even common – to receive "unmatched" invoices that do not correspond to a known load.

When a carrier invoice is created in the TMS, the first thing the system does automatically is determine whether the invoice is matched to an existing load. If the invoice is unmatched, it will be up to a user to find (or create) a match eventually, or to dispute or reject the invoice.

Carrier invoice records have a field named "Matched," automatically set to true or false, which can be viewed in reports:

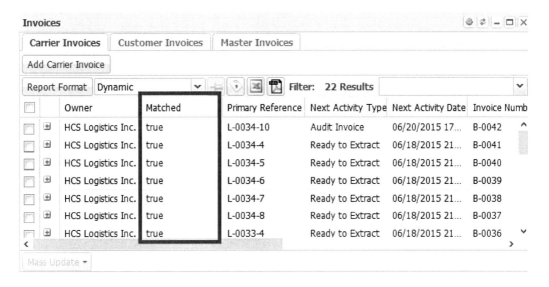

Fig. 9-2: 'Matched' field available in invoice report format.

The system searches based on a combination of the carrier's SCAC code and an identifying number that exists on both the load and the invoice.

Unmatched - Manual Creation

Users can deliberately create unmatched invoices from the TMS menu (Edit > Add > Unmatched Invoice), or from the "Add Carrier Invoice" button in the invoice portlet. This might be the case when users are entering a paper invoice for a load that does not exist yet in the system and we expect to match later.

Unmatched invoices created this way are placed on "dummy" loads in the TMS with their own primary reference numbers. Once an invoice is matched, it moves from the dummy load to its true owning load.

Matching

We have two options for matching an unmatched invoice:

- Using a "Find Match" blue-button activity that has been created automatically on the invoice.
- Using the "Match Invoice" mass-update option from the invoices portlet, which a user can select any time.

A dynamic ruleset places a "Find Match" activity on an unmatched invoice. The button will appear in the expanded invoice detail in the invoices portlet:

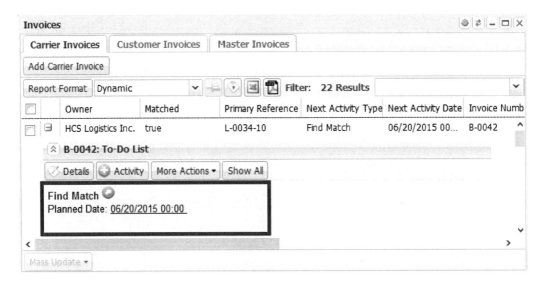

Fig. 9-3: Unmatched invoices are assigned a 'Find Match' blue button by the system.

Clicking the 'Find Match' button opens a window to look for potentially matching loads. The window opens with a filter with existing values from our invoice such as carrier SCAC, origin, or destination. We can search for loads that share these values to look for the match.

The result is a list of potentially matching loads (Fig. 9-4). Selecting a load in the list matches it with the invoice. (The default load report is just a list of load numbers – use the "Report Format" button to display more fields to help identify the right load.)

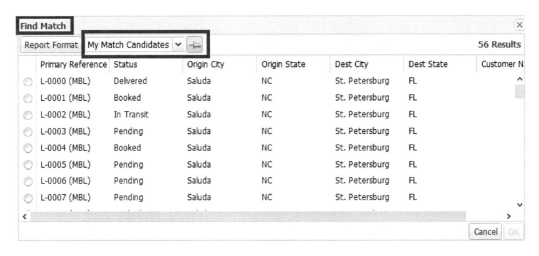

Fig. 9-4: Result of a load search from the 'Find Match' invoice blue button. Choose a load from the list to match it with the invoice. Notice the load list report format – this report shows additional information about origin and destination to help users identify the load.

Mass Update Option

Another way to match invoices to loads is the "Match Invoice" command from the mass-update menu of the invoice portlet. This command re-attempts the system matching previously tried, in the event that a matching load has since been created. If successful, the "Matched" field changes from false to true.

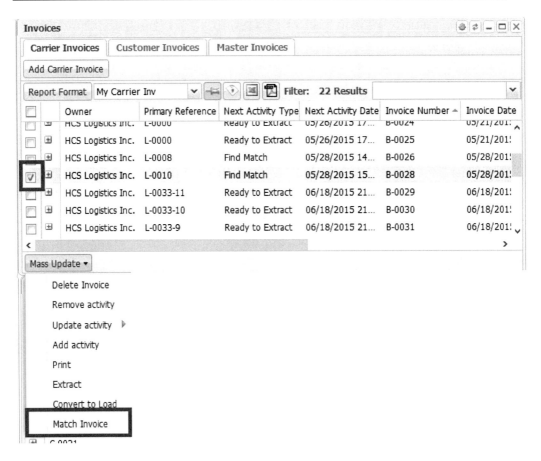

Fig. 9-5: The 'Match Invoice' command from the portlet's mass-update menu will run against any invoices in the portlet that have been selected by their left-hand checkbox.

Create Load from Unmatched

Yet another option for dealing with unmatched carrier invoices is simply to create loads that match them. After all, the invoice already tells us most of what we need to know to create a load - freight, origin, destination, dates and carrier. Doing it this way means we assume that we really did move the load and owe the money. But some TMS clients routinely create their loads off the receipt of carrier invoices.

From a list of unmatched carrier invoices, we use the mass update option "Convert to Load" for all unmatched carrier invoices that we have selected from the list (Fig. 9-6):

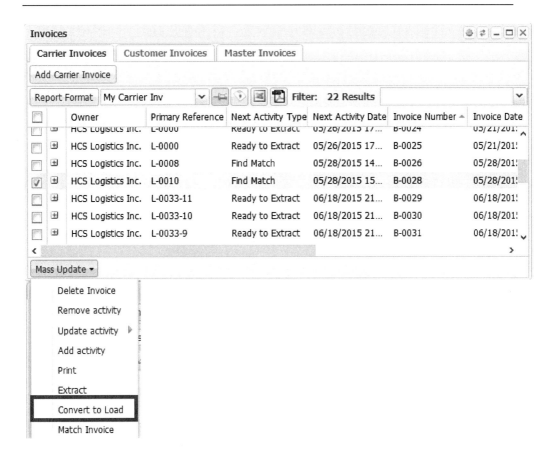

Fig. 9-6: Mass-update command to convert the selected unmatched invoices to a load.

Next Step: Duplicate Check

After determining an invoice's matched or unmatched status, the TMS usually is set up to test for whether a new carrier invoice is a duplicate or a second invoice on the same load.

A duplicate invoice is an exact copy (or close enough, according to system settings) of an invoice that we already have. We don't owe the same money twice, so we need to cancel, dispute, or otherwise deal with the duplicate.

A second or multiple invoice (usually just called a "second invoice") is an invoice for a load that already has at least one invoice. Maybe an additional charge came in late. But we want to make sure that we really owe it, and again that we're not paying the same charges twice.

Invoices that fail these tests are automatically assigned an "Audit Duplicate" or "Audit 2nd Invoice" blue button activity in the invoices portlet. Both blue buttons open a version of the audit screen that we'll learn about in a bit.

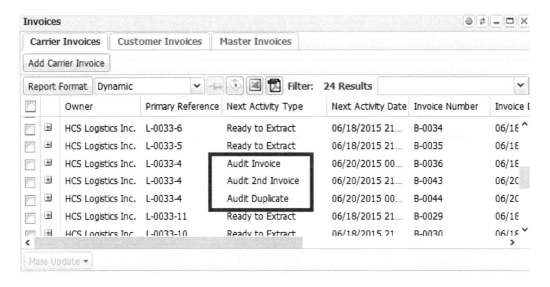

Fig. 9-7: We have three carrier invoices for the same load. The extra invoices have been assigned activities of "Audit Duplicate" and "Audit 2nd Invoice" by the system.

Next Step: Tolerance Check

If an invoice is matched to a known load, and if it has not been flagged as a duplicate or second invoice, next we test to make sure its charges are within acceptable limits.

This step is known as a tolerance check. "Tolerance" means that we will accept charges as long as they do not vary from expected rates by more than a certain amount or percentage, according to system settings.

If the invoice charges are too different from the expected rates then an "Audit Invoice" activity/blue button is placed on the invoice for us to handle.

Audit Process

Auditing an invoice means opening a window to compare its charges against expected rates. Users can approve or reject invoices, or dispute their charges.

Clicking any of the audit blue buttons opens a user screen for viewing invoice charges and acting upon them. Depending on various settings, a user may:

- Approve the invoice.
- Approve the invoice and allocate its charges (share them across customer shipment/loads).
- Open a dispute process with the carrier.
- Reject the invoice outright.
- Reject the invoice and create a new one.
- Re-rate the invoice, if its rates came from a contract rating.
- Request a review of the contract used to rate the load.
- Cancel the invoice.
- Cancel the invoice and create a new one.
- Close the window, leaving the audit pending.

System settings determine which load statuses (Rated, Booked, In Transit, Delivered, etc.) allow an invoice to be audited, and also defines what happens after the audit step is completed.

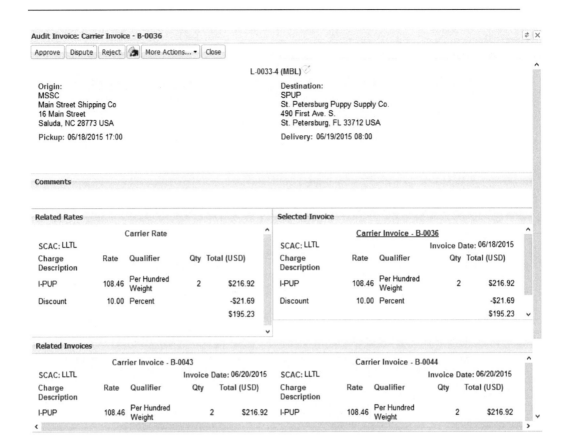

Fig. 9-8: Invoice audit screen. Users compare rates on the load to actual invoice amounts, and can compare the invoice being audited to any other invoices that exist for this load. Users can approve, reject, or dispute the invoice, among other actions.

About the audit screen:

- The top toolbar is visible only if the owning load is in a status that allows auditing, as determined by settings.
- The "Approve" and "Reject" buttons appear if the user's role permissions allow those actions.
- The "Dispute" button appears if a "dispute" activity has been named in the settings.
- The re-rate icon appears if the load's selected carrier pricesheet is a contract rate.
- Any pending contract-review activity is noted in the upper-right of the audit screen.
- For a consolidated invoice there may be several related rates.

- "Selected invoice" is the invoice that owns the blue button clicked.
- "Related Invoices" are of the same type (carrier / customer) owned by the same transport / shipment (but not the 'current' invoice you clicked).
- The "Comments" section, if enabled, displays comments added by users, along with a user id and timestamp.
- The collapsible "Dispute History" section contains a history of dispute messages (see dispute process below).

Audit Approval

Clicking the "Approve" button opens a window for selecting a reason and entering an optional comment (Fig. 9-9). Reason codes are an important part of the process. They help us understand why variations get approved.

Fig. 9-9: Window opened by 'Approve' button click in the invoice audit screen.

Depending on each company's processes, an invoice approved in the 'Audit Invoice' process might undergo re-rating from the audit screen or by dynamic ruleset. Your company also might require that an approved invoice go through a final audit by accounting ("Audit by Accounting" or "2nd Audit" are frequently used blue-button names).

Lastly, the invoice might move to an "Approve Invoice" blue button, or even be set to be send to the external accounting system (see "Ready to Extract" section below).

Rejection

Rejecting the invoice from the "Audit Invoice" screen leaves the activity in "Rejected" status for manual handling. A "Rejected Invoice" activity and blue button might be assigned back to the audit-invoice screen for the next reviewing user. Again, assigning a reason code for the rejection is important.

'Dispute' Process

A "Dispute" button might be present as an option in the top toolbar of the audit screen. Clicking "Dispute" creates a dispute activity on the invoice and opens a window for editing a message, with a reason code and a comment/message field.

For each dispute message, a document is created and attached to the record of the dispute activity in the system.

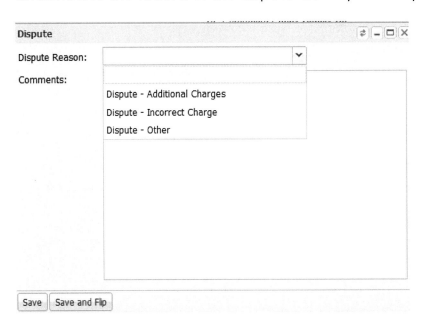

Fig. 9-10: Window opened by 'Dispute' button for specifying a reason and entering optional comments. The user can save the record for further editing, or 'flip' it to a carrier user logging into the system to handle disputes.

Users can edit their comments until the "Save and Flip" button is clicked to turn the dispute process over to a carrier/customer user for response via their own portlet. This assumes that carrier-users have been set up with TMS logins and assigned portlets. The history of the dispute and comments is available as an expandable section of the audit screen (Fig. 9-11).

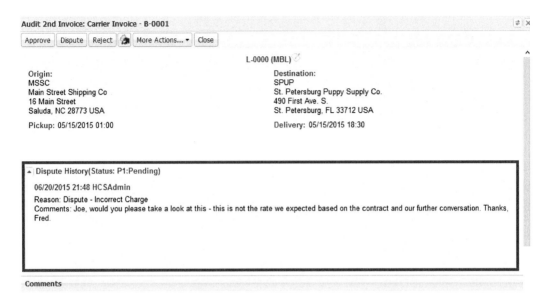

Fig. 9-11: Dispute history displayed as an expandable/collapsible section in the invoice audit screen.

Following the carrier user's response, the user may cancel and reject the carrier invoice, changing the status of the Dispute activity to complete, and potentially requiring the carrier to re-submit. As an alternative to canceling the invoice, the user may click the Dispute button anew.

Instead of trading dispute comments with a carrier, a company also might be set up simply to have an invoice report named "Dispute Invoice" with a list of all invoices with a dispute blue-button activity, intended for a user's manual handling. This might be the case when a TMS client does not provide TMS logins to its carriers.

'Review Contract' Process

From the audit screen, a user also can request a supervisor review of the underlying contract (if the rate is a contract rate) by selecting "Review Contract" from the "More Actions" menu. Once a review activity has been created, the activity and its status are noted in the upper-right corner of the audit window:

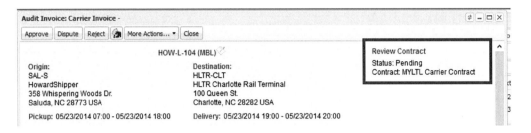

Fig. 9-12: User is notified of a pending 'Review Contract' activity in the invoice audit window.

'Approve Invoice'

To reach the approval stage, an invoice either has passed all its automatic tests (match, duplicate check, tolerance check), or a user has approved it in an audit screen. At this point an "Approve Invoice" activity/blue button might be placed on an invoice. Or your company might move it directly to a "Ready to Extract" activity – see that section below.

Validation Process

We mentioned earlier that a TMS client or customer might require certain documents such as a proof of delivery or bill of lading, with the invoice. In the TMS we can test to make sure those documents have been received and attached to the record before sending.

If any required data is missing, the user sees a "Ready to Extract" blue button on the invoice that has a status of "Missing Required Data." (You can click on the link of the blue button's planned date to inspect its status.)

The "Comments" section of the activity window tells you which kinds of documents or references are missing:

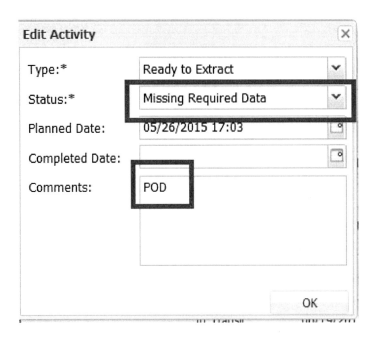

Fig. 9-13: One of the loads related to this invoice is missing a required proof of delivery.

Your company setup might allow you to add any missing documents or data later once you get them, triggering a new check. If successful, the "Ready to Extract" activity now is placed in "Pending" status - the invoice is ready to be extracted.

Ready to Extract/Extract Process

When you see a "Ready to Extract" activity or blue button on an invoice in "Pending" status, it means the invoice is either:

(1) Waiting to be sent automatically to the accounting system at the next scheduled interval, or
(2) Ready to be sent manually by a user.

An <u>extract</u> is the transmission of a TMS invoice to an external accounting system. Extracts can be performed manually by mass update from the invoice portlet, or automatically if the company is set up to do so. After extraction the "Ready to Extract" activity is automatically set to "Complete" status.

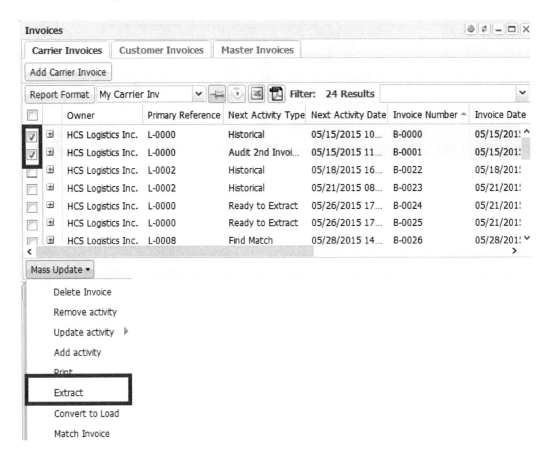

Fig. 9-14: Choosing "Extract" from the Mass Update menu sends the selected invoices to the external system.

Post-Extract

It is not good practice to change invoice values in the TMS after the invoice has been sent to the external system, without certain safeguards. System settings determine which editing actions, if any, can occur after extract.

In the invoice portlet, extracted invoices are marked with a red checkbox (Fig. 9-15):

Fig. 9-15: Detail of invoice portlet showing non-editable status of invoices already extracted.

Customer Invoices

So far we have talked mostly about carrier invoices on execution loads. <u>Customer</u> invoices instead belong to the records of shipments or customer loads in the system. The TMS handles customer invoices a little differently, because we might need to revisit them for customer disputes down the road.

An activity of type "Historical" simply means the invoice has been handled. Users might use a report of "Historical" activities just to find an invoice for a later customer credit. An activity of type "Credit" or "Credit and Rebill" might be placed on the invoice by the system, left in "Pending" status in case of a future credit or credit and rebill request by the customer.

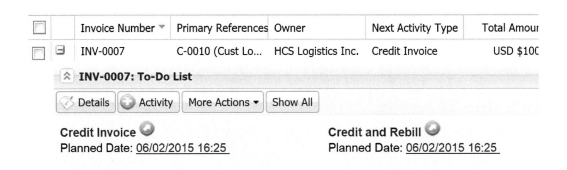

		Invoice Number ▼	Primary References	Owner	Next Activity Type	Total Amou
☐	⊟	INV-0007	C-0010 (Cust Lo...	HCS Logistics Inc.	Credit Invoice	USD $10C

⌃ **INV-0007: To-Do List**

[Details] [Activity] [More Actions ▼] [Show All]

Credit Invoice 🔵
Planned Date: 06/02/2015 16:25

Credit and Rebill 🔵
Planned Date: 06/02/2015 16:25

Fig. 9-16: Customer invoice with available "Credit Invoice" and "Credit and Rebill" blue buttons.

The "Credit Invoice" blue button uses a variation on the Audit Invoice screen, with the addition of a "Credit" button, and a dropdown menu of reasons for issuing the credit.

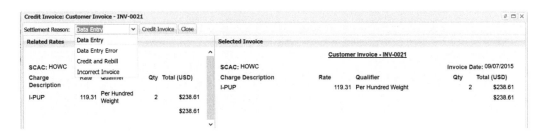

Fig. 9-17: Credit-invoice screen.

Clicking the "Credit Invoice" button generates a "reversal" invoice of the original amount, with a suffix of "R" added to the invoice number. Partial credits are not allowed – the correct practice is to reverse the invoice to be credited, and rebill.

A reference of type "Reversal Invoice" with a value of "true" is placed on the reversal invoice. A "Ready to Extract" activity in "Pending" status is created automatically on the reversal invoice. The reversal invoice therefore is captured in the next scheduled report and extracted.

After a credit invoice, both the original and reversal invoices are present on the shipment/customer load. The settlement reason field for the <u>original</u> invoice is set to "Credit and Rebill." The reason selected for the credit is stored as a reference on the original invoice as well.

Margins

A margin is the difference between customer rates (or invoices) and carrier rates (or invoices). Margins are needed to calculate commissions for agents. A margin column is available in report formats.

System settings determine how margins are calculated. Business practice varies widely as to what is included or excluded. Some businesses calculate margins based on rates, and others wait to calculate margins based on actual invoices.

Margins can be calculated for an overall TMS route across its related loads. Because a route can involve execution and customer loads in different stages of the process, a route financial can consist of "blended" information between rates and invoices.

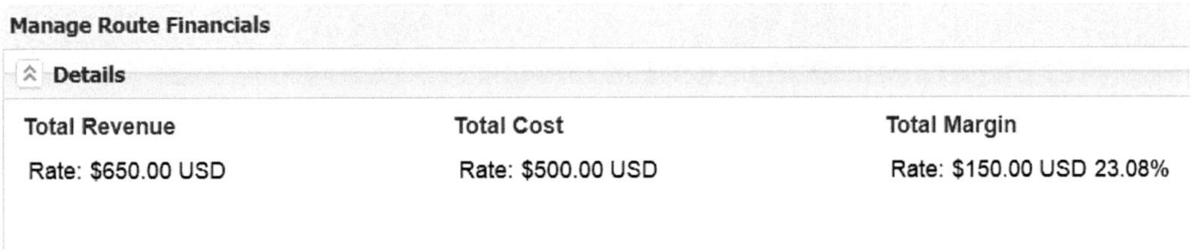

Manage Route Financials		
☆ Details		
Total Revenue	Total Cost	Total Margin
Rate: $650.00 USD	Rate: $500.00 USD	Rate: $150.00 USD 23.08%

Fig. 9-18: 'Manage Route Financials' window opened from a route record.

Margin will not calculate if certain information is missing, such as rates or invoices for all legs. Margin calculations also require the use of a "normalized currency" in system settings to create apples-to-apples calculations. If the margin calculation fails, an activity of type "Margin Issue" will be created, and the summary section of this activity will contain an error message.

Commissions

Up to four sales or agent commissions can be generated on a load if the system is set up to do it. The payment of commissions to agents for procuring a load is common in the brokerage environment.

Commissions are created automatically by dynamic ruleset, or by user click of a blue button. Commissions can be generated on a customer load, on an execution load, or both. If they are generated on a customer load, the action also will generate any commissions for its related execution load.

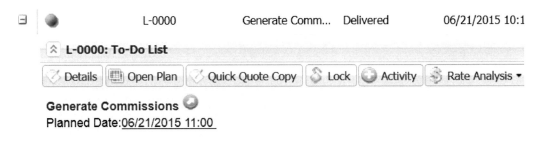

Fig. 9-19: 'Generate Commissions' blue button.

Using commissions requires several system settings and a margin for the load that can be calculated. Clicking the "Generate Commissions" blue button automatically calculates a new margin. If the commissions invoice generation fails, an activity of type "Commission Issue" will be created, and the summary section of this activity will contain an error message.

MercuryEdge and Invoice Audit

One of MercuryGate's other, downloadable applications is named MercuryEdge. It is a spreadsheet-style application that can be used to conduct further analysis on TMS data. For basics on installation and usage, see the textbook appendix.

One possible use of MercuryEdge is to look for open settlement liability, or simply loads for which invoices were never received. In MercuryEdge, this is simple enough: Open a load report for the specified period, open a carrier invoice report, merge them on primary reference and tell the application to keep rows without a match – that's what we're looking for.

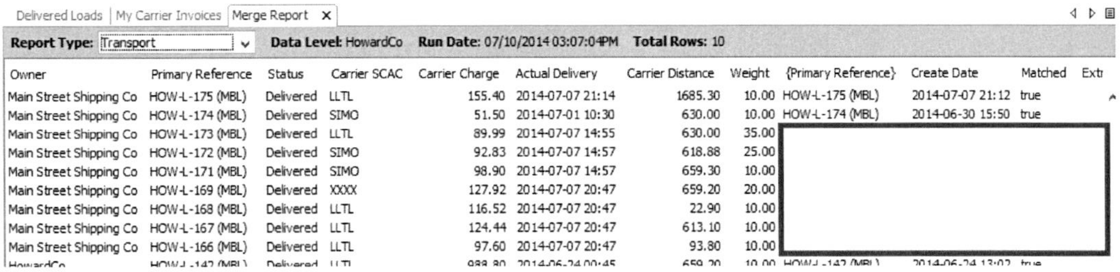

Delivered Loads | My Carrier Invoices | Merge Report ×

Report Type: Transport **Data Level:** HowardCo **Run Date:** 07/10/2014 03:07:04PM **Total Rows:** 10

Owner	Primary Reference	Status	Carrier SCAC	Carrier Charge	Actual Delivery	Carrier Distance	Weight	{Primary Reference}	Create Date	Matched	Extr
Main Street Shipping Co	HOW-L-175 (MBL)	Delivered	LLTL	155.40	2014-07-07 21:14	1685.30	10.00	HOW-L-175 (MBL)	2014-07-07 21:12	true	
Main Street Shipping Co	HOW-L-174 (MBL)	Delivered	SIMO	51.50	2014-07-01 10:30	630.00	10.00	HOW-L-174 (MBL)	2014-06-30 15:50	true	
Main Street Shipping Co	HOW-L-173 (MBL)	Delivered	LLTL	89.99	2014-07-07 14:55	630.00	35.00				
Main Street Shipping Co	HOW-L-172 (MBL)	Delivered	SIMO	92.83	2014-07-07 14:57	618.88	25.00				
Main Street Shipping Co	HOW-L-171 (MBL)	Delivered	SIMO	98.90	2014-07-07 14:57	659.30	10.00				
Main Street Shipping Co	HOW-L-169 (MBL)	Delivered	XXXX	127.92	2014-07-07 20:47	659.20	20.00				
Main Street Shipping Co	HOW-L-168 (MBL)	Delivered	LLTL	116.52	2014-07-07 20:47	22.90	10.00				
Main Street Shipping Co	HOW-L-167 (MBL)	Delivered	LLTL	124.44	2014-07-07 20:47	613.10	10.00				
Main Street Shipping Co	HOW-L-166 (MBL)	Delivered	LLTL	97.60	2014-07-07 20:47	93.80	10.00				
HowardCo	HOW-L-142 (MBL)	Delivered	LLTL	988.80	2014-06-24 00:45	659.20	10.00	HOW-L-142 (MBL)	2014-06-24 13:02	true	

Fig. 9-20: Where are the invoices for these long-delivered loads?

Another example is the use of MercuryEdge to identify "rogue spend," or unauthorized carrier spend on a non-contract basis.

The process is similar – open a list of loads for the target period, making sure the report includes the carrier SCAC for each load. Now open a contract report that also includes carrier SCAC and merge your two reports, again keeping the unmatched rows – those are the ones we're looking for.

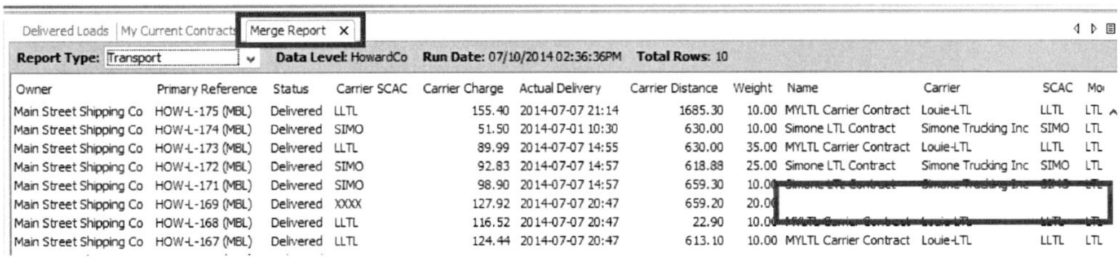

Delivered Loads | My Current Contracts | Merge Report ×

Report Type: Transport **Data Level:** HowardCo **Run Date:** 07/10/2014 02:36:36PM **Total Rows:** 10

Owner	Primary Reference	Status	Carrier SCAC	Carrier Charge	Actual Delivery	Carrier Distance	Weight	Name	Carrier	SCAC	Mo
Main Street Shipping Co	HOW-L-175 (MBL)	Delivered	LLTL	155.40	2014-07-07 21:14	1685.30	10.00	MYLTL Carrier Contract	Louie-LTL	LLTL	LTL
Main Street Shipping Co	HOW-L-174 (MBL)	Delivered	SIMO	51.50	2014-07-01 10:30	630.00	10.00	Simone LTL Contract	Simone Trucking Inc	SIMO	LTL
Main Street Shipping Co	HOW-L-173 (MBL)	Delivered	LLTL	89.99	2014-07-07 14:55	630.00	35.00	MYLTL Carrier Contract	Louie-LTL	LLTL	LTL
Main Street Shipping Co	HOW-L-172 (MBL)	Delivered	SIMO	92.83	2014-07-07 14:57	618.88	25.00	Simone LTL Contract	Simone Trucking Inc	SIMO	LTL
Main Street Shipping Co	HOW-L-171 (MBL)	Delivered	SIMO	98.90	2014-07-07 14:57	659.30	10.00	Simone LTL Contract	Simone Trucking Inc	SIMO	LTL
Main Street Shipping Co	HOW-L-169 (MBL)	Delivered	XXXX	127.92	2014-07-07 20:47	659.20	20.00				
Main Street Shipping Co	HOW-L-168 (MBL)	Delivered	LLTL	116.52	2014-07-07 20:47	22.90	10.00	MYLTL Carrier Contract	Louie-LTL	LLTL	LTL
Main Street Shipping Co	HOW-L-167 (MBL)	Delivered	LLTL	124.44	2014-07-07 20:47	613.10	10.00	MYLTL Carrier Contract	Louie-LTL	LLTL	LTL

Fig. 9-21: No contract for the carrier that got this load. Why?

For further analysis you could use MercuryEdge to re-rate these "rogue" loads to determine the least-cost contract rating in effect at the time, and find out whether such loads are costing you or saving you money.

For more usage examples and instruction on using MercuryEdge, consult the appendix and the <u>*MercuryEdge User Manual*</u>.

Chapter Discussion

(1) Why is aggressive management of invoicing on both the carrier (payable) and customer (receivable) side so important for a logistics services provider?

(2) Why is invoicing more complicated than just getting a bill and paying it, as we are used to doing in our own daily lives?

(3) What are some of the most common dangers in invoicing, and what kinds of steps can we take to protect ourselves?

(4) Why is it a bad idea to allow further editing to invoices once they have been sent to the external accounting system?

Chapter 10: Rewarding Your Best Carriers

In the invoicing chapter we stressed the importance of active, aggressive management of invoices. In this chapter we'll stress the importance of active management of carriers and carrier records.

For a logistics provider, carriers are not just entries in a static list, to be entered once and thereafter taken for granted. Carrier records are a living, ever-changing database that requires constant vigilance and instant response. As just one example, if a carrier's insurance expires at midnight, we need to know about it before we tender even one more load.

And as we saw in the "Finding Capacity" chapter, one of our goals should be to reward our "best" carriers with our loads – not out of the goodness of our hearts, but because our best carriers give us the best chance to do our best business.

In this chapter we'll take a look at some carrier records management, then devote ourselves to answering two questions:

(1) How do I identify my "best" carriers?
(2) What kinds of things can I do with that knowledge?

Basic Carrier Records

Carrier records in the TMS, which contain basic information, are adequate for many clients. You can see a list of your carriers from the toolbar "Carrier" icon, or from the menu: View > Rating > Carriers. From the resulting carrier list, click the carrier's details icon (the "piece of paper" icon) to open a carrier record.

All			Name	SCAC		Modes
☐	📄	🐾	Lyndon Trucking	LYND	TL, Truckload	
☐	📄	🐾	Louie-LTL	LLTL	LTL	
☐	📄	🐾	Delta	DL	Air	
☐	📄	🐾	HLT Railway	HLTR	Rail	
☐	📄	🐾	Howard Nationwide Drayage	HDRY	Drayage	
☐	📄	🐾	HowardCo	HOWC	Drayage, Intermodal, LTL, Rail, TL	
☐	📄	🐾	GLS Carrier	GLSC	LTL	
☐	📄	🐾	Simone Trucking Inc	SIMO	Drayage, LTL, TL	

Report Format "Dynamic"

Fig. 10-1: Carrier list in the TMS. Click the details (piece of paper) icon to open a carrier record.

A TMS carrier record includes:

- Carrier name.
- True/false flag for whether this carrier should be considered active. (Rating results and carrier data can be filtered by active carrier status.)
- The carrier's federally assigned Standard Carrier Alphanumeric Code (SCAC).
- Modes available from this carrier, selected by checkbox.
- Primary location.
- Unique carrier ID used in the TMS.
- Federal employer identification number.
- US DOT number.
- MC number, issued by the Federal Motor Carrier Safety Administration allowing this carrier to engage in interstate commerce.
- Carrier's default currency to use in the absence of other determining factors.
- Types of hazardous materials that can be handled by this carrier.
- Whether this carrier can be issued cash advances, and if so, the limits and fees associated with those advances.
- A list of references attached to the carrier.

Edit Carrier

Carrier Details				
Name	Lyndon Trucking			
Active	Yes ⌄			
SCAC	LYND			
Modes	☐ Air		☐ Air Freight	
	☐ Bulk		☐ Drayage	
	☐ Expedited		☐ FCL	
	☐ Intermodal		☐ International	
	☐ LCL		☐ LTL	
	☐ Last Mile		☐ Letter	
	☐ Mixed		☐ Ocean	
	☐ Other		☐ Parcel	
	☐ Parcel Carton		☐ Rail	
	☐ Service Mode		☐ Small Package	
	☑ TL		☑ Truckload	
Primary Location	Lyndon Terminal, Smithfield, NC, 27577 ⌄			
Carrier ID	HOW5757			
Federal EIN				
D-U-N-S Number	0000000			
USDOT	6666666			
MC Number	zzzzz			
Oversize Factor				
Currency	USA, Dollars (USD) ⌄			
Hazmat	☐ Flammables		☐ Corrosives	

Fig. 10-2: First part of TMS carrier record with basic identifying fields, modes and hazmat.

Insurance Information

There's also a section about the carrier's insurance information. The basic carrier record has separate fields for three categories of insurance: cargo, general, and liability:

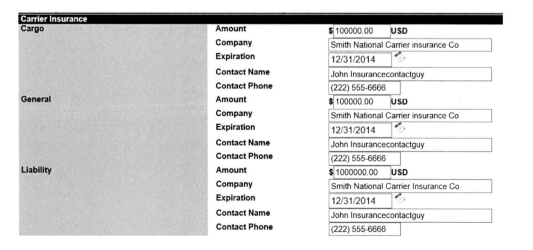

Fig. 10-3: Basic insurance records in a TMS carrier record, with expire dates.

The last sections on the carrier screen are the contact methods defined for tendering a load, request a quote, or requesting a status check.

One simple reporting strategy in the TMS is to show a list of carriers nearing their insurance expiration date in the next 30 days (or any desired period). From a carrier list, click the "Report Format" button and create a report with filter values like this:

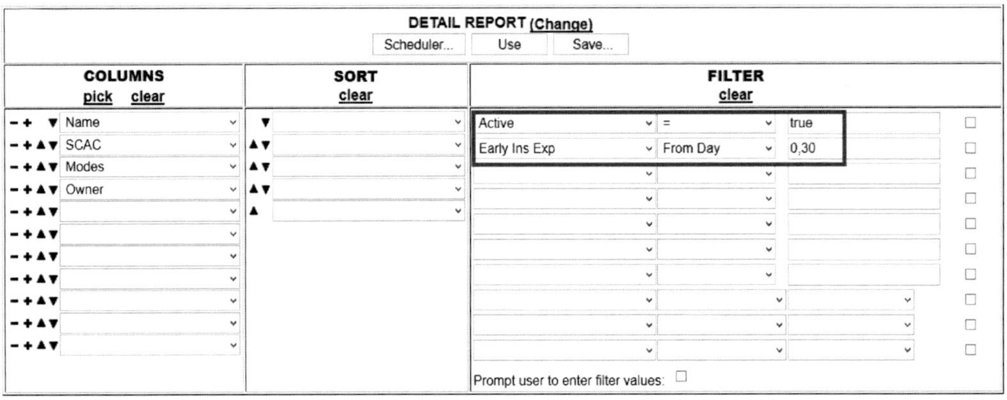

Fig. 10-4: *A carrier report that captures currently active carriers with an insurance expiration date within the next 30 days.*

SAFER

We can view a carrier's record with the federal Safety and Fitness Electronic Records (SAFER) system. This is a command available from the "Carrier" menu that appears in the menu bar when a carrier detail window is open (Carrier > SAFER).

The carrier must have a valid MC Number in the carrier record detail page to retrieve the information. Information returned from the query can be saved to the TMS carrier record.

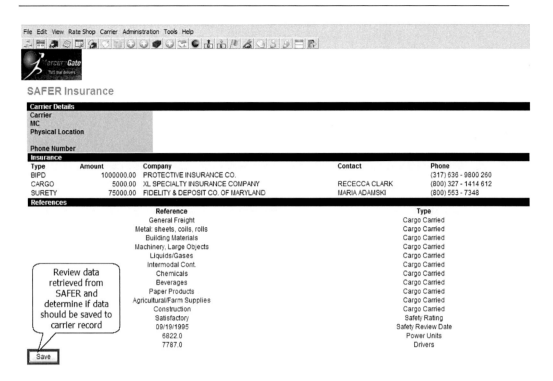

Fig. 10-5: Carrier information returned from the SAFER database.

Carrier Management Systems (CMS)

Basic carrier records are not enough for many modern logistics providers. Sophisticated carrier management is an essential part of their daily business. Large shops have entire carrier-management teams or departments.

These clients need frequent updates (even every few minutes) from federal and commercial carrier databases about expirations of insurance and authority. They need the latest safety ratings from government agencies. They need current hazmat capacity, up-to-the-minute performance assessments, and detailed information about carrier equipment and assets. Lastly, for clients of both a carrier-management system and a TMS, they need records to flow easily between the two systems.

MercuryGate's separate, proprietary carrier management system is named <u>Carma</u> (from "carrier records management") and is an additional software service to clients. TMS users can also have logins to Carma, and the system can be set up to allow automatic, seamless access by users from the TMS to Carma. Users so enabled will see a "Login to Carma" item in their TMS power-button menu:

Fig. 10-6: Access to Carma carrier records system from the TMS.

Carma, like the TMS, has a "dashboard" or home screen that presents the user with a "power button" list of menus. For the purpose of this chapter we're most interested in the Carma menu labeled "Carriers," from which we'll open a carrier list:

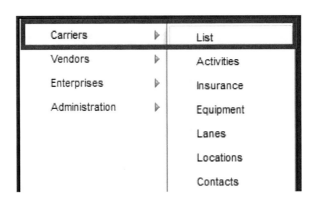

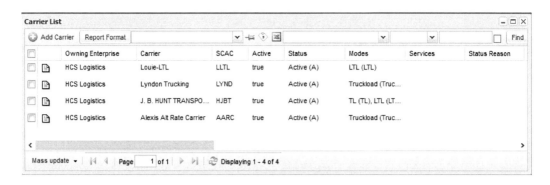

Fig. 10-7: A carrier list in Carma. As in the TMS, clicking a details icon opens a record for the individual carrier. The carrier list can be filtered by report format and a Quick Find search.

Clicking a carrier's editing icon in the list opens a window that gives us access to extensive detail of the carrier's record (Fig. 10-8). Note the series of tabs running down the left-hand side of the carrier window – each tab leads to a different screen of information.

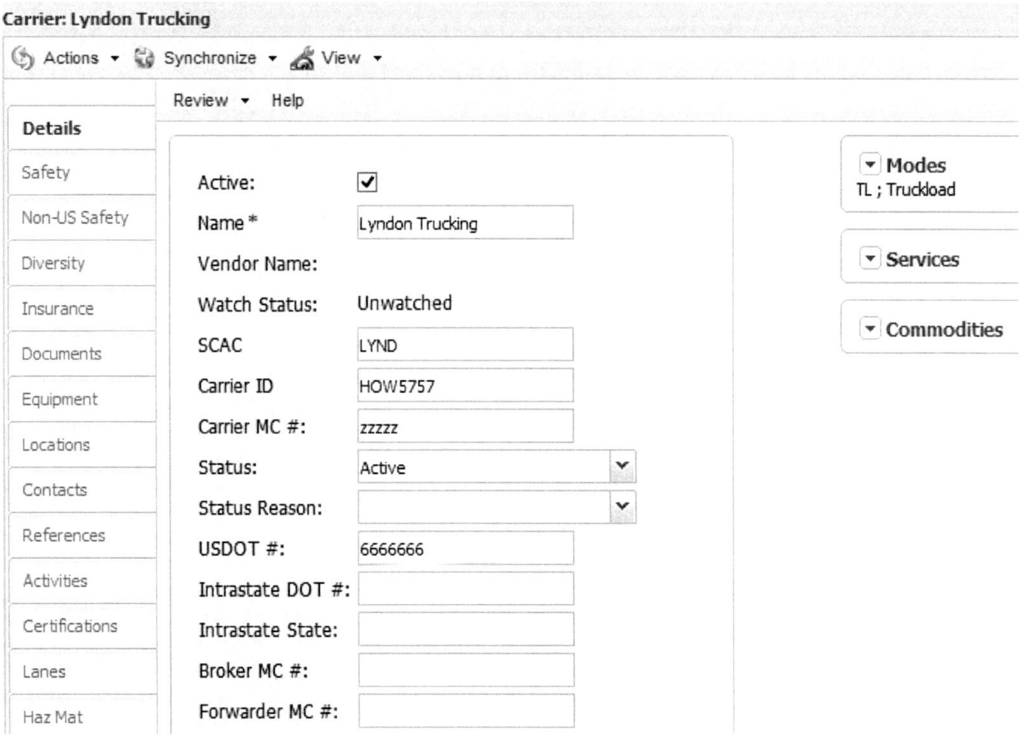

Fig. 10-8: Carrier detail window in Carma. Each left-hand tab leads to a subscreen of records for that area.

The "Details" tab contains basic identifying information. "Safety" contains information (usually updated from an external data source, see below) about the carrier's safety rating, incident counts, and relative percentile ranking among all carriers.

"Insurance" is one of the most important tabs, of course. Information about policies, coverage and expirations are kept here. Other tabs track the carrier's diversity certifications, stored documents, available equipment, associated locations, contacts, lanes, and hazardous material certifications.

Carma integrates with various external commercial <u>carrier data sources</u> to provide online updates of carrier data. These updates (which require a user account for the external system) can occur by explicit user action, or, more usually, by a scheduled automatic execution.

Carma carrier records are synched with the TMS at regular intervals, according to certain triggers in the system, or by manual user command, ensuring that TMS execution always is based on the current carrier data.

'Active Carrier' Flag

We saw that every carrier in the TMs has an "active" flag:

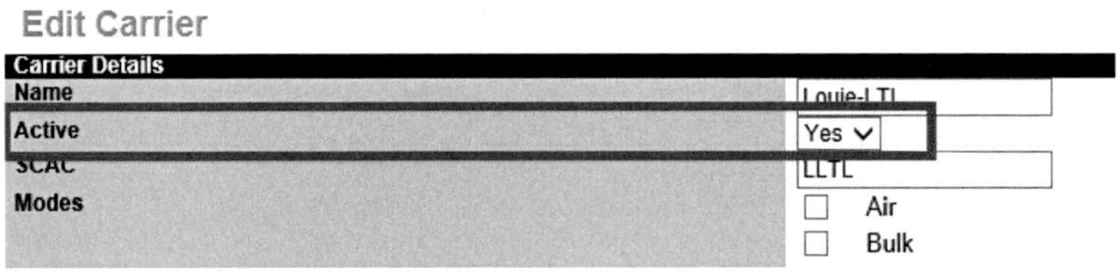

Fig. 10-9: The 'Active' flag is one of the most important fields in a TMS carrier record.

We use this flag in a variety of ways, the most obvious being to filter our displayed carrier reports to show only active carriers. Active status also can be used to control TMS rating – there's a system setting to limit rating results only to rates from carriers that we consider active.

However, even if you have only 100 carriers – or 50, or even 25 – setting their active status in a manual process is an unnecessary inconvenience. One of the strengths of Carma is that each client can design its own set of conditions to test for whether a carrier should be considered active.

Clients run this "carrier active" test on a regularly scheduled basis, and then synch to the TMS to set all carrier statuses automatically. Users can start each workday with an active-carrier list guaranteed to be based on the latest information.

Measuring Performance

Active carrier management also includes the ability to gather, view and respond to key performance indicators about how our carriers are doing their jobs. Some examples include:

- On-time pickup and delivery percentage
- Tender accept/reject/expire ratios
- Average delay for status updates
- Billing timeliness & accuracy

In the TMS, the starting point for this kind of data is a window called the Carrier Scorecard Portlet.

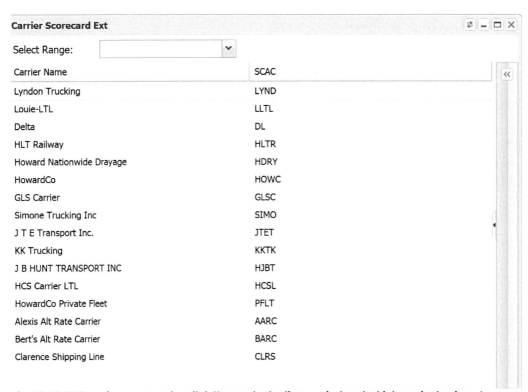

Fig. 10-10: TMS carrier scorecard portlet. Users select a time period and which carrier to view. An arrow on the right expands a display of statistics about the selected carrier (see next image).

Carrier Scorecard: ▮▮▮▮▮▮▮▮▮▮
03/01/2015-03/31/2015

Load Count: 1
Spend: $75.00

ON TIME METRICS	Pickup	Delivery
Total	42	51
Late	31 (73.81%)	45 (88.24%)
Goal %		

FREIGHT CLAIMS	Open	Closed
Count	0	0

TENDER EFFICEINCY	Accepted	Rejected	Expired
EDI	0	0	0
Email	3	0	0
Other	0	0	0
%	100.00%	0.00%	0.00%
Goal %			

STATUS UPDATES - Avg Hours to Update	Pickup	Delivery
imdemo	Count: 1 Avg. Hours: 2.75	Count: 1 Avg. Hours: 0.01
Goal Hours		

Print

Fig. 10-11: Statistics available from carrier scorecard portlet.

The information displayed in this portlet includes:

- Total count of actual loads (i.e. loads with actual pickups). Actual pickup date of the load is used for time period filtering.
- Total amount spent (total of all carrier rates).
- On Time Metrics:
  - Total number of pickups / deliveries - target early date of the event is used for time period filtering
  - Number of late pickups / deliveries - target early date of the event is used for time period filtering

- % of late pickups/deliveries - colored red if above goal maximum, green if under goal minimum, yellow if in between (configurable)
  - Goal % of late pickup / deliveries
- Tender Efficiency:
  - Number of accepted EDI / Email / Other tenders, rejected EDI / Email / Other tenders, expired EDI / Email / Other tenders - date of tendering response is used for time-period filtering
  - % of each type - accepted is colored red if under goal minimum, green if above goal maximum, yellow in between. Rejected / Expired is red if above goal maximum, green if under goal minimum, yellow in between (configurable).
  - Goal % of each type
- Status Updates - all information is per user:
  - Number of received pickup/delivery status messages - create date of status message is used for time-period filtering
  - Average number of hours between actual event time and corresponding status message time - color red if above goal maximum, green if under goal minimum, yellow in between (configurable)
  - Goal hours
- Freight Claims:
  - Number of opened and closed "Manage Claim" activities - Create Date and Complete date of the activity is used respectively for time period filtering

Another source of carrier metrics is the "Analytics" tab of a carrier record in Carma, which displays statistics for pickup/drop, freight spend and tender rejection ratio:

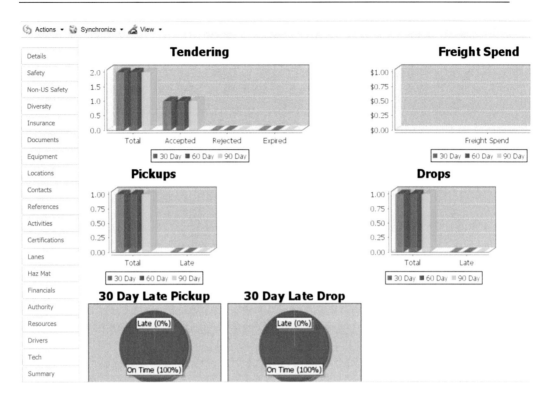

Fig. 10-12: 'Analytics' tab in a Carma carrier record.

Billing Timeliness and Efficiency

Two other frequently used carrier metrics relate to billing efficiency. How good is a carrier at getting out its bills on time, and how accurate do they tend to be? As we saw in our chapter on invoice management, sometimes we might get billed indifferently, inaccurately -- or even not at all.

This can be a significant management problem on our end, especially when we finally do get invoices and they vary from expected rates. Not knowing exactly how much you owe, or when you are going to owe it, is the enemy of good planning. The questions of timely and accurate billing from our carriers therefore are good subjects for measuring carrier performance.

One tool for doing this is MercuryEdge, the data-analysis application that we've seen used in other chapters. (For the basics of MercuryEdge, see the appendix.) You can follow the general idea even if you haven't used MercuryEdge yet. It operates like a kind of spreadsheet.

We're going to calculate an average for days elapsed between load delivery and invoice date. First, we open a list of carrier invoices from the TMS in MercuryEdge. Our TMS invoice report should include columns for the fields "Invoice SCAC," "Actual Delivery" and "Invoice Date."

There's a "Filter" command in MercuryEdge we can apply to any list. In this example we want to filter our invoice list to use only loads that have been delivered and invoiced. (All we're measuring in this example is the time lag between those two kinds of events.)

Invoices ×									
Report Type: FreightBill	v	**Data Level:** HCS Logistics Inc.	**Run Date:** 06/21/2015 02:22:33PM	**Total Rows:** 20					
Owner	Primary Reference	Invoice Number	Load Status	Actual Delivery	Invoice Date	Invoice SCAC			
HCS Logistics Inc.	L-0033-11 (MBL)	B-0029	Delivered	2015-06-20 09:00	2015-06-18 00:00	LLTL			^
HCS Logistics Inc.	L-0033-4 (MBL)	B-0044	Delivered	2015-06-19 08:00	2015-06-20 00:00	LLTL			
HCS Logistics Inc.	L-0033-4 (MBL)	B-0043	Delivered	2015-06-19 08:00	2015-06-20 00:00	LLTL			
HCS Logistics Inc.	L-0033-4 (MBL)	B-0036	Delivered	2015-06-19 08:00	2015-06-18 00:00	LLTL			
HCS Logistics Inc.	L-0033-5 (MBL)	B-0035	Delivered	2015-06-19 08:00	2015-06-18 00:00	LLTL			
HCS Logistics Inc.	L-0033-6 (MBL)	B-0034	Delivered	2015-06-19 08:00	2015-06-18 00:00	LLTL			
HCS Logistics Inc.	L-0033-7 (MBL)	B-0033	Delivered	2015-06-19 08:00	2015-06-18 00:00	LLTL			
HCS Logistics Inc.	L-0033-8 (MBL)	B-0032	Delivered	2015-06-19 08:00	2015-06-18 00:00	LLTL			
HCS Logistics Inc.	L-0033-9 (MBL)	B-0031	Delivered	2015-06-19 08:00	2015-06-18 00:00	LLTL			

Fig. 10-13: TMS invoice report as opened in MercuryEdge, showing delivery vs. invoice date with carrier SCAC.

Next we use the MercuryEdge command to add a "calculated column" that subtracts delivery date from invoice date for each row, to get an elapsed time for each invoice. The time is expressed in hours, so we'll add one more column to divide the value by 24 to get a value expressed in days. Finally, we'll use the "Summarize" command to calculate an average for each carrier SCAC in the report (Fig. 10-14):

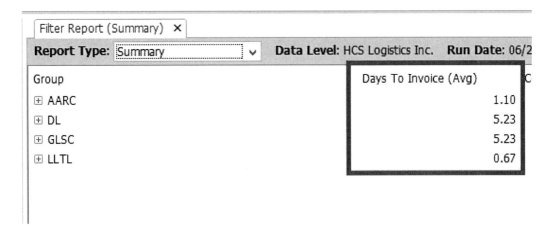

Fig. 10-14: Using MercuryEdge, we've calculated an average time in days between delivery and invoice date, by carrier SCAC.

We can perform comparable steps to design a calculation for billing accuracy. A simple example is a post-audit of each load's carrier initial rate versus its final invoice amount. Or maybe we want to look for carriers who tend to send multiple invoices with added charges.

Armed with this kind of data, MercuryGate clients in practice have had success in encouraging their carriers to produce more timely and accurate billing data. For example:

- Client X created a "grading" system for billing timeliness, and informed carriers that grade "A" carriers would be paid on an expedited basis, grade "B" carriers on a somewhat less expedited basis, and grade "C" carriers according to ordinary time limits. Their carrier billing timeliness improved noticeably.

- Client Y created a ranking system for carriers based on billing accuracy, and instituted a system of carrier-users with access to TMS carrier portals to ensure the accuracy of their own invoices. Again, carrier performance increased dramatically.

Audit Logs and Carrier Measurement

The Audit Logs feature of the TMS contains helpful information that we can pull into our own "home-cooking" version of data in the Carrier Scorecard portlet.

We create TMS audit-log reports (with the Report Format button) that look for entries with the key phrases, such as "Tender Expired" and "Tender Rejected."

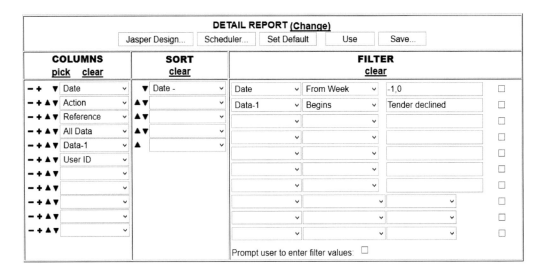

Fig. 10-15: Audit log that pulls a list of rejected tenders for the past week.

We pull these reports into MercuryEdge and, using the same kind of steps described above, create calculations of tender accept/reject ratios from carriers.

Route Guides

One way to put our findings about carrier performance to good use is by applying route guides to our rating and carrier-award decisions.

Route guides allow us to use additional guidelines besides sheer least cost for awarding loads to carriers. Getting the lowest rate might not be the main factor in assigning a load if you know the carrier is less likely to accept the tender, or if the carrier has the worst on-time performance

So a route guide, which is a spreadsheet uploaded to the TMS, lets us award loads on lanes by ranking our preferred carriers for that lane, or by allocating loads on the lane across a set of carriers based on a certain distribution formula.

Figure 10-16 shows a simple rating result returned from a TMS route-guide rating process, shown in a load detail screen, waiting for us to choose a carrier rate:

Carrier Rates

	Selected	Seq	Reason	Total	Norm. Total	Carrier	SCAC	Mode	Allo
	☐	1		$180.80 USD	$180.80 USD	Lyndon Trucking	LYND	TL	
	☐	2		$187.03 USD	$187.03 USD	Simone Trucking Inc	SIMO	LTL	
	☐	3		$162.72 USD	$162.72 USD	Louie-LTL	LLTL	LTL	

Fig. 10-16: Rates returned by a route guide, ranked by preference, in a load detail screen.

Notice in the above example, the "Lyndon" carrier is ranked first, even though it is not the lowest rate. The "Simone" carrier is ranked next, even with the highest rate– and "Louie" is ranked last, even with the lowest. Clearly some other consideration went into the route guide rankings.

Route guides can be set up to recommend a simple ranking of carriers on a lane. But they also can be used to allocate carriers on a lane dynamically, on either a numerical or percentage basis.

E	F	G	H	I
rier SC	Carrier Mc	Carrier Service	Carrier Score	Carrier Cc DI
ID	TL	Standard	PCT:50	
L	LTL	Standard	PCT:40	
O	LTL	Standard	PCT:10	

Fig. 10-17: Lane allocations in a route guide spreadsheet, uploaded to the TMS.

Allocations can be performed by the week, by the month, or by the quarter, according to system settings. The rating results returned from such a setup are based on dynamic calculations of which carrier is "due" to get the next load, according to the distribution formula.

Example: carrier "Lyndon", which gets 50 percent of the loads on a lane, comes in ranked first and we select it for a load:

Carrier Rates	Lyndon Trucking(LYND), LYND01 Carrier Contract TL Standard, $180.80 USD						Carrier Goal: $0.00	
⊕	Selected	Seq	Reason	Total	Norm. Total	Carrier	SCAC	Mode
✖✎✓	☑	1		$180.80 USD	$180.80 USD	Lyndon Trucking	LYND	TL
✖✎✓	☐	2		$162.72 USD	$162.72 USD	Louie-LTL	LLTL	LTL
✖✎✓	☐	3		$187.03 USD	$187.03 USD	Simone Trucking Inc	SIMO	LTL

Fig. 10-18: Carrier 'Lyndon' should get 50 percent of the loads on this lane by route guide allocation.

For the next load that comes up on the lane, our route guide recognizes that the carriers "Louie" and "Simone" each get 25 percent, and this time ranks them first and second. We'll select Louie.

Carrier Rates	Louie-LTL(LLTL), LLTL Carrier Contract LTL LTL Standard, $162.72 USD						Carrier Goal: $0.00 P/M	
⊕	Selected	Seq	Reason	Total	Norm. Total	Carrier	SCAC	Mode
✖✎✓	☑	1		$162.72 USD	$162.72 USD	Louie-LTL	LLTL	LTL
✖✎✓	☐	2		$187.03 USD	$187.03 USD	Simone Trucking Inc	SIMO	LTL
✖✎✓	☐	3		$180.80 USD	$180.80 USD	Lyndon Trucking	LYND	TL

Fig. 10-19: Route guide now ranks 'Louie' first for the next load.

For the next load on this lane, now the route guide knows it's Simone's "turn." The route guide is keeping score correctly – over time it will assign 50 percent on loads on this lane to Lyndon, and 25 percent apiece to Louie and Simone.

Carrier Rates								
⊕	Selected	Seq	Reason	Total	Norm. Total	Carrier	SCAC	Mode
✖✎✓	☐	1		$187.03 USD	$187.03 USD	Simone Trucking Inc	SIMO	LTL
✖✎✓	☐	2		$180.80 USD	$180.80 USD	Lyndon Trucking	LYND	TL
✖✎✓	☐	3		$162.72 USD	$162.72 USD	Louie-LTL	LLTL	LTL

Fig. 10-20: Route guide gives carrier 'Simone' a turn in the rotation, despite having the highest rate.

A route guide is a useful way to adjust rating results based on preferred carriers on a lane. However, it's not the only way.

We might use MercuryEdge to create our own adjustments to rate tables that weight a carrier based on performance examples. For example, given an automated report measuring on-time performance, we could:

- Rank our carriers by performance.
- Assign a "weight" or factor to the worst performers.
- Put that factor into a rate table open in MercuryEdge. Add a calculated column to adjust the actual contract rate by the weight factor, and use that result as the "rate" to be returned for this carrier on this lane.

In this sense, thinking of ways to apply what we can learn about carrier performance is a creative endeavor.

Chapter Discussion

1. Why is carrier management important for a logistics provider? Why is there more involved than just making a list of carriers and their email addresses?
2. What are some examples of carrier information that should be updated regularly? What are the consequences of not updating that information?
3. What is the function of carrier records management software, and why is it important? How are carrier records actually updated?
4. Name some of the ways we can judge carrier "performance." Why is this important, and what can we do about it? What are ways for to account for a carrier's track record in our decision-making?

Chapter 11: Optimization

The first job of being a logistics provider is finding a truck. But the first step toward becoming a <u>better</u> logistics provider is to ask: Was it the <u>best</u> truck?

Was it the best rate? Did the route make the most sense? Did it meet all my needs, or was I forced to make tradeoffs? Could I have consolidated shipments differently for a better result?

What if our company is handling hundreds of transactions a day, or even thousands? How good a job did we do of consolidating them? Did we save enough money, enough miles, enough time? How do we even know?

Questions like these are related to the subject of <u>optimization</u>, which we might loosely define as "building loads in a way intended to get an improved result."

Historically, the building and consolidation of loads was based on seat-of-the-pants experience, eyeball judgments or one-size-fits-all, conventional wisdom – like the paper route guide stapled to a bulletin board.

Even today, a lot of providers still do it more or less the same way. Maybe instead of the printed route guide tacked to the bulletin board, they use an Excel spreadsheet. But the underlying circumstance is the same – they "know" how to build the best loads themselves.

Many companies still select carriers based on inflexible route guides - or, to be blunt about it, they just choose the carriers they find easier to work with. They might select mode based on a simplistic criteria such as weight breaks (parcel up to X, LTL up to Y, truckload above Y), which even can lead to an even worse solution.

Types of Optimization

Notice that we defined optimization very generally as the art of building loads in a way "to get a better result." This leads to a logical question: "Better" than <u>what</u>? What are we trying to accomplish?

The answer is - it depends. "Optimization" can mean different things depending on a company's needs and goals. In fact we might speak of a few different types of optimization.

<u>Rate optimization:</u> Rate optimization is the most obvious goal, of course – moving freight at the lowest possible cost, while still achieving what we need in terms of service, volume, timetable and carrier performance.

<u>Route optimization:</u> Route optimization means constructing routes, pickups and drops in the most efficient way possible. Most of the time this dovetails with rate optimization – but not always. Take a look at Fig. 11-1, a result churned out by a software optimizer:

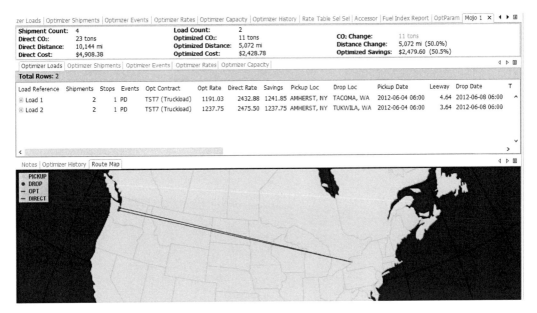

Fig. 11-1: Why send shipments separately across the country on the same day, when they would fit on the same truck?

In the above illustration, the software decided to send shipments on two separate trucks to almost the same spot, at the same time and on the same day, all the way across the country. You can almost hear spreadsheet users snickering.

But in this case the optimizer relentlessly made its decision based on the fact the two-truck <u>solution was the least-cost solution.</u> A fine example of "rate" optimization versus "route" optimization!

Load optimization: We can approach the problem from the aspect of <u>load</u> optimization, with our focus on maximizing weight, cube or pallet count on as few trucks as possible. One of our main goals here is realizing the benefit of break ranges that give us an incentive to fill the truck.

Network optimization: Finally, <u>network</u> optimization can be the major factor for a lot of companies. "Network" optimization means you are driven by the needs of your structure. Maybe you have a pool-point system, warehouses or distribution centers. Maybe Product X has to go through Facility Y and not Facility Z. We might need to consider facility costs, operating hours and labor availability as we build our routes.

We've just named four "philosophies" or approaches to optimization – rate, route, load and network. Sometimes you'll be pursuing one to the exclusion of all the others, and sometimes you'll naturally be achieving more than one kind of optimization at once.

Optimization 'Constraints'

If we're just organizing a few shipments, a few destinations and a few ship dates, then maybe any of us could do just about as well putting them together.

But let's add one more factor – let's say that some of our shipments have to be refrigerated, and some don't.

Now how about another factor? Let's say some of our freight types have to be on the same load, and others <u>can't</u> be on the same load.

Next - some of the facilities that you need for your pickups, drops and pools have a variety of operating hours, and you have to keep track of them all versus your calculated transit times, to make sure you never show up too early or too late.

And you really need to use carrier WYXZ, which often will have the best routes, but you'll have to be mindful that the carrier's contract has limits on the order and number of stops on a route.

Meanwhile, you definitely want to use carrier ABCD, but you have to respect the fact that carrier ABCD has only a certain number of trucks available each day, varying by lane.

You get the idea. Even if you had just 100 shipments, it would be a huge if not impossible undertaking even to sort out even the few requirements that we just named,

The limitations, requirements and limits that we need to respect in optimization are known collectively as <u>constraints</u>. And without question, collectively, constraints are the main issue in optimization. Here are just a few kinds of constraints (and the list could be a lot longer than this):

Location constraints	Operating hours, limits on service, mode, carrier
Route constraints	Required order of events (pickup/drop), max "out-of-route" limits (zig-zagginess)
Vehicle constraints	Max weight, quantity, cube
Driver constraints	Duty/driving limits
Freight constraints	Incompatible cargo types
Carrier constraints	# vehicles available per lane/day
Dock constraints	# facilities, operating hours
Pooling constraints	Required/preassigned pool locations

It's no wonder that historically, and especially in the pre-digital age, many logistics providers simply did the best they could by relying on arbitrary practices.

Software Optimization Tools

MercuryGate's name for its optimization tool is <u>Mojo</u>. Mojo builds loads at the least cost while respecting any number of constraints. Fig. 11-2 shows a screen of Mojo results:

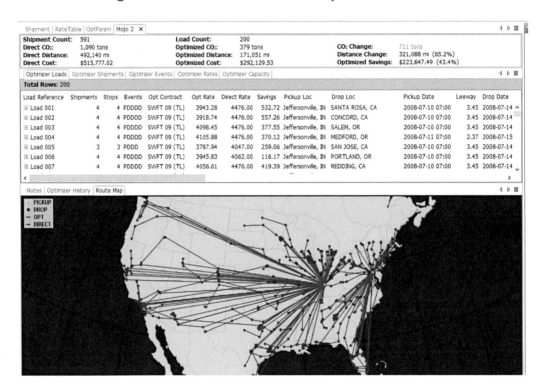

Fig. 11-2: Results of a Mojo optimization result, consolidating 591 shipments into 200 recommended execution loads, at a considerable cost and mileage savings versus non-consolidated direct ship.

In this results window, Mojo presents a series of tabs with the lists of loads that it recommends, a breakdown of the shipments on those loads, and lists of events, rates, and carrier capacity used by day over the time window of the routes listed. The map shows the load list in graphical form; clicking on a route in the map highlights the load in the list, and vice-versa.

Mojo users employ its results both for analysis and for real-world execution. One of the commands available after a Mojo run is the instruction to create Mojo's recommended loads as actual loads in the TMS, where they can be tendered and executed.

Mojo is not a standalone program, but runs inside the MercuryEdge application that we've already discussed in several chapters. A password called a "Mojo key" is installed in the MercuryEdge system preferences window, which unlocks Mojo-related commands. See the appendix.

Typical Optimization Run

At a minimum, all that Mojo needs to optimize is two kinds of data: a list of shipments, and a table of carrier rates, both of them open as reports (spreadsheet tabs) in MercuryEdge.

Shipment data must contain at least:

- A unique identifying field for each shipment.
- Origin and destination information.
- Pickup and delivery time window.
- Weight.

Shipment data can be much more extensive, and include information about pallet count, quantity, cube, equipment and services, and many other possible fields. But those listed above are the minimum for optimization.

The other requirement is a rate table. Each line in a rate table declares the lane for which that rate is applicable, the rate calculation method, and one or more break ranges to which the rate applies. For example, a rate might be effective on a lane for weights up to 100 pounds, a different rate for 100 pounds to 200 pounds, and so forth.

One way to get a rate table is to open a TMS contract report in MercuryEdge, and then choose the command labeled "Open Rate Table Report" to open a usable rate table from those contracts. The structure and fields of a MercuryEdge rate table are described in the appendix.

A user launches Mojo with a command in MercuryEdge labeled "Route optimizer…" from a menu of commands that can be run against a shipment report:

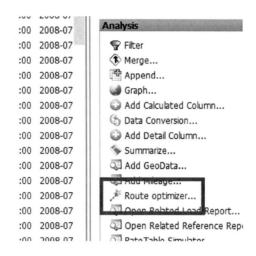

Fig. 11-3: The command to launch Mojo is found in the 'Analysis' task window on the right side of the screen.

Each time Mojo runs, it presents the user with a series of four screens filled with options for the run. These screens are known collectively as the "Mojo Optimization Wizard" and we'll refer to them as "wizard screens."

Their main function is to map the columns of the shipment report, and to set the constraints that the user needs the optimizer to obey. Fortunately, we don't have to set every single setting every time – Mojo remembers the settings from past runs, and we can save and recall them as well.

The first Mojo screen (Fig. 11-4) asks the user to "map" the columns from the shipment data to the columns that Mojo expects. This allows flexibility in the data; we can use somebody's outside Excel file, but still optimize with Mojo by correctly mapping the source columns.

For origin and destination, the only required fields are Country and a "Geo" value. This is a latitude and longitude code, and if it is not already present in your shipment data, MercuryEdge will add it via a command.

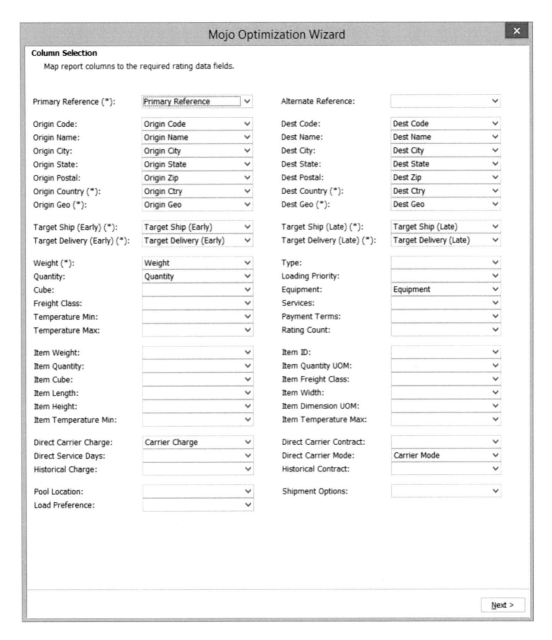

Fig. 11-4: First screen of the Mojo Optimization Wizard, used to map columns from the shipment data.

"Weight" is the only field required to describe the load. But we can map columns for quantity, cube, freight class and other descriptive information, if that's what we need for our rating.

The "Direct" columns toward the bottom refers to historical values that Mojo will try to "beat" in conducting its optimization. If we're using historical shipment data and we know how much we actually paid, we can map those columns in the wizard, and Mojo will know that's the rate it's trying to improve upon.

Remaining Wizard Screens

The second, third and fourth screens deal primary with setting constraints – the "rules" for the optimization that Mojo will be forced to respect. This is where Mojo truly shines. At the end of this chapter we'll show the screens and the lists of things that can specified for each Mojo run. But here's a sample:

- Hypothetical changes in fuel costs
- Maximum permitted "out-of-route" ratio (zig-zag of a route)
- Max truck weight, quantity, cube, max stops per route
- Compatible and incompatible freight types
- Service times (load/unload)
- Operating hours of pickup/drop locations
- Date window flexibility
- Driver duty limits
- Carrier vehicle availability (# per day, lane, etc.)
- Dock capacity limits by location
- Pooling strategy – whether to use pool points and how
- Whether to enforce services and equipment requirements
- Pickup and drop clustering where possible

After a user has set all desired constraints, he or she clicks "Finish" on the final wizard screen and Mojo will optimize. The user also can check a checkbox to save these settings for further use. At any rate, Mojo will "remember" the settings for the current session.

Working with Mojo Results

When Mojo completes an optimization, the results of the run are displayed in a "Mojo" tab in MercuryEdge. At the top of this panel there are overall statistics for number of shipments, number of loads created, and savings estimates for cost, mileage and carbon emissions (Fig. 11-5).

Shipment Count:	591	Load Count:	200	CO₂ Change:	711 tons
Direct CO₂:	1,090 tons	Optimized CO₂:	379 tons	Distance Change:	321,088 mi (65.2%)
Direct Distance:	492,140 mi	Optimized Distance:	171,051 mi	Optimized Savings:	$223,647.49 (43.4%)
Direct Cost:	$515,777.02	Optimized Cost:	$292,129.53		

Fig. 11-5: Detail of Mojo results showing overall statistics and savings calculations.

Below the summary data is a sub-panel that has separate tabs breaking out the results of the optimization according to load, shipment, events, rates and capacity (Fig. 11-6). Each entry in a list can be expanded to view drill-down information. For example, for each load we can see its list of consolidated shipments. For each shipment, we can even see a list of reasons that Mojo chose the load that it chose.

	Optimizer Loads	Optimizer Shipments	Optimizer Events	Optimizer Rates	Optimizer Capacity						◁ ▷ ▤

Total Rows: 200

Load Reference	Shipments	Stops	Events	Opt Contract	Opt Rate	Direct Rate	Savings	Pickup Loc	Drop Loc	Pickup Date	Leeway	Drop Date
⊞ Load 001	4	4	PDDDD	SWFT 09 (TL)	3943.28	4476.00	532.72	Jeffersonville, IN	SANTA ROSA, CA	2008-07-10 07:00	3.45	2008-07-14 ⌃
⊞ Load 002	4	4	PDDDD	SWFT 09 (TL)	3918.74	4476.00	557.26	Jeffersonville, IN	CONCORD, CA	2008-07-10 07:00	3.45	2008-07-14
⊞ Load 003	4	4	PDDDD	SWFT 09 (TL)	4098.45	4476.00	377.55	Jeffersonville, IN	SALEM, OR	2008-07-10 07:00	3.45	2008-07-14
⊞ Load 004	4	4	PDDDD	SWFT 09 (TL)	4105.88	4476.00	370.12	Jeffersonville, IN	MEDFORD, OR	2008-07-11 07:00	2.37	2008-07-15
⊞ Load 005	3	3	PDDD	SWFT 09 (TL)	3787.94	4047.00	259.06	Jeffersonville, IN	SAN JOSE, CA	2008-07-10 07:00	3.45	2008-07-14
⊞ Load 006	4	4	PDDDD	SWFT 09 (TL)	3945.83	4062.00	116.17	Jeffersonville, IN	PORTLAND, OR	2008-07-10 07:00	3.45	2008-07-14
⊞ Load 007	4	4	PDDDD	SWFT 09 (TL)	4056.61	4476.00	419.39	Jeffersonville, IN	REDDING, CA	2008-07-10 07:00	3.45	2008-07-14

Fig. 11-6: Mojo results viewable by shipment, load, events, rates and carrier capacity statistics.

In the bottom subpanel there's an interactive map of the loads recommended by Mojo – click on a load in the list and it is highlighted in the map, and vice-versa.

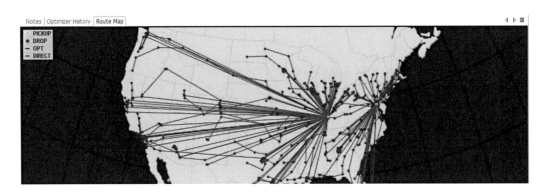

Fig. 11-7: Interactive map of Mojo's recommended loads.

Two other tabs in the bottom subpanel are labeled "Notes" (Fig. 11-8) and "Optimizer History" (Fig. 11-10).

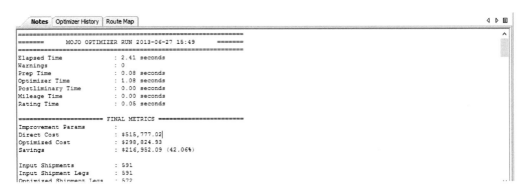

Fig. 11-8: The 'Notes' tab of a Mojo results screen contains much valuable information about why Mojo produced the results it did.

The Notes tab for each run will contain detailed statistics about the run, number of shipments, the various calculations made, and a list of the parameters that were set for the run. Figure 11-9 is an interesting snippet from a Notes tab:

```
Limiting Constraints
    Max Out-of-Route        : 35,837
    Truckload Max Stops     : 21,658
    Shipment Type           : 0
    Temperature Range       : 0
    Vehicle Loading (LIFO)  : 2
    Vehicle Max Weight      : 0
    Vehicle Max Quantity    : 4,136
    Vehicle Max Cube        : 0
    Loading Priority        : 0
    Time Window/Loc Hours   : 2,635
    Optimized Rate          : 45
    Carrier Capacity        : 0
    Pickup/Drop Clustering  : 0
```

Fig. 11-9: Mojo reports the most common reasons that it had to reject certain load combinations, based on the constraints supplied by the user.

The History tab (Fig. 11-10) contains a row for each Mojo run conducted so far, which parameters were changed between runs, and a comparison of the results.

Notes	Optimizer History	Route Map										◁ ▷ ▣

Total Rows: 3

#	Run Date	Elapsed	Savings/Sec	Direct Cost	Opt Cost	Savings	% Sav	Input Ship Legs	Opt Ship Legs	PL Adj	Total Loads	Opt Loads	Direct Miles
1	2013-06-27 14:56:38	3.96	55911.87	515777.02	292129.53	223647.49	43.36	591	571	0	200	180	492139.71
2	2013-06-27 15:49:26	2.41	72317.36	515777.02	298824.93	216952.09	42.06	591	572	0	202	183	492139.71
		-1.55	+16405.49		+6695.40	-6695.40	-1.30		+1		+2	+3	

Fig. 11-10: History tab shows the result of each run to date.

Each time you re-optimize your results, Mojo remembers what you have done before, and keeps a record of each run in this tab. To restore a previous run, double-click on its entry and the Mojo Optimization Wizard will launch with those values loaded.

This feature is extremely useful when you want to experiment with changing one or more parameters. In the illustration above, for instance, the change made for the second run actually resulted in smaller savings – we were better off the first time.

Using Mojo Results

Once we have the results of a Mojo run we can:

- Save them for future re-use or share them.

- Select any subset of shipments and run them as a separate optimization.

- Graphically view timetables, load configurations, and statistics.

- Modify our settings, re-run the optimization and compare results.

- Filter our results as needed.

- Send our Mojo results back to the TMS to create loads on the server for execution in the real world.

When a Mojo results tab is active in MercuryEdge, all of these tasks and more will be available in the Tasks Window on the right-hand side of the screen.

Mojo Example – Pooling Scenario

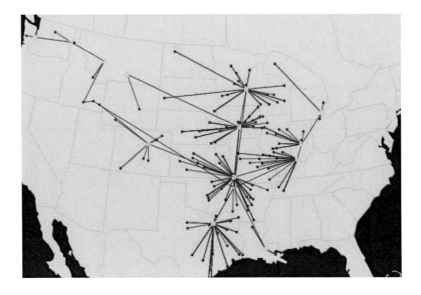

Fig. 11-11: Loads built by Mojo under a pool-point scenario.

Mojo can be instructed to build loads under several different pooling scenarios:

- Do not use pool points.
- Require the use of preassigned pool points that are supplied in the shipment data.
- Require that all shipments be pooled, but choose the best pool point from a supplied list of locations.
- Just consider whether pool points are the best solution, choosing from a supplied list of locations.

Where Mojo has discretion, we also set an overall strategy – choose a pool point nearest to the destination, nearest to the origin, located on the straightest path to delivery, and so forth.

Mojo Example – Zone-Skip Scenario

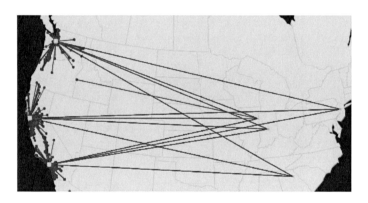

Fig. 11-12: Loads built by Mojo under a zone-skip scenario.

The intent of zone-skip is to save money by avoiding charges related to moving parcel through multiple zones. Notice that our shipments are routed in a straight shot by truckload to one of a handful of designated pool points, and only then sent out by parcel to the destination.

We achieved the above results by telling Mojo to allow only one stop per leg (origin to pool point, pool point to destination) with an "out of route" or zig-zag factor of 1.0 – that is to say, a straight line. Then we told Mojo to choose pool points from a list, in each case choosing the pool point closest to the final destination.

Mojo Live! and Mojo 'Scripting'

The latest generation of optimization include two new features: (1) The ability to run Mojo in the TMS itself, a feature known as "Mojo Live!" (2) The ability for advanced users to write their own scripts that actually reach into Mojo's decision-making.

Mojo Live! runs from the TMS' "Load Builder" portlet. Users can choose a list of candidate shipments or loads and select a new option to optimize with Mojo. All the parameters and settings for the optimization have been set up in advance and stored in the TMS.

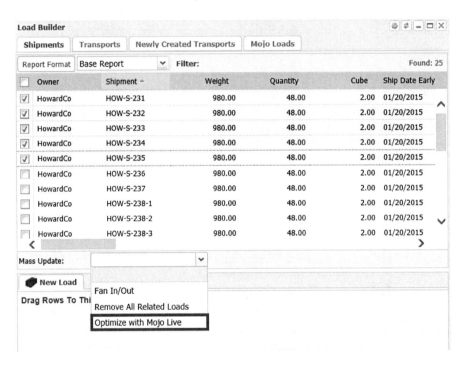

Fig. 11-12: Command to launch Mojo from the TMS Load Builder portlet.

Mojo scripting allows authorized users to write JavaScript that defines actions to execute at specified points during optimization. Scripts can be saved as part of a Mojo package, and shared with other users who can run them.

Scripts consist of functions triggered at key stages, with access to the fields of Mojo records such as shipments, loads, locations, events and rates.

For examples of script usage, we can:

- Reject a proposed load only when certain conditions about it are true.
- Create our own calculation of location hours, beyond the capacity of Mojo parameters.
    Example: If shipping from a pool, delivery must be on Wednesday or Thursday, else it can be any day.
- Conduct a customized evaluation of dates.
- Conduct a custom calculation of carbon emissions.
- Build reports using a specialized format.

Once the scripting function is unlocked, the scripting option appears on the last page of the Mojo Optimization Wizard. The possible values for the wizard parameter are "Off" and "JavaScript."

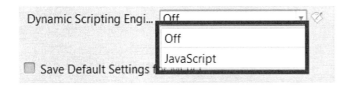

Fig. 11-13: Enabling the scripting engine in the Mojo Optimization Wizard.

Clicking the editing icon next to the parameter opens a window for editing and saving the script (Fig. 11-14):

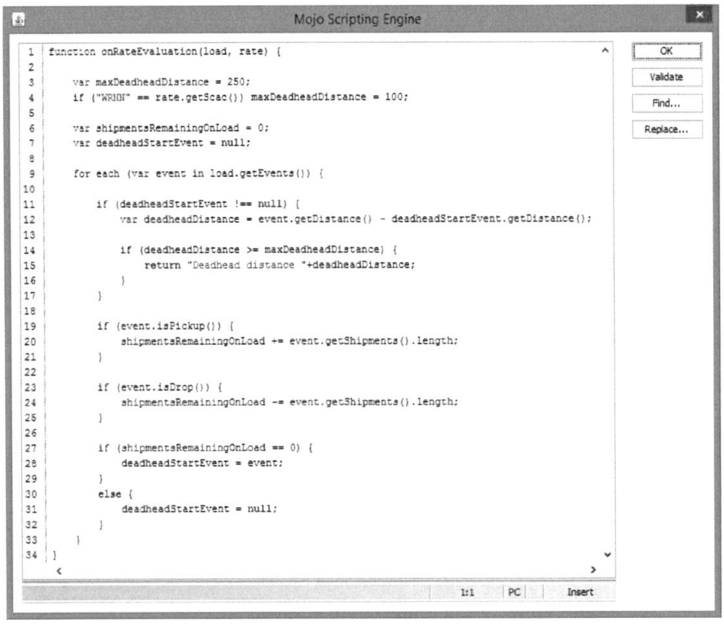

Fig. 11-14: Mojo scripting editing window.

Once Mojo scripting is unlocked, authorized programmers will have access to the application programming interface (API) needed to describe its functions and Mojo field names.

Chapter Discussion

1. What are the distinctions between "rate" optimization, "route" optimization, "load" optimization and "network" optimization? Is it possible to achieve more than one at a time? Is it possible to achieve one kind of optimization at the expense of another?

2. What are "constraints" on optimization? What are examples of constraints? Is it possible to consider every constraint for a large number of loads and still build loads that respect them all?

Chapter Addendum - Mojo Optimization Wizard

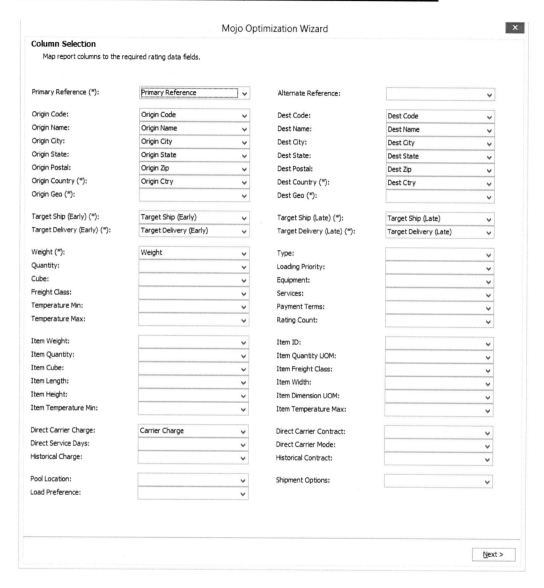

Primary Reference: Maps to a column containing a unique identifier for each shipment. May be supplied by a TMS report or by user-defined imported data. Non-unique entries are treated as items within the same shipment. Improper duplicate values can affect optimization.

Alternate Reference: Maps to a column containing user-defined contents that may be used for any purpose.

Location Codes (Origin Code, Dest Code): Maps to columns containing a unique TMS location code for each location. Use highly recommended. Duplicate codes for different locations will result in shipments omitted from optimization.

Origin Name and Destination Name, City, State, Postal, Country, Geocode: Of these only country and geocode are required for optimization but individual rate tables may require the others. MercuryEdge uses ZIP codes (if present) or valid city-state combinations (if ZIP not present) to generate geodata. Edge does not confirm ZIP codes match the city and state.

Target Dates (Target Ship Early, Target Ship Late, Target Delivery Early, Target Delivery Late): All required. For historical data missing some values, the same column can be mapped more than once, then adjusted with the use of window extensions. Typical date format is yyyy-mm-dd hh:mm; however, MercuryEdge/Mojo usually can parse other formats.

Shipment Information (Weight, Quantity, Cube, Freight Class, Temperature Min, Temperature Max): Any or all can be used with any unit of measure (lb, kg, cu-ft, cu-m) consistent with the rate table. Quantity can be mapped to a column with a number of units of any package type (pallets, effective pallets, cartons, shipments). If SMC modules will be used for rating a freight-class column needs to be mapped. For adding a freight class column, see Weight/Quantity/Cube/ Freight Class/Dimension/Temperature . Any consistent unit of measure for temperature is accepted. A minimum, maximum or both may be defined. Mojo will not consolidate shipments with incompatible ranges.

Type: Maps to a column with a user-defined value that allows Mojo to separate incompatible shipments, e.g. dry vs. frozen, hazmat vs. non-hazmat. This column can be used any way the user prefers, for example, mapping a destination state into this field to separate shipments. For additional fine-tune control of types, a report can control the compatibility/incompatibility of specific types. See "Type Compatibility Method" and "Type Compatibility List" under the second wizard screen.

Loading Priority: Maps to a column in the shipment data that numbers a shipment in ascending order of priority. With no priority a shipment can be loaded in any order. Only enforced if the "Vehicle Loading" parameter is set on a later wizard screen.

Equipment/Services: Maps to columns in the shipment data that specify required equipment/services. Rate tables may define optional accessorials in a contract lane. Non-optional equipment might be specified in a "Carrier Equipment" column. Both of these options must be enabled in a setting later in the wizard to be enforced.

Item fields: Maps columns with information about individual items in a shipment, such as when items exist on individual lines in the shipment report. If the rate table being used for the optimization uses an "ItemCount" rating method, then Mojo expects to find any values that it needs for quantity, weight or cube to be mapped in these fields.

Direct Carrier Charge/Contract: Maps to columns showing the charge and/or timeframe for actual or historical values that Mojo is trying to beat. The contract field is simply a contract identifier for reference purposes. "Direct Carrier Mode" maps to a column to allow mode to be determined when using external or synced rates. The "Historical Charge" and "Historical Contract" columns, if used, should contain the actual charge for the item and an identifier for the contract used.

Pool Location: Maps to a column containing unique location code for pooling this shipment. Required for pre-assigned pooling scenarios. For no pre-assigned pool locations, do not map this column. For a mix of pre-assigned and non-pre-assigned, leave the non-pre-assigned blank. Entries with the word "none" will not be assigned. Non-pre-assigned pool locations exist in a Pool Location report.

Load Preference: Maps to a column in the shipment data containing a user-defined load preference for each shipment. Shipments with matching preferences will be consolidated. Load Preference may be enforced in various ways – only one preference in a load, a load may contain shipments with more than one preference, etc. – with the wizard parameter Load Preference .

Shipment Options: Maps to a column containing a predefined code that overrides certain global Mojo settings for that shipment only. The codes are in a comma-delimited list. Current possible values are:

-WindowExtension	*Do not use time-window extensions for this shipment*
-WindowExtensionP	*No extensions for pickups only*
-WindowExtensionD	*No extensions for delivery only*
-NonTLConsol	*Prevent use of non-TL consolidations*
-NonTLConsolP	
-NonTLConsolD	

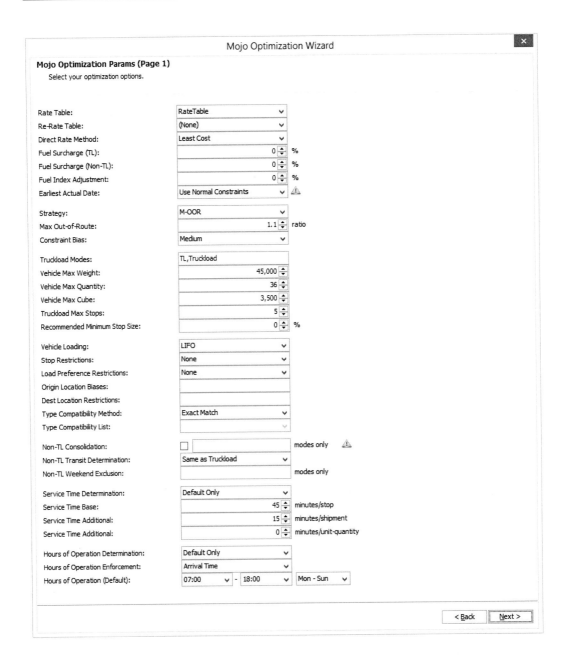

Rate Table: The name of the rate table open in MercuryEdge to use in the optimization.

Re-Rate Table: Advanced optional feature to specify a second rate table to conduct re-rating after the initial optimization. For example, we might run a "light" optimization in a MercuryEdge rate table, then conduct a more intensive server-based rating.

Direct Rate Method: The method Mojo should use to calculate the direct rate it should try to improve upon. Usually set to "Least Cost."

Fuel surcharges: A percentage uplift for quick calculations of what-if impacts of fuel-cost changes.

Fuel Index Adjustment: A global offset to apply to any fuel indexes associated with rate tables being used for rating.

Earliest Actual Date: Used to prevent Mojo from building live loads with pickup dates in the past. Example: pickup windows in shipments from Monday to Wednesday with optimization occurring on Tuesday.

Strategy: Adjusts Mojo's fundamental optimization strategy. The two most common options are M-OOR (Max-out-of-Range) and NOGGIN. Others include SPARR and STOCHAT. The first three have an "Hz" variant for unusual geographic features. Consult MercuryGate for uses other than M-OOR or NOGGIN.

Max-Out-of-Route: This number is a ratio of the sum of the legs in a load against the direct distance between origin and final destination. A zigzag route would have a higher ratio. Although the maximum possible value is 25, as a practical matter carriers may reject the tenders of loads with ratios higher than 1.4. See also Max Out-of-Route M-OOR looping option.

Constraint Bias: Values of high/medium/low reflect how likely Mojo is to use already-provisioned vehicles instead of new vehicles. Comes into play when the potential savings is negligible. Mojo can be instructed to run multiple constraint-bias scenarios; see Constraint Bias.

Truckload Modes: Enter a comma-delimited list of terms that Mojo should use to recognize a truckload mode, such as "TL,Truckload." Some rate tables may use other terms that should be included here.

Vehicle Max Weight/Quantity/Cube, Truckload Max Stops: Self-explanatory. These settings WILL BE OVERRIDEN BY THE RATE TABLE if the rate table's values are smaller. Besides reflecting real-world limits, these values can be adjusted to study the effect of what-if scenarios, such as carrier capacity.

Recommended Minimum Stop Size: Tells Mojo to avoid placing relatively small drops on the same multi-stop route as relatively large ones. The actual ratio is known as "relative effective stop size." Each drop is calculated as a percentage of vehicle capacity by weight, quantity or cube (whichever is largest). Then these ratios are compared against each other. Example: stop 1 is 3.3% of capacity, stop 2 is 95%, so the size of the first relative to the second is 3.3%/95% = 3.5%. If this figure is below the parameter setting, Mojo is discouraged from putting the two drops on the same route.

Vehicle Loading: This parameter enforces the "Loading Priority" column mapped from the shipment data. The options are "LIFO" (Last In First Out) and "Any Order." Using the LIFO setting makes loads with other, conflicting constraints subject to LIFO violations and not being optimized.

Stop Restrictions: Applies only to multi-pick/multi-stop loads. The options are None, No Multi-Pick, No Multi-Drop, No Pickups After 1st Drop, Drop Bias. Choosing "Drop Bias" tells Mojo to schedule drops before pickups when the distance is not significantly farther. In effect, this biases Mojo toward continuous moves.

Load Preference Restrictions: This setting enforces the "Load Preference" column mapped from the shipment data. The options are None, Enforce (Single Only), Enforce (Allow Groups), Bias (Normal) and Bias (Strong). The single-only option means only shipments with the same load preference may be consolidated. The allow-groups option allows shipments with different preferences to be on the same load. The bias options may split shipments with matching preferences for greater savings; a strong bias generally is more likely to leave them together.

Vehicle Speed: Self-explanatory. To adjust for average speed around congested areas such as city centers use instead the "Service Time Base" parameter Service Times.

Origin Location Bias: Enter a comma-delimited list of location codes that indicate a preference for first/earlier pickup; e.g., two warehouse locations in the same city. Only applicable to multi-pick loads. Biases Mojo toward the outcome but does not force it.

Dest Location Restrictions: Comma-separated list of location codes that must be last on a route. If a route does not have a location that is restricted, all normal routing rules apply. If a route has more than one location that is restricted, the route is invalid ("DestRestriction-constrained"). If a route has one restricted location, the last drop will be at the specified location.

Type Compatibility Method: Shipments can be consolidated according to type by requiring an exact match, or else use of a "compatibility list" or "incompatibility list" that specifies compatibility by individual types.

Type Compatibility List: If the previous field specifies use of a list, this field contains a dropdown menu list of compatibility reports open in MercuryEdge. The report type must be "OptConstraint." The report contains two columns labeled "Type 1" and "Type 2". In a compatibility list, the report specifies which types can be consolidated with each other. In an incompatibility list, shipments can be consolidated with any type *not* specified in the report. Types with blanks are treated as wildcards that can be consolidated with any other type.

Non-TL Consolidation: By default Mojo only considers "truckload" vehicles. If this option is enabled you can enter a comma-delimited list of other, non-TL modes to consider, e.g., "LTL,Parcel." Or you can enable the option and leave the list empty, meaning all contracts are eligible for consolidation.

Non-TL Transit Determination: Determines non-TL (single-stop) transit time either in the same manner as for truckload contracts or by an alternate method as follows:

- Using the Direct Service Days column mapped from the shipment data.

- Using two optional columns in the Edge rate table with the headings "Transit Method" and "Transit Value." If the entry contains the value "Service Days," Mojo uses the value (1-99) in the value column. If the method column contains the value "Zone Days," then the value column contains a value relative to the calculated zone. Example: Column = 3, value = -1, Mojo uses a value of 2 for service days.

- If neither of these options is used, Mojo uses a value returned from a TMS contract.

Non-TL Weekend Exclusion: By default weekend days are excluded for <u>all</u> carriers. This behavior can be overridden in this field by entering a comma-delimited list of <u>only</u> the modes for which weekends should be excluded (for non-listed modes, weekends will be included). In general, most LTL carriers will keep the exclusion; in general most intermodal carriers will include weekends; parcel tends to depend on additional contract information. This field is enabled when the previous parameter, Non-TL Transit Determination, is set to "Use Specified Values."

Service Times: The options for the "Service Time Determination" parameter are "Default Only" and the names of any Load/Unload Service Time reports open in MercuryEdge. The default-only setting uses the next three settings (Service Time Base, Service Time Additional) as global values. Shipments with a location code not listed in the report will default to the global values. The fields of a Load/Unload Service Time report are:

Location Code (mandatory)   *String*
Service Time Base   *Numeric*
Service Time Per Shipment   *Numeric*
Service Time Per Quantity   *Numeric*
Delivery Idle Time   *Numeric*

Hours of Operation Determination: The possible values are Default Only, Use Shipment Hours, and the names of any Location Hours reports open in MercuryEdge. The default-only setting applies the default settings of the next two parameters globally. The shipment-hours setting uses the hours specified in the shipment data. The hours of operation for each location specified in a Location Hours report will be used instead of the default. The fields of a Location Hours report are:

Location Code (mandatory)   *String*
Days   <Constant>
Hours   hh – hh, hh:mm – hh:mm

Example formats for location hours:

Mon-Fri, Mon-Sat,Mon-Sun
Mon,Tue,Wed,Thu,Fri,Sat,Sun
Date: 12-25
Date: 2012-11-22

Specific dates are considered before recurring dates; weekly or day-of-week after that. Hence a location might be open Mon-Fri except on Dec. 25. Location codes also may include *DEFAULT* (with asterisks) for all locations not listed in the report, or *GLOBAL* applying to all locations if not overridden.

Hours of Operation Enforcement: The "Arrival" option in this setting allows any arrival before a facility's closing time. "Arrival/Departure" means arrival, unloading and departure before closing.

Mojo Optimization Wizard

Mojo Optimization Params (Page 2)

Select your optimization options.

Extend Early Ship Window:	0	days
Extend Late Ship Window:	0.5	days
Extend Early Delivery Window:	0.5	days
Extend Late Delivery Window:	0	days
Input Date Adjustment:	0	days
HOS / Speed Determination:	Default Only	
Vehicle Speed:	50	mph
Driver Duty Limit:	14	hours
Driver Driving Limit:	11	hours
Driver Off-Duty Rest:	10	hours
Route Duty Limit:	70	hours
Allow Off-Duty Extension:	☐ 84	hours max
Carrier Capacity Strategy:	Off	⚠
Carrier Capacity Enforcement:	Optimized Loads Only	
Carrier Capacity Default:	10	
Dock Capacity Strategy:	Off	
Dock Time Requirements:	Full Service Time	
Dock Capacity Default (Pickup):	3	docks/location
Dock Capacity Default (Drop):	3	docks/location
Private Fleet Strategy:	Off	
Private Fleet SCAC:	PFLT	
Backhaul Bias:	Off	
International Stop Restrictions:	None	
Pool Strategy:	Off	
Pool Locations:		
Pool Assignment:	Pre-assigned Only	
Max Pool Hold Time:	2	days
Equipment Enforcement:	☐ ⚠	
Services Enforcement:	☐ ⚠	

< Back   Next >

Extend Early Ship/Late Ship/Early Delivery/Late Delivery Window: Allows Mojo to be flexible in its time windows for pickup and delivery, in increments of half-days at a time. Mojo reports how much of the available extension that it used in the "Pickup Window" and "Delivery Window" columns of the Optimizer Shipments tab. Time extensions often are used to optimize historical data where only one date (e.g., ship-by) is available. Another common tactic is to extend the inner windows (late pickup, early delivery) to achieve better results. Individual shipments may override these extension settings in a "Shipment Options" column.

Input Date Adjustment: A global adjustment that can be applied against times in the shipment data. One example of usage would be to adjust historical shipments into the effective period of a contract for rating. Clicking the field adjusts the offset in increments of seven days, recommended to comport with any location service days constraints.

HOS/Speed Determination: If this parameter is set to "Use Lane Info," then Mojo uses the "Transit Method" column of a MercuryEdge rate table. The value in each row of the rate table should have the format: "HOS: #1/#2/#3/#4/#5" where #1 = Vehicle Speed, #2 = Driver Duty Limit, #3 = Driver Driving Limit, #4 = Driver Off-Duty Rest, #5 = Route Duty Limit. For example, "HOS: 50/14/11/10/70" for typical USDOT single-driver. An alternate form is simply "HOS: #1" where #1 = vehicle speed, with driver and route limits using wizard-based defaults in the following parameters.

Driver constraints: The defaults are set to USDOT regulations but are configurable, for instance in a tandem-driver scenario. Mojo uses these values in calculating transit times.

Allow Off-Duty Extension: Allows Mojo to include off-duty driver time as part of its calculations. Important, for example, for shipments with a short transit time that might arrive before a facility's operating hours. Off-duty extensions/Hours violations.

Carrier Capacity Strategy: By default Mojo assumes carrier capacity is infinite. Other available options in this setting are:

Vehicles available per origin or destination per day
Vehicles available per origin/destination pair per day
Vehicles available per contract per lane per day
Vehicles available per carrier per origin or
    destination per run, or dest per run
Vehicles available per carrier per origin/destination pair per run
Vehicles available per contract per lane per run

Carrier Capacity Enforcement: Option to enforce carrier capacity limits even on non-optimized (i.e., direct) loads. If this option is enabled and a violation occurs, a "Capacity Violation" flag is raised on the load. If it is not enabled, non-optimized loads are is assigned the direct rate automatically.

Carrier Capacity Default: If the capacity strategy is not "Off," sets the default number of vehicles available. Detailed values for carrier capacity can be specified using a "Capacity" column in the RateTable itself.

Dock Capacity Strategy: Either off, or tied to a Dock Capacity report open in MercuryEdge. Names of open reports appear in the dropdown menu of this parameter. A dock-capacity report has the required columns Location Code, Pickup Docks, Drop Docks. With no dock restrictions Mojo will schedule the first route pickup as early in the day as possible. A dock capacity limits the number of vehicles that can be unloaded/loaded at the same time.

Private Fleet Strategy/Private Fleet SCAC: Options are "Off" and, if using a private fleet, "Return Vehicle." The SCAC of the carrier should be in the "Private Fleet SCAC" parameter. This strategy may be used with or without backhaul bias. Use the "Origin Location Bias" parameter Origin Location Bias to specify a fleet origin, which must also be a shipment origin. The final return leg is identified by an "R" or "Return" in event-related fields in Mojo results.

Backhaul Bias: This parameter determines how likely Mojo is to allow a route with a partial or complete return toward its origin. Settings are Off, Low, Medium, High. Lower bias results in fewer backhauls allowed in Mojo's results; higher bias, more backhauls.

International Stop Restrictions: "None" or "No Backtracking," in which routes may not return across a border once a stop is completed.

Pool Strategy: Options are Off, Consider Pools, Consider Hybrid, Force Pools. Strongly recommended to use "Force Pools" first with new data because errors such as missing rates will be flagged in results. With the "consider" options Mojo simply does not assign a pool location. The final wizard screen has an improvement option called "Consider Pools Depth" Consider Pools Depth .

Pool Locations: Will contain a dropdown list of any Pool Location reports open in MercuryEdge. A pool-location report is required for an optimization involving pools. The only required columns in a Pool Location report are Location Code and Geo, but other possible columns include Name, City, State, Country, Drop Modes, Drop SCACs, Pickup Modes and Pickup SCACs.

Pool Assignment: Controls the way Mojo assigns pool locations. The options are:

Pre-assigned Only:	Uses "Pool Location" column defined in mapping screen
Best Rate (Predictive):	Assign a pool loc with the

	lowest predicted rate.
Best Rate (Introspective):	In-depth analysis; significantly longer than predictive
Nearest to Ratetable Origin	
Nearest to Ratetable Dest	
Nearest to M-OOR Origin	Nearest pool that passes the M-OOR constraint, if one is available
Nearest to M-OOR Dest	
Nearest to Origin	

Max Pool Hold Time: Limits time allowed for a shipment at a pool location. Increasing hold time generally improves optimization opportunities. This global setting can be overridden for individual locations with a "Max Pool Hold Time" column in a Pool Locations report.

Equipment/Services Enforcement: When enabled, these options enforce the equipment and/or services column mapped from the shipment data in the first screen of the wizard Equipment/Services. Equipment and services in the rate table are specified in columns headed "Carrier Equipment" and "Carrier Services."

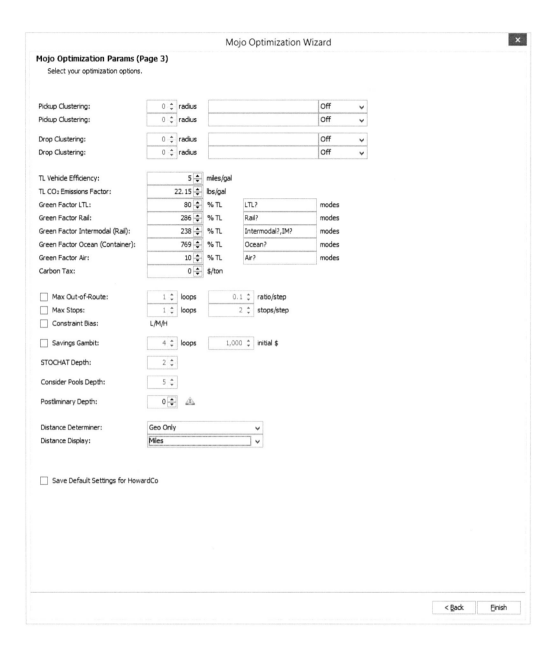

Pickup/Drop Clustering: Allows pickup and/or drop events to be limited by specified radius/radii. Pickup radius determined by first pickup location. Drop radius determined by last drop location. Limits may be defined by SCAC or mode (use comma-separated lists). Up to four distinct limits may be defined.

Green Methodology/CO2: For calculating estimated CO2 savings, sets a truckload baseline and calculates other modes as a percentage relative to the baseline. Enter a comma-separated list of modes in the right-hand column to which this calculation should apply. (The question marks in the default values exist to prevent interference with any existing calculations. Remove them if you want the calc to apply to that mode.) "Carbon Tax" adds a "CO2" accessorial on all ratetable-derived rates based on CO2 usage. Typical values are $10-$50 per ton. For the sources of the default values and a disclaimer on fleet assumptions, see the user manual topic.

Max Out-of-Route: Tells Mojo to run multiple M-OOR scenarios with the specified number of loops and the increment to use in each loop. Example: the Max Out-of-Route parameter on the second wizard screen is set to 1.4, then on this screen the settings are 3 additional loops with an increment of 0.1. Mojo runs loops at values of 1.4, 1.3, 1.2 and 1.1 The best option will be listed in the "Notes" tab of Mojo results.

Max Stops: Tells Mojo how many times to consider a new maximum-stop value and how much to increase that value on each loops.

Constraint Bias: Conduct multiple runs with each possible constraint bias, low, medium and high. Constraint Bias.

Savings Gambit: Potentially finds fewer loads but an overall savings is not guaranteed. At initial settings of 4 loops and initial value of $1,000, Mojo finds loads that each save a minimum of $1,000, then $667, then $333, then finally all remaining loads with any savings.

STOCHAT Depth: Sets Mojo's depth when using the "STOCHAT" strategy STOCHAT Depth. Valid range is 1-4 with default of 2.

Consider Pools Depth: How deep to search in pooling scenarios. Possible values are 1-10 with a default of 5. At a setting of 2, Mojo considers only two runs, all shipments forced through a pool and none forced through a pool. Intermediate settings reflect additional combinations of pooled and non-pooled shipments.

Postliminary Depth: How deep to look overall. Possible values range from 0 to 100. A value of 0 performs no adjustments to Mojo's original solution. Values between 10 and 20 usually provide the best compromise between optimizer time and overall savings. Large datasets (>5000 shipments) will most likely perform unacceptably with values above 5.

Distance Determiner: Tells Mojo whether to use server-based or cached distance calculations instead of its faster, default geocode-based calculation, which is usually sufficient. Options are Geo Only, Distance Table Cache (zip-to-zip distances), Server-Lite (combination of server and non-server distances) and Server (slowest option).

Distance Display: Set to miles or kilometers. Distance columns are labeled "Distance." To revert to earlier label of "Mileage," use optimization parameter "outputversion=2" or lower.

Save Default Settings: All wizard settings are saved for the current company. Remember that saving Mojo results as a Mojo package also preserves the settings used for the run.

Finish: Tells Mojo to conduct an optimization based on the settings chosen in the wizard.

Chapter 12: Managing Inbound Freight

The ability to manage inbound freight – taking control of the movement of goods coming to us from our suppliers - is not something most of us do as individuals. We can buy a shirt online, but we don't get to book the truck that brings it to us.

On a larger business scale, however, active management of inbound freight, as a seamless part of the overall transportation mix, is one of the great opportunities of modern logistics. With active inbound management we have the chance to achieve savings and consolidations that otherwise would simply not exist.

The extent to which we can exercise this management is a function of our contractual terms and relationships with suppliers. But it would not be possible to the extent it is today without the visibility and control that our systems afford us.

The more control that we gain over our inbound freight, the more opportunity we have for efficiency and cost savings.

The Historical Model (Or, How Not To Do It)

In the pre-digital era inbound freight was closer to the "passive consumer" model - it arrived when it arrived, and you paid what you were told. Transportation costs were embedded in the cost of the goods and as the buyer you had limited visibility of those transportation costs (or no visibility at all).

There was no opportunity to consolidate inbound shipments because there was no control over them. There was no linkage between purchase orders to vendors and any records of the shipments that they generated in response. There was no opportunity to gain efficiency by scheduling and management of inbound facilities.

In this all-manual, non-integrated world, ship dates often were inaccurate and there was little ability to verify item and ship unit information. Shipment status or expected delivery information was not easily available.

Each supplier operated within its own, isolated "silo" and incurred whatever transportation costs it saw fit to incur – with freight as a profit center, and with the consignee (us) ultimately footing the bill.

The Modern Model: Visibility and Control

The contrast with modern inbound management is dramatic. A strong system involves visibility and up-to-the-second information flowing between supplier and consignee. The information flow includes the use of EDI messages (purchase orders, status updates), XML extracts and imports, and updates that can be made directly by supplier-users with their own logins into a TMS.

Other hallmarks of the modern system include centralized planning and consignee control of ship date and carrier mode. That means now we have access to our entire universe of inbound shipments in the TMS, where we can consolidate and optimize them to our benefit. The net effect is overall lower transportation spend.

Figure 12-1 illustrates the multi-directional flow of information in inbound freight management:

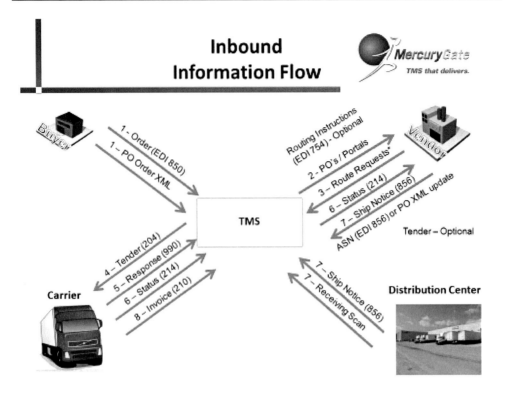

Fig. 12-1: Multidirectional information flow in a modern inbound freight-management system. Purchase orders come into the TMS from the buyer/consignee and accessed by suppliers, who in turn create shipments/routing requests to fulfill them. Loads created in the TMS are tendered to carriers and executed.

Most importantly, the modern inbound system involves actively managed partnerships between vendors and consignees, with a clear understanding of the responsibilities of the two roles. The terms of the relationship are laid out in the customer agreement.

This relationship is built on communication and cooperation. At the same time, the technology gives consignees more information than ever for managing supplier compliance and performance based on metrics such as timely fulfillment, claims, order accuracy, and proper record-keeping.

A Shipper Model

For an example of active inbound freight management, we can look to the standard shipper model of a TMS. Here's how it works:

- The TMS client creates purchase orders in the system representing goods to be supplied by its vendors. Purchase orders can be created by an external system integrated with the TMS, or they can created manually by internal users.

- Suppliers have their own logins to the TMS client's enterprise. They view their purchase orders and fulfill them by creating shipments/customer loads in the system.

- Internal TMS users see the supplier's new shipments in the system as part of the overall transportation flow. All shipments are available for consolidation into efficient carrier loads.

- As loads are created, operations users manage them on load boards through booking, tracking, delivery and invoicing, through the regular life cycle.

Purchase Orders

A purchase order is a record of a request to buy a quantity of goods from a supplier. TMS purchase orders often are created via integration with an external system such as an ERP system or an order management system.

TMS users create a purchase order in a manner similar to that of a shipment, specifying the supplier, desired destination, items and quantities. Purchase orders are the starting point for our management of an inbound movement. Suppliers will create records of shipments/customer loads in fulfillment of the orders.

When a supplier creates a shipment In response to a purchase, one of three things is true:

(1) The created shipment is a partial fulfillment of the order, which remains available until it is fulfilled.
(2) The shipment fulfills the purchase order, which moves in the system to a "Fulfilled" status and no longer appears as an option to suppliers.
(3) The supplier provides a "fill and kill" response, proposing to satisfy the order with a lesser quantity. The buyer retains approval rights over such actions.

Figure 12-2 is the detail of a purchase order record that shows not only the original order, but the records of shipments created in the system in response.

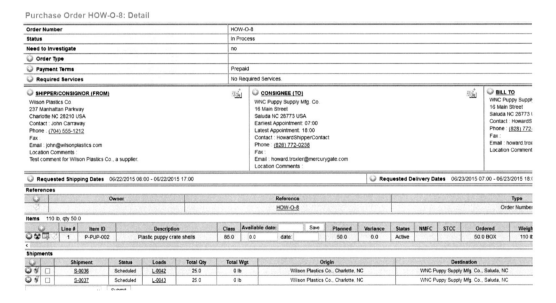

Fig. 12-2: A TMS purchase order record showing requested shipper, destination, item and quantity information, and shipments to date that have been created in fulfillment.

Purchase Order Portlet

Once purchase orders are created they are viewed in their own TMS portlet (Fig. 12-3).

Purchase Orders (Internal)

		Next Activity Type	Owner	Next Activity Planne	Order Number	Status	Create Date
☐	⊞	Request Routing	Wilson Plastics ...	06/22/2015 11:55	HOW-O-7	Pending	06/22/2015 11
☐	⊞	Request Routing	Wilson Plastics ...	06/22/2015 14:21	HOW-O-8	Pending	06/22/2015 14
☐	⊞	Request Routing	Specialty Wire P...	06/22/2015 14:32	HOW-O-10	Pending	06/22/2015 14
☐	⊞	Request Routing	Specialty Wire P...	06/22/2015 14:32	HOW-O-11	Pending	06/22/2015 14

Report Format: HCS PO — Filter: 4 Results

Mass Update ▾

Fig. 12-3: Purchase order portlet, internal user's view – all purchase orders for all suppliers are visible.

Internal users see all pending purchase orders in the portlet. External users representing suppliers are set up in the system to view only the orders that are owned by their own company or family of related companies.

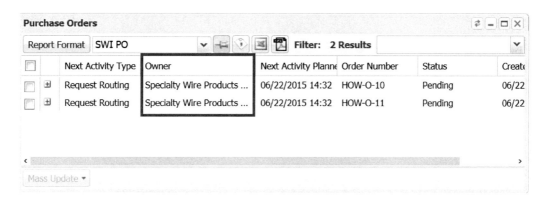

Purchase Orders

		Next Activity Type	Owner	Next Activity Planne	Order Number	Status	Create
☐	⊞	Request Routing	Specialty Wire Products ...	06/22/2015 14:32	HOW-O-10	Pending	06/22
☐	⊞	Request Routing	Specialty Wire Products ...	06/22/2015 14:32	HOW-O-11	Pending	06/22

Report Format: SWI PO — Filter: 2 Results

Mass Update ▾

Fig. 12-4: A user representing a supplier sees only his/her own company's purchase orders.

Clicking an entry in the list expands more information about that purchase order. In the example below we see that the order has a pending activity named "Request Routing."

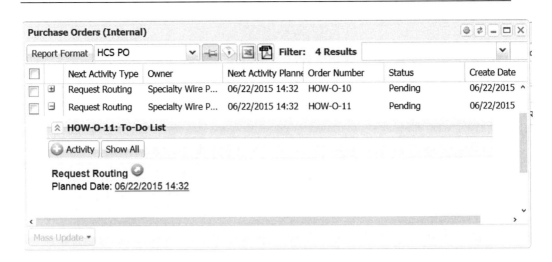

Fig. 12-5: Expanded purchase order display with a pending 'Request Routing' activity.

Routing

The supplier-user's job is to create shipments that fulfill the routing request. To do this, the user selects one or more purchase orders in the portlet by the left-hand checkbox, and selects the command "Route" from the mass-update menu at the bottom of the portlet.

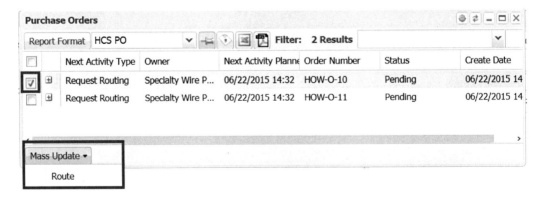

Fig. 12-6: The supplier's TMS user starts the process by selecting one or more purchase orders in the list, and choosing 'Route' from the portlet's Mass Update menu.

The "Route" command takes the supplier-user through a series of screens for creating a shipment. The exact sequence and fields displayed are configurable – TMS clients can allow as much or as little leeway as they wish to their suppliers.

The first screen (Fig. 12-7) asks the user to select the items/ship units from the selected purchase order(s) to be routed:

Fig. 12-7: Supplier selects the item(s) from the purchase orders to fill.

On the next screen the supplier might be asked to confirm origin-destination information:

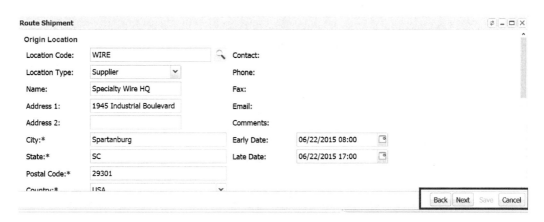

Fig. 12-8: Supplier confirms origin and destination information. This step can be omitted.

The following screen allows the user to specify required services or equipment, and finally the actual items being shipped (Fig. 12-9):

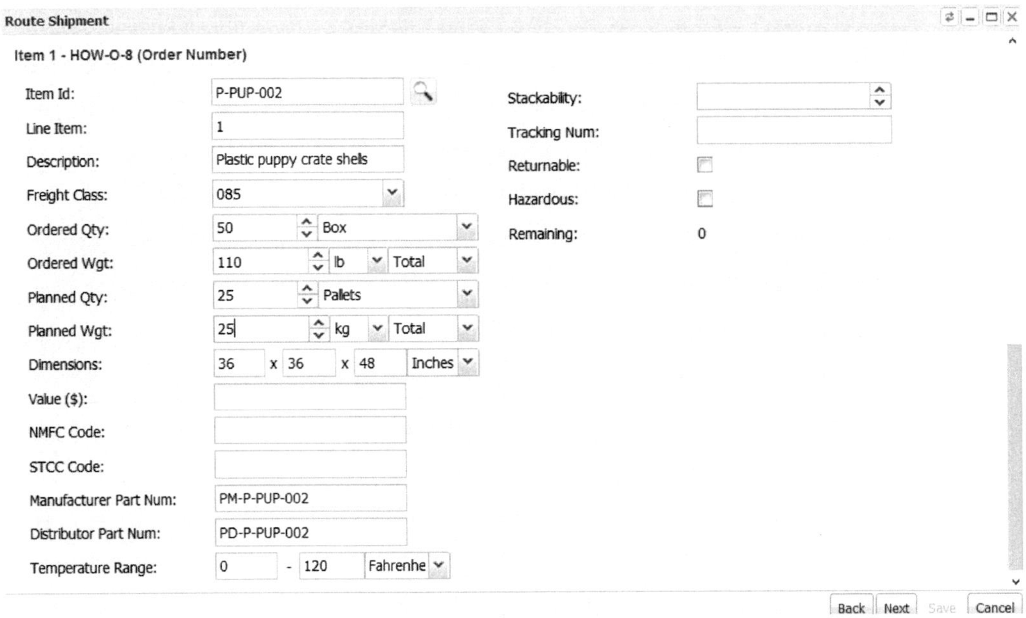

Fig. 12-9: Specifying item information in the creation of the shipment.

"Ordered quantity" is the total quantity of the purchase order. "Planned quantity" refers to the quantity of this shipment, which allows either a partial or entire fulfillment of the order.

The remaining screens that the supplier-user might or might not see include special instructions, contact information, bill-to information and acceptance of terms and conditions. However, every screen and option is configurable – the TMS client might want the supplier to perform only a minimum number of these steps.

Upon clicking "Save" the user sees a pop-up showing that the shipment has been created. Once a purchase order is completely fulfilled, it drops off the list shown in the purchase order portlet.

Shipments and Loads

The routing requests created by vendor-users feed into the pool of all available shipments/customer loads in the TMS for load-building and consolidation.

Depending on the company's practices, "inbound" shipments could even be consolidated with "outbound" shipments if it makes sense to put them on the same truck.

Our model offers two ways of consolidating shipments into carrier loads that might contain several shipments. The first is through Mojo, MercuryGate's optimization tool, discussed in an earlier chapter.

Given a list of shipments, a list of carrier rates, and a list of constraints on how to build the loads, Mojo will arrive at a list of proposed carrier loads (Fig. 12-10).

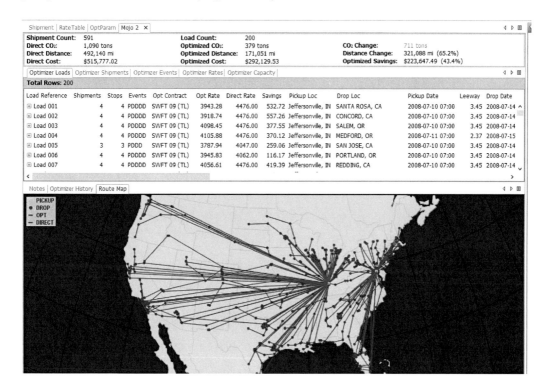

Fig. 12-10: Screen of Mojo results showing shipments consolidated into recommended carrier loads.

As an alternative to Mojo, many TMS clients consolidate manually in a TMS portlet called the "Load Builder." Users click and drag shipments down from a shipment list (or existing loads from a load list that they want to re-combine) into a new tab to create a proposed load. From there users can create the load and obtain a carrier rating.

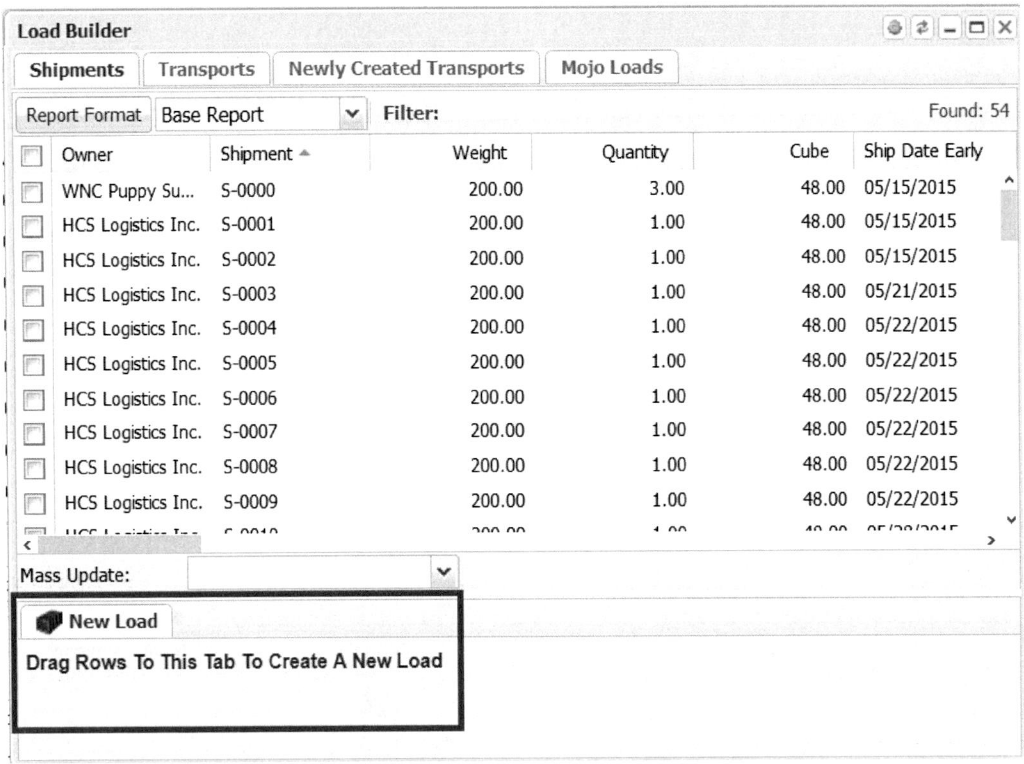

Fig. 12-11: Load Builder portlet. Users click and drag entries from the list to the "New Load" tab to consolidate.

Select, click and drag the shipments to consolidate to the "Create New Load" tab at the bottom of the screen. The candidate shipments now populate the proposed new load, showing their origin, destination and other information. Users can create the load, obtain a rating, edit the proposed events, view the shipments in detail or find a possible matching transport.

After a load has been created, it is managed on the load board via the familiar blue-button workflow.

Conclusion

The TMS architecture of purchase orders, supplier-users with their own logins, and fulfillment gives the enterprise final control over the management of inbound freight.

Not only is the process visible from the start, with up-to-the-minute information available at all times, but TMS enterprises have the opportunity to benefit from consolidation, rate management, and the other advantages of controlling their own freight.

Chapter Discussion

Why does inbound freight management present us with opportunities for cost savings? What are the main ways by which those savings are realized?

Chapter 13:   Private Fleet vs. Common Carrier

Some providers also arrange the movement of freight on their own assets – their own drivers, tractors, trailers, equipment and facilities. They might be using such assets exclusively, or they might be working them into the mix.

One example would be a large retail shipper routing its own trucks to move goods from distribution centers to retail locations. Another example might be a large carrier that also operates its own brokerage.

We'll use the term <u>private fleet</u> to describe owned assets. Private fleets can be used in various ways:

- Exclusively, for all loads.
- As the required or preferred carrier for specific locations, geographic areas or load types (but see the warning about this below).
- As a backup or last resort when other options are unavailable or undesirable.
- As an everyday alternative, selected on a case-by-case basis.

There are two points to stress about the topic of private assets:

(1) Almost any arbitrary rule for asset usage – based on weight, mileage, geography or number of stops – should be avoided in favor of a true evaluation of options. Arbitrary and inflexible rules mean loss of efficiency and loss of money.

(2) Intelligent decisions about private assets depend on one key question. The question might seem simple, but it isn't. Yet unless

we have a good answer, we can't fairly evaluate private assets vs. common carriers – which means we cannot make correct decisions.

The key question is:

How much does a private fleet <u>really</u> cost?

'Total Cost of Ownership'

Many small and mid-sized owners of private assets do not really know how much their assets cost to own and operate. Instead the decision to deploy them is made on the basis of sentiments such as:

"We've already paid for them, so our only expenses are fuel and drivers." Or: "We invested in them, so it would be a waste not to use them." The first of those two statements is never true. The second is not necessarily true.

At the other extreme, some owners of large corporate fleets go to elaborate lengths to construct a true cost model that captures expenses that are not immediately obvious. Their goal is to arrive at a fair estimate of a figure known as "total cost of ownership."

The obvious expenses are the cost of the equipment itself, maintenance and drivers. (Fuel is an expense too, but remember we're paying a fuel surcharge to carriers anyway.) But here are some other costs that might need to be considered:

- Insurance.
- Regulatory, permitting and licensing expense, including required training.
- Depreciation.
- Financing expense.
- Administrative costs.
- Allocation of common expenses.

Some advanced models go even further and calculate the "opportunity cost" of owning fleet assets in the first place. In other words, would the company have been better off putting the money into a growing profit center instead, even if it meant somewhat higher third-party transportation costs?

These are hard questions to answer, which means that easy answers don't work. So the statement, "My only expenses are fuel and drivers" is untrue. As for not wanting to "waste" assets that have been bought and paid for – think of the familiar saying, "throwing good money after bad."

The decision of whether to invest in a private fleet has already been made, for better or worse. The question at hand is whether to use it, and that decision should be made purely on business considerations. It's tough to a mothball a truck if you're the one who made the decision to buy it, and it's your name in big letters on the side. But a heartless mega-corporation will do it the instant that it makes financial sense.

None of the above should be taken as a claim that private fleets are always a bad idea. They can provide least-cost efficiency in the right circumstance. And there might be other extremely important reasons for having control over your own operations.

Private Fleet Strategy

In the TMS, we set up private assets to be treated as a "carrier" to be selected for loads like any other. We'll then use the optimization tool to designate a private fleet strategy in which these assets compete for loads during optimization.

The Mojo tool allows us to consider a private fleet as part of any optimization scenario. The main setting is found on the third screen of the Mojo Optimization Wizard:

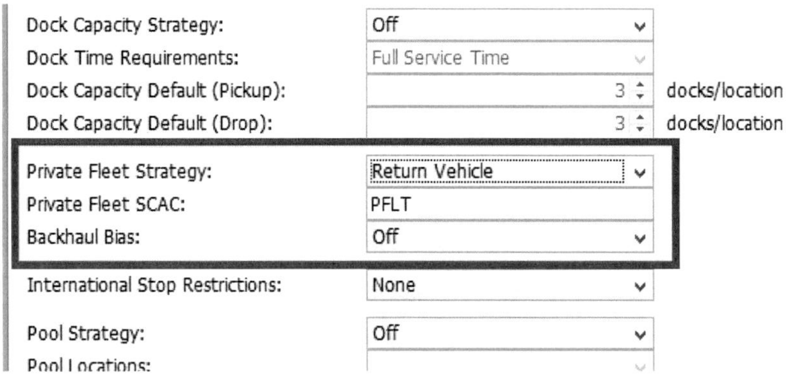

Fig. 13-1: Enabling a private-fleet strategy in the Mojo Optimization Wizard.

There are two possible values for the parameter labeled "Private Fleet Strategy": "Off" and "Return Vehicle." If this is set to "Return Vehicle," then Mojo will calculate return-to-origin mileage for the carrier designated by the next setting, "Private Fleet SCAC."

The purpose of including return-to-origin mileage is to acknowledge that our trucks have to get home. When we're hiring somebody else's truck, our relationship ends at the delivery, and that carrier has already covered its expenses in the rates it charges us. But if it's <u>our</u> truck we can't just pretend that it magically re-appears at home at no cost.

Even in TMS rating, an option exists to include return to origin mileage in rating a contract for private fleet assets (Fig. 13-2):

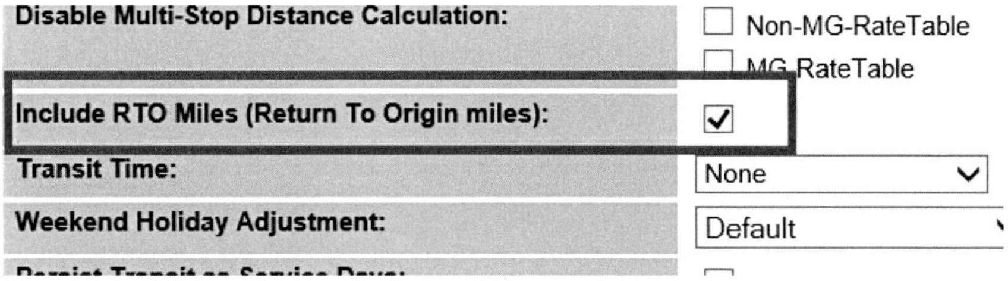

Fig. 13-2: Setting in a TMS contract telling the system to include Return to Origin miles in its calculations.

In Mojo, there are two other settings we use in conjunction with a private fleet strategy: Designating a fleet origin location, and including an accurate model of private fleet cost in our Mojo rate structure.

Fleet Origin

If your intention is to create multi-pick loads, then the Mojo parameter labeled "Origin Location Bias" on the previous (second) wizard screen should be set to the fleet's origin location code. Now routes that originate from that code will return to it after the final drop event.

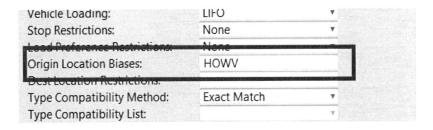

Fig. 13-3: Specifying fleet origin in Mojo parameters.

When Mojo builds loads and routes that employ the private fleet, and they originate from the fleet origin, then Mojo will return those trucks to the origin. In the event sequence of the Mojo load, return events are represented with an "R":

Fig. 13-4: Example of a route built with a return leg to fleet origin.

Return legs are displayed on the map as dotted lines:

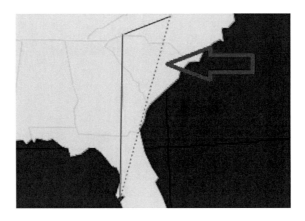

Fig. 13-5: Return leg displayed on Mojo results map.

When Mojo knows it is using return routes, it has the freedom to sequence events differently. Here's a route built without return to origin:

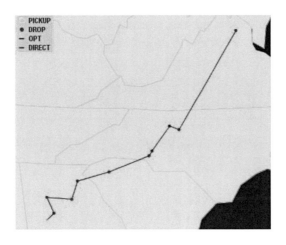

Fig. 13-6: Multi-drop load, but without return leg.

But knowing we're heading back, Mojo is able to take advantage of the return to smooth things out:

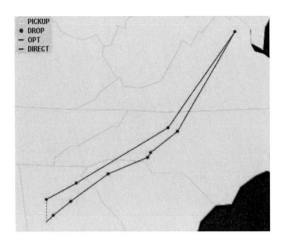

Fig. 13-7: Mojo uses return leg to smooth out load events.

Private Fleet Rates

The private fleet's rates must be identified by a SCAC in the Mojo rate table and associated with a per-mile rate. This is how the return-to-origin expense ordinarily is captured.

As we discussed earlier, developing an accurate rate model for the private fleet is crucial – if you underestimate true expense, then the private fleet "looks too good" compared to other carriers, and Mojo will wrongly favor it.

One solution is to create a rate table using a cost-per-mile estimate derived from Total Cost of Ownership divided by mileage. However, you also could create lanes that apply higher or lower rates by location code, city, state, or any other factor, to fine-tune the estimated cost.

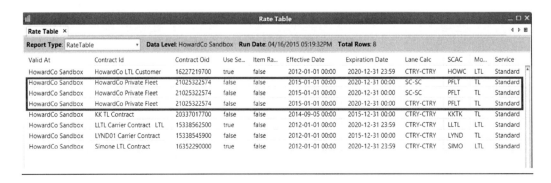

Valid At	Contract Id	Contract Oid	Use Se...	Item Ra...	Effective Date	Expiration Date	Lane Calc	SCAC	Mo...	Service
HowardCo Sandbox	HowardCo LTL Customer	16227219700	true	false	2012-01-01 00:00	2020-12-31 23:59	CTRY-CTRY	HOWC	LTL	Standard
HowardCo Sandbox	HowardCo Private Fleet	21025322574	false	false	2015-01-01 00:00	2020-12-31 00:00	SC-SC	PFLT	TL	Standard
HowardCo Sandbox	HowardCo Private Fleet	21025322574	false	false	2015-01-01 00:00	2020-12-31 00:00	SC-SC	PFLT	TL	Standard
HowardCo Sandbox	HowardCo Private Fleet	21025322574	false	false	2015-01-01 00:00	2020-12-31 00:00	CTRY-CTRY	PFLT	TL	Standard
HowardCo Sandbox	KK TL Contract	20337017700	false	false	2014-09-05 00:00	2015-12-31 00:00	CTRY-CTRY	KKTK	TL	Standard
HowardCo Sandbox	LLTL Carrier Contract LTL	15338562500	true	false	2012-01-01 00:00	2020-12-31 23:59	CTRY-CTRY	LLTL	LTL	Standard
HowardCo Sandbox	LYND01 Carrier Contract	15338545900	false	false	2012-01-01 00:00	2015-12-31 00:00	CTRY-CTRY	LYND	TL	Standard
HowardCo Sandbox	Simone LTL Contract	16352290000	true	false	2012-01-01 00:00	2020-12-31 23:59	CTRY-CTRY	SIMO	LTL	Standard

Fig. 13-8: Private fleet treated as a 'carrier' with rates in a Mojo rate table.

By requiring return miles, it might appear we have tied a heavy stone around the neck of our private fleet in the "race" with other carriers – we are making it travel a lot more miles in the rating. However, there are other factors to take into consideration:

(1) As noted earlier, the true cost of the third-party carrier's operation already is built into its carrier rates, so we're actually finally putting our private fleet on an apples-to-apples comparison.

(2) Charging ourselves full mileage for a return to origin and assuming no revenue to show for it is not necessarily realistic either. In practice, logistics providers go to a great deal of trouble to keep their trucks busy. In Mojo, we have the chance to build backhaul legs that take advantage of the direction we're heading. We'll talk about backhauls next.

Mojo and Backhaul Bias

In the least favorable case described above, our truck makes its last drop, and now turns to go home, empty and unused – while still burning fuel and money. In our rate table, we're charging ourselves the full cost of these "empty" miles.

Wouldn't it make sense to try to get something on the truck for part or all of the return leg? Of course. Every such backhaul that we can arrange produces revenue for all or part of a distance that we were going to travel anyway.

We can instruct Mojo to look for backhaul opportunities with another wizard setting – right below the private fleet settings – labeled "Backhaul Bias."

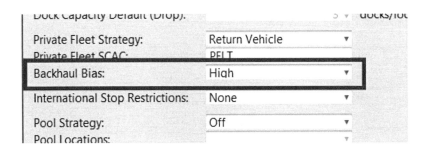

Fig. 13-9: Setting for the likelihood Mojo will built backhauls.

The available settings are high, medium, low, and off. The higher the setting, the more likely Mojo is to create backhauls.

Fig. 13-10: On the left: Backhauls not allowed. The Tampa Bay to Columbia shipment is treated as a separate load. On the right: With backhauls allowed, Mojo can use the Tampa-Columbia leg as a backhaul toward the origin. Now our final return leg from last drop to origin is much shorter.

Using backhauls helps produce a more accurate overall optimization, allows us to apply revenue against otherwise empty return legs, and reduces the number of routes and amount of total freight spend.

Requiring Asset Use

We can use Mojo's parameters to make sure that private fleet equipment is used in a specific way desired by the client. Let's say we want to make sure private assets are used for all refrigerated loads. The equipment is requested in the TMS shipment report, and therefore in the shipment report opened in MercuryEdge:

Mojo Shipments ×								
Report Type: Shipment ▾	Data Level: HCS Logistics Inc.	Run Date: 06/24/2015 02:35:23PM		Total Rows: 58				
Owner	Primary Reference	Equipment	Origin Code	Origin Name		Origin City	Origin State	Orig
HCS Logistics Inc.	S-0013 (BOL)	48 Ft Reefer (48R)	MSSC	Main Street Shipping Co		Saluda	NC	287
Wilson Plastics Co.	S-0037 (BOL)		WILS	Wilson Plastics Co.		Charlotte	NC	282

Fig. 13-11: Shipment report – this shipment requires refrigeration.

Meanwhile our private fleet's rate table should include a "Carrier Equipment" column (the column name must be exact) that states that this carrier does indeed provide the equipment type:

ents **Rate Table** × Mojo 11									◁ ▷ ▦
RateTable		Data Level: HowardCo Sandbox	Run Date: 04/17/2015 02:45:07PM		Total Rows: 8	Selected Rows: 1			
ak 2 ... Break 3 F...	Break 3 ...	Break 3 ...	Max S...	Transit Meth...	Transit V...	Notes	Accessorial Pr...	Carrier Equipment	
						SMC			
			11.00	Service Days	3.50			48 Ft Reefer (48R)	
			4.00	Service Days	1.50			48 Ft Reefer (48R)	
			4.00	Service Days	2.50			48 Ft Reefer (48R)	
			11.00	Service Days	2.25				

Fig. 13-12: Rate table – these lanes in the rate table provide refrigeration.

The final piece of the puzzle is turning on equipment enforcement in the Mojo Optimization Wizard. On the first wizard screen make sure that the shipment report's "Equipment" column is properly mapped. At the bottom of the third screen, make sure we actually are enforcing the equipment requirement.

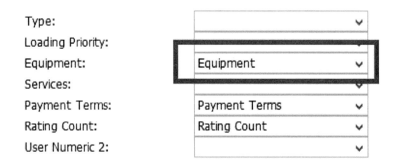

Fig. 13-13: Detail of Mojo wizard first screen, mapping 'Equipment column from shipment report.

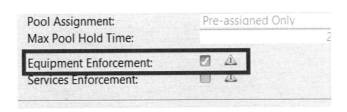

Fig. 13-14: Detail of third wizard screen, instructing Mojo to enforce equipment requirements.

Upon optimization, Mojo obeys the requirement and assigns refrigerated shipments to the private-fleet carrier with the equipment:

Load 21	1	1	PD	Simone LTL Contract (LTL)	445.90	445.90	0.00	St. Petersburg, FL
Load 22	1	1	PD	HowardCo Private Fleet (TL)	2698.56	2698.56	0.00	48 Ft Reefer (48R)	Saluda, NC

Notes Optimizer History Route Map

Fig. 13-15: Mojo obeys its instructions and assigns shipments that require refrigeration to the private fleet lanes that provide it.

Instead of equipment, we could just as easily require services that only the private fleet provides. We could use all-purpose, user-defined fields in shipment reports to match them with rate tables. Finally, in using location reports in Mojo, we have the option to restrict any location by SCAC, including the private fleet's:

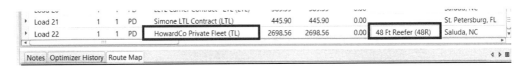

	A	B	C	D	E	F	G	H	I
	Location Code	Address1	City	State	Country	Postal Code	Geo	Drop SCACs	Pickup SCACs
2	POOL_CA	3855 N Lakewood Blvd	Long Beach	CA	USA	90846-0003	33.817400,-118.150900		
3	POOL_PA	1 Main St	Carlisle	PA	USA	17013-3713	40.204600,-77.199400		

Fig. 13-16: Ability to restrict a facility by carrier SCAC.

Posting Unused Capacity

One other possibility we should mention is sharing our remaining, unused return-to-origin capacity with public boards, as discussed in the "Finding Capacity" chapter.

In that scenario, we were looking for capacity that others had posted. But if we have access to the boards, we become the "carrier" posting our own private-fleet capacity for others to see. Every dollar so gained is a bonus.

Chapter Discussion

1. What is the biggest challenge to setting up a comparison of private fleet assets versus hiring outside carriers? What are some of the costs associated with operating private fleet assets that are often overlooked?
2. What does the Mojo "Private Fleet" option do? Why is it fair to put this requirement on private fleet rating? What are the ways that we can compensate for it?
3. Define "backhauls" and explain their relevance to offsetting private fleet costs.

Chapter 14: Mobile Solutions

We need mobile access to our logistics data from portable devices whether smartphone or tablet. We need to be able to execute actions at the level of individual records. But we also need mobile access to an overview of what's happening in our system.

Drivers in the field should be able to send the system updated status and call check information, and to supply required materials such as proof of pickup and proof of delivery. In return we should be able to post loads that carriers can view and accept in real time.

Not too long ago, figuring out how to get this kind of access at all was one of the "challenges" of logistics management. The challenge today, with mobile access as a fact of life, is exploring everything that we can do with it.

Among the capacities we'll discuss:

- Searching carrier and customer rates on the fly.
- Tracking loads in transit.
- Viewing TMS reports of shipments and loads.
- Status and call check updates from the field.
- Providing proof of delivery materials.
- Sharing news and information to mobile users.

A Mobile TMS Application

Fig. 14-1 TMS Mobile home screen for internal users.

The "TMS Mobile" application seamlessly applies the user permissions and settings that are already determined in the TMS. Mobile users are able to see the same data and perform the same functions that they can on the desktop TMS

Rate Carrier

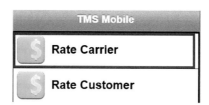

Use the "Rate Carrier" command to perform an informational contract rate inquiry. Clicking the "Rate Carrier" demand displays a screen asking the user to specify an origin and destination zip, a weight and a freight class. The information is rated against contracts in the system and a list of rate results is returned.

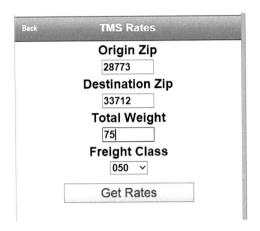

Fig. 14-2: Mobile carrier rating.

Clicking an entry in the list expands it to show any additional available details, and clicking again hides the details.

Louie-LTL
LLTL Carrier LTL SMC   **$115.13**
LTL
(Class: 50.0) $54.78
SMC Minimum Adjustment $73.14
Discount   -$12.79

Fig. 14-3: Detail of expanded carrier rate.

Rate Customer

Rate Carrier

Rate Customer

Track Shipment

The "Rate Customer" command works the same way as Rate Carrier, but searches rates against available customer contracts in the system. For example, a customer contract might be based on an uplift of a rate from a carrier contract.

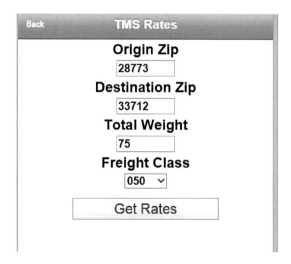

Back   **TMS Rates**

Origin Zip
28773
Destination Zip
33712
Total Weight
75
Freight Class
050 ⌄

Get Rates

Fig. 14-4: Mobile rating of customer contracts.

Track Shipment

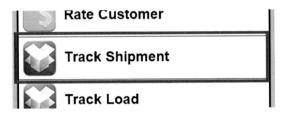

The "Track Shipment" command asks the user to enter the primary reference number of a shipment and provides a read-only display of the shipment status. (The next command, "Track Load," allows users the update the status of the owning load.)

Fig. 14-5: Mobile tracking of customer shipment by reference number.

Track Load

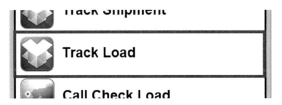

"Track Load" asks the user to enter an execution load number, then displays a status screen:

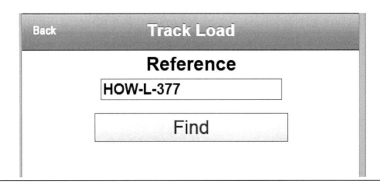

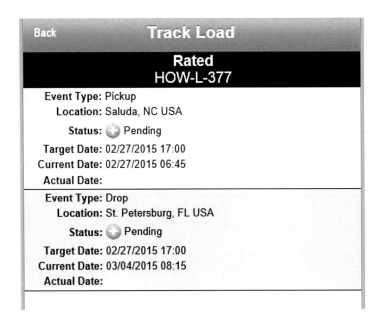

Fig. 14-6: Mobile tracking of carrier load, with ability to update event status.

Notice the " 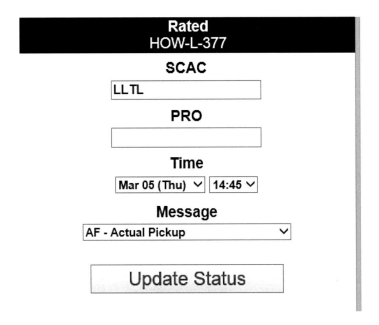 " icon next to the "Pending" status for both the pickup and drop event. Either an internal TMS user, or a driver-user with a login, can update the load status by clicking the add icon:

Fig. 14-7: Status message update via mobile device.

The "Message" field contains a dropdown list of status message codes used by the company:

Fig. 14-8: Status message select dialog.

The status message is added and the updated information is visible both in TMS Mobile, and back in the TMS under the load's record.

Fig. 14-9: Load status is updated in mobile view and in the TMS.

Proof of Delivery

After the addition of a delivery message, the user has the opportunity to add Proof of Delivery information, such as the image of a document, or a signature.

Clicking the "pencil" icon opens a window for adding a signature:

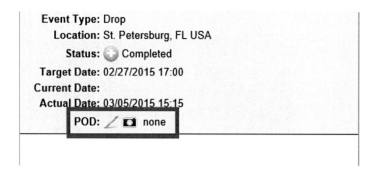

Fig. 14-10: Adding a POD signature via mobile screen.

Or clicking the "camera" icon lets the user capture an image of the POD document with the smartphone, or choose an existing image file, and upload it to the TMS load.

Call Check Load

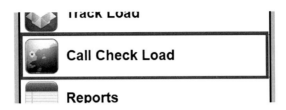

This command allows the user (whether in-house or driver) to enter the record of a call check on the load.

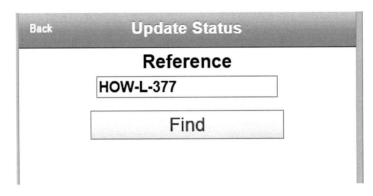

Fig. 14-11: Option to enter status check for a load in transit.

The "Add" button allows the user to add the call check. A smartphone user might be asked if the application can use the current location and populate the values, but the user can enter them as well:

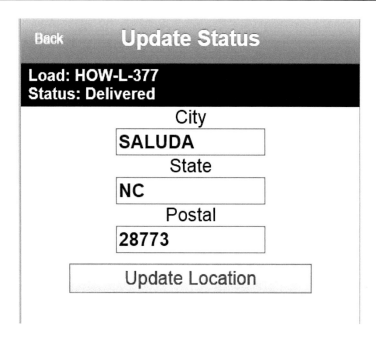

Fig. 14-12: Status check entry screen.

Clicking "Update Location" adds the call check to the load, with the current local timestamp:

Location: SALUDA, NC 28773
As of: 03/05/2015 16:02
User ID: Howard

Reports

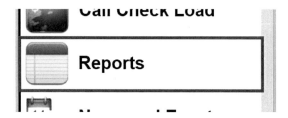

The Reports command leads to a menu of report types, for lists of records in the TMS system: purchase orders, shipments, carrier loads, tracking messages, carrier and customer invoices, or log messages.

Fig. 14-13: Report types available from 'Reports' option of mobile app.

For example, Figure 14-14 shows the submenu from clicking the Load report option. The entries in the list correspond to report formats available to the user the TMS:

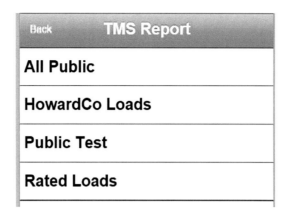

Fig. 14-14: TMS load reports available to this mobile user.

Clicking a report opens its contents:

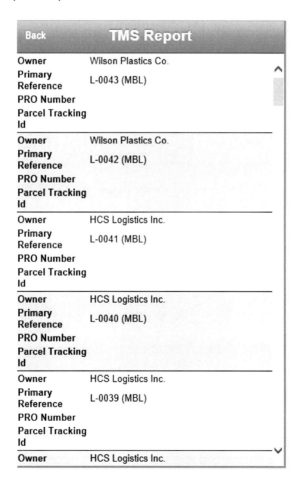

Fig. 14-15: TMS execution load report open in mobile app.

Here's a list of recent tracking messages available to the user:

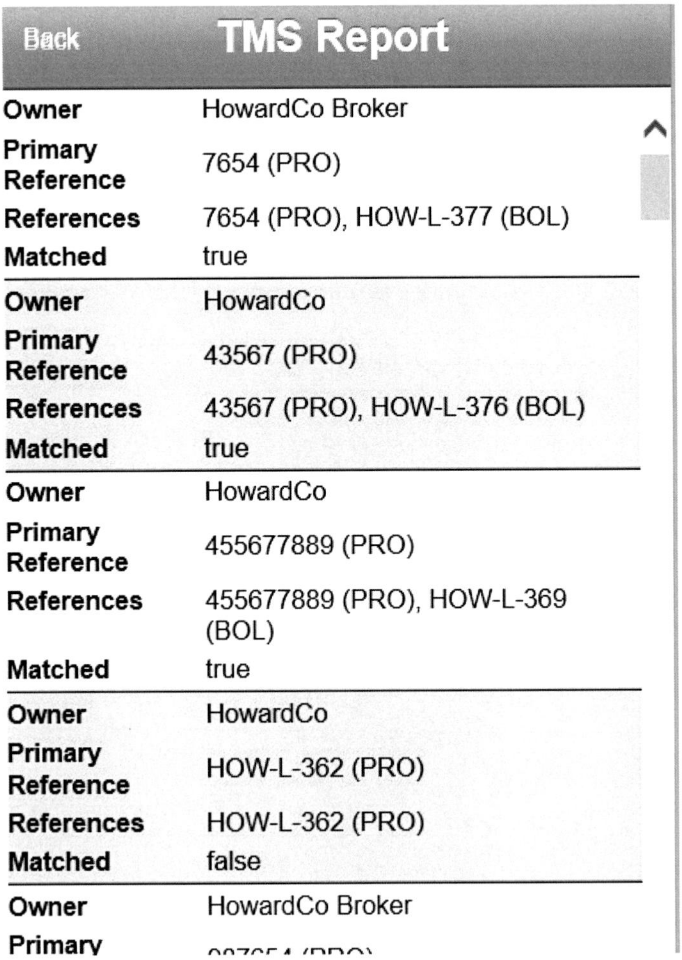

Back	TMS Report
Owner	HowardCo Broker
Primary Reference	7654 (PRO)
References	7654 (PRO), HOW-L-377 (BOL)
Matched	true
Owner	HowardCo
Primary Reference	43567 (PRO)
References	43567 (PRO), HOW-L-376 (BOL)
Matched	true
Owner	HowardCo
Primary Reference	455677889 (PRO)
References	455677889 (PRO), HOW-L-369 (BOL)
Matched	true
Owner	HowardCo
Primary Reference	HOW-L-362 (PRO)
References	HOW-L-362 (PRO)
Matched	false
Owner	HowardCo Broker
Primary	007654 (PRO)

Fig. 14-16: TMS tracking message report shown in mobile app.

Clicking on a tracking message reveals more detail:

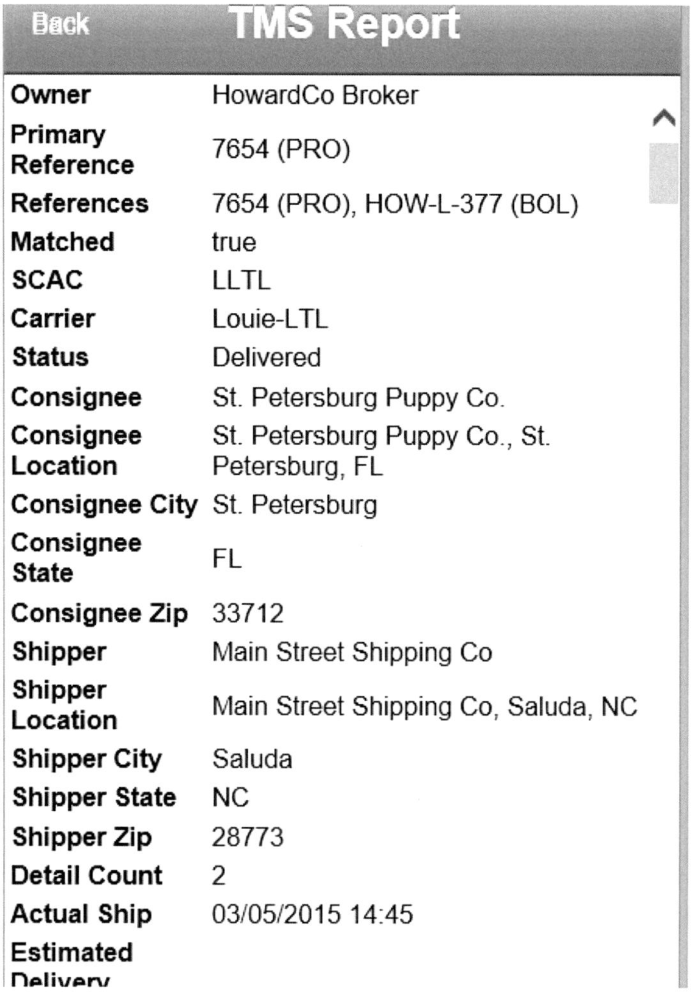

Back	TMS Report
Owner	HowardCo Broker
Primary Reference	7654 (PRO)
References	7654 (PRO), HOW-L-377 (BOL)
Matched	true
SCAC	LLTL
Carrier	Louie-LTL
Status	Delivered
Consignee	St. Petersburg Puppy Co.
Consignee Location	St. Petersburg Puppy Co., St. Petersburg, FL
Consignee City	St. Petersburg
Consignee State	FL
Consignee Zip	33712
Shipper	Main Street Shipping Co
Shipper Location	Main Street Shipping Co, Saluda, NC
Shipper City	Saluda
Shipper State	NC
Shipper Zip	28773
Detail Count	2
Actual Ship	03/05/2015 14:45
Estimated Delivery	

Fig. 14-17: Clicking a tracking message in the list expands to a screen of details. Clicking again collapses the entry.

Other Options

"News and Events" shows any news items currently posted for the enterprise. This can be a useful way to get information across to users who need it.

Fig. 14-18: News and event view in mobile app.

"Switch Company" displays a list of the companies in the hierarchy to which this user has access. The list is determined in the TMS user setting labeled "Quick Enterprise Change List."

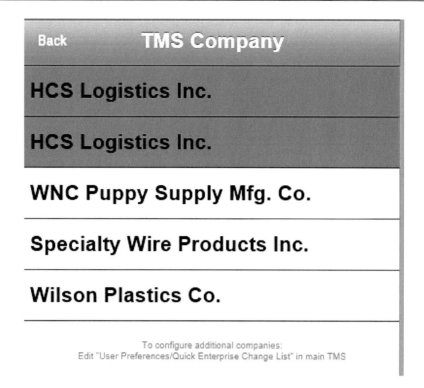

Fig. 14-19: Navigating the TMS hierarchy in mobile app.

Carrier Users

Carrier users see different options on the mobile home screen. Figure 14-20 shows a typical carrier screen. The driver can enter status messages via "Track Load," create call checks via "Call Check Load," or respond to pending bid requests via "Load Board." However, some options are not present that would be available to an internal operations users, such as "Rate Carrier" or "Rate Customer."

Fig. 14-20: TMS Mobile home screen for carrier users.

Besides the ability to track and call check loads as described earlier, the screen's "Load Board" option for carrier-users displays a screen to search for any loads in a geographic area that have been posted for bid by the TMS enterprise:

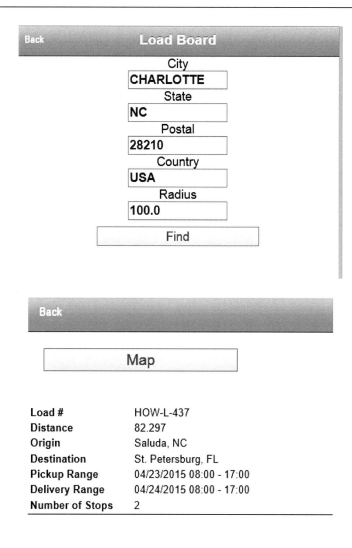

Fig. 14-21: Carrier users can search a geographic area for loads posted for bid.

In the results list, clicking the "Map" button displays the listed loads on a map.

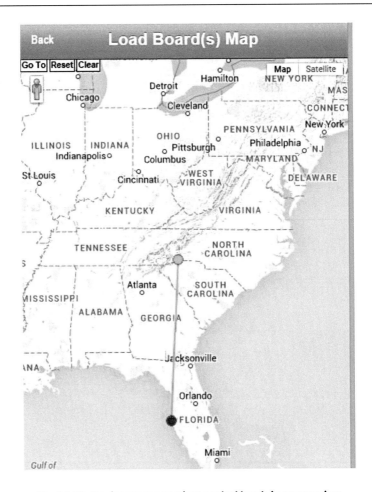

Fig. 14-22: Carrier users can view posted loads in a map view.

Tablet Application

Fig. 14-23: View of MercuryTouch dashboard.

In the tablet application shown, the home screen is a dashboard of configurable charts and graphs showing an overall picture of what's happening with the TMS enterprise.

Notice the five categories at the bottom of the screen that govern what's being displayed – graphs, maps, TMS reports, shipment tracking, or a settings screen.

Graphs

The dashboard upon login starts with the Graphs screen as shown in Fig. 14-23. In the illustration we see graphs for:

- Customer Revenue
- Carrier Cost

- Loads vs. Quotes
- Customer Revenue By Mode
- Carrier Mode by Mode
- Load Counts
- Average Carrier Cost
- Timeliness (Days)
- Average Customer Revenue
- Loads Total

The "Choose Group" button at the top left of the windows opens a dropdown menu of selection for other graph types to display: Costs, Lane Averages, Shipment Counts, Invoice Extracts and Weekly Fuel.

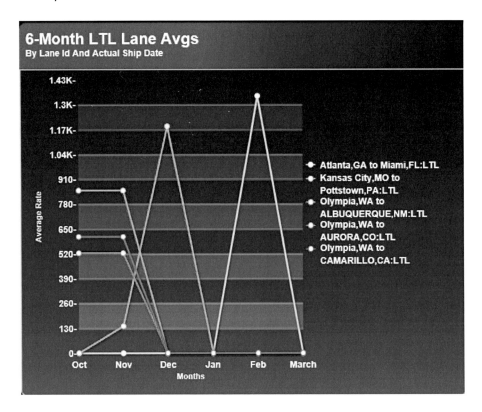

Fig. 14-24: 'Lane Averages' graph, configurable by mode.

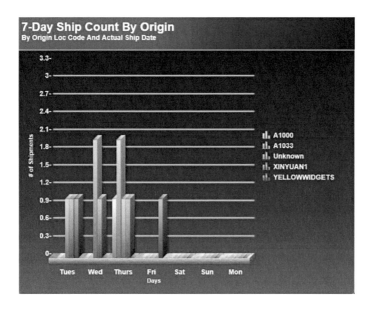

Fig. 14-25: Shipment count graph by origin. Other options include by status, by creating user and by mode.

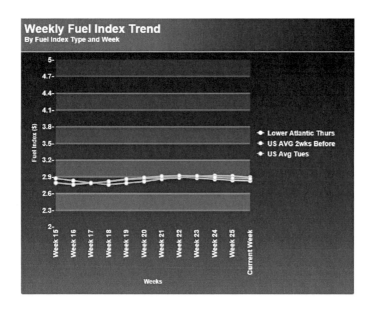

Fig. 14-26: Weekly fuel trend graph.

Maps

This command maps shipments in the currently selected shipment report from the TMS. (The choice of initial report to display is chosen in the application's settings.)

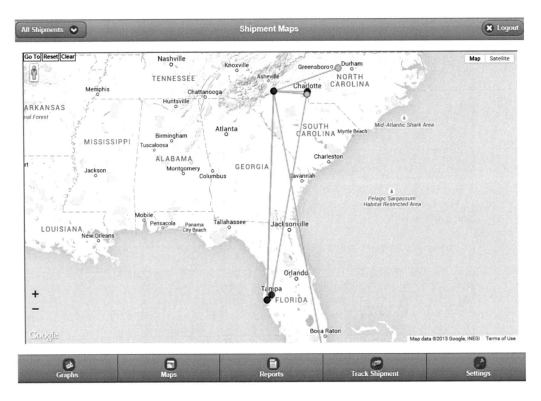

Fig. 14-27: Map displays shipments in the currently selected report. Different reports in the TMS can be mapped by choosing a new report from the upper left selection menu.

Reports

The "Reports" button shows a dropdown menu of available report types from the TMS: purchase order, shipment, load, tracking message, carrier invoice, customer invoice or activity log.

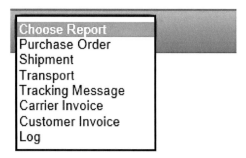

Choosing a report type displays a list of all available TMS reports of that type. For example, we ask for a list of all execution load reports and see in this case that there are three (Fig. 14-28):

Fig. 14-28: Any load reports in the TMS are available in the tablet application.

Owner	Primary Reference	PRO Number	Parcel Tracking Id
Wilson Plastics Co.	L-0043 (MBL)		
Wilson Plastics Co.	L-0042 (MBL)		
HCS Logistics Inc.	L-0041 (MBL)		
HCS Logistics Inc.	L-0040 (MBL)		
HCS Logistics Inc.	L-0039 (MBL)		
HCS Logistics Inc.	L-0038 (MBL)		
HCS Logistics Inc.	L-0037 (MBL)		
HCS Logistics Inc.	L-0036 (MBL)		
HCS Logistics Inc.	L-0035 (MBL)		
HCS Logistics Inc.	L-0034-11 (MBL)	MG12740	
HCS Logistics Inc.	L-0034-10 (MBL)	MG12741	
HCS Logistics Inc.	L-0034-9 (MBL)	MG12742	
HCS Logistics Inc.	L-0034-8 (MBL)	MG12743	
HCS Logistics Inc.	L-0034-7 (MBL)	MG12744	
HCS Logistics Inc.	L-0034-6 (MBL)	MG12745	

Fig. 14-29: Choosing a report displays its individual load records.

Track Shipment

As with the smartphone application, this command asks the user to specify a shipment number and then provides detailed information:

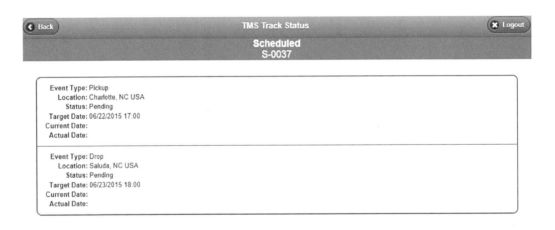

Fig. 14-30: Status lookup of a TMS shipment in the tablet application.

Conclusion

Mobile access to TMS data allow us to look from "either end of the telescope." At the detail level, we should be able to access TMS reports and individual records, with the ability to track and update status. Carrier-users in the field should be able to update status, call checks and load documents. At the control-tower level, however, we want mobile access that gives us a strategic overview of our system's performance.

Chapter 15: Analyzing Future Costs

Modeling the impact of future cost changes on the way we arrange the movement of freight is not a cut-and-dried proposition. It is not necessarily a simple reckoning – "If fuel goes up by X, we'll just raise our customer rates by Y. "

Instead we need to consider how changes in various cost centers could affect our overall mix – our mix of mode, of contract versus spot rates, of pooling versus non-pooling scenarios, and how we consolidate customer loads onto execution loads.

We saw in the chapter on optimization that the Mojo optimization tool could be used for simple what-if scenarios:

- What if fuel goes up X percent?
- What if I use this other carrier's rate structure instead?
- What happens if I move my distribution center to another city?
- What should happen to my mode mix if truckload rates go up?

In the simplest sense, we already are analyzing "future cost changes" any time we that change one of several parameters in the Mojo Optimization Wizard, re-run the optimizer, and then compare one result to the next.

For example, on the second screen of optimization settings we can tell Mojo to apply a hypothetical bump to fuel prices, by specific truckload versus non-truckload mode, or to bump any fuel index that our rate tables are using (Fig. 15-1):

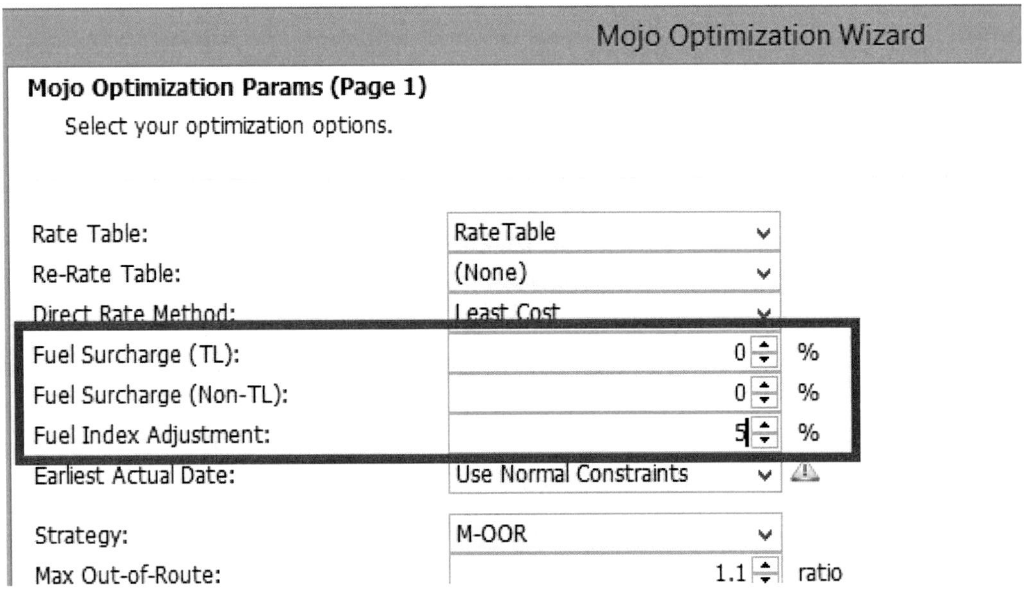

Fig. 15-1: Ability to bump fuel surcharge assumptions in Mojo optimization scenarios, either by truckload vs. non-TL mode, or by overall bump in fuel index.

In the "Optimizer History" tab, we get a line-by-line comparison of how our assumptions changed, and the result (Fig. 15-2):

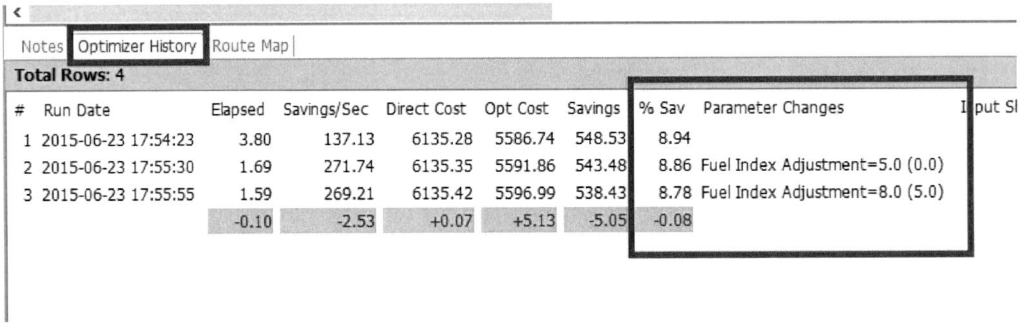

Fig. 15-2: Mojo's 'History' tab reports changes in optimized savings based on changed assumptions about increase in fuel index.

These comparisons are fine for changes in a single assumption. However, there is a more comprehensive modeling tool built into Mojo for analyzing any number of parameter changes projected over time. This feature is known as "Mojo Futures."

'Mojo Futures'

After we have completed an initial Mojo run to use as our baseline, notice in the right-hand "Analysis" tasks that there is now a command named "Mojo Futures" (Fig. 15-3):

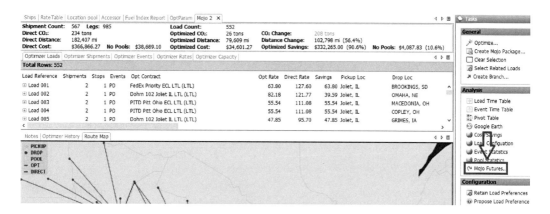

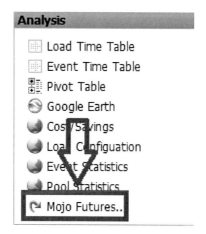

Fig. 15-3: 'Mojo Futures' command after an optimization run.

Clicking this command re-launches the Mojo Optimization Wizard – but with an interesting difference.

The wizard now skips its first screen (which mapped the columns from our shipment data). In the remaining screens, <u>only the numerical parameters</u> are available for adjustment. The remaining parameters are grayed out.

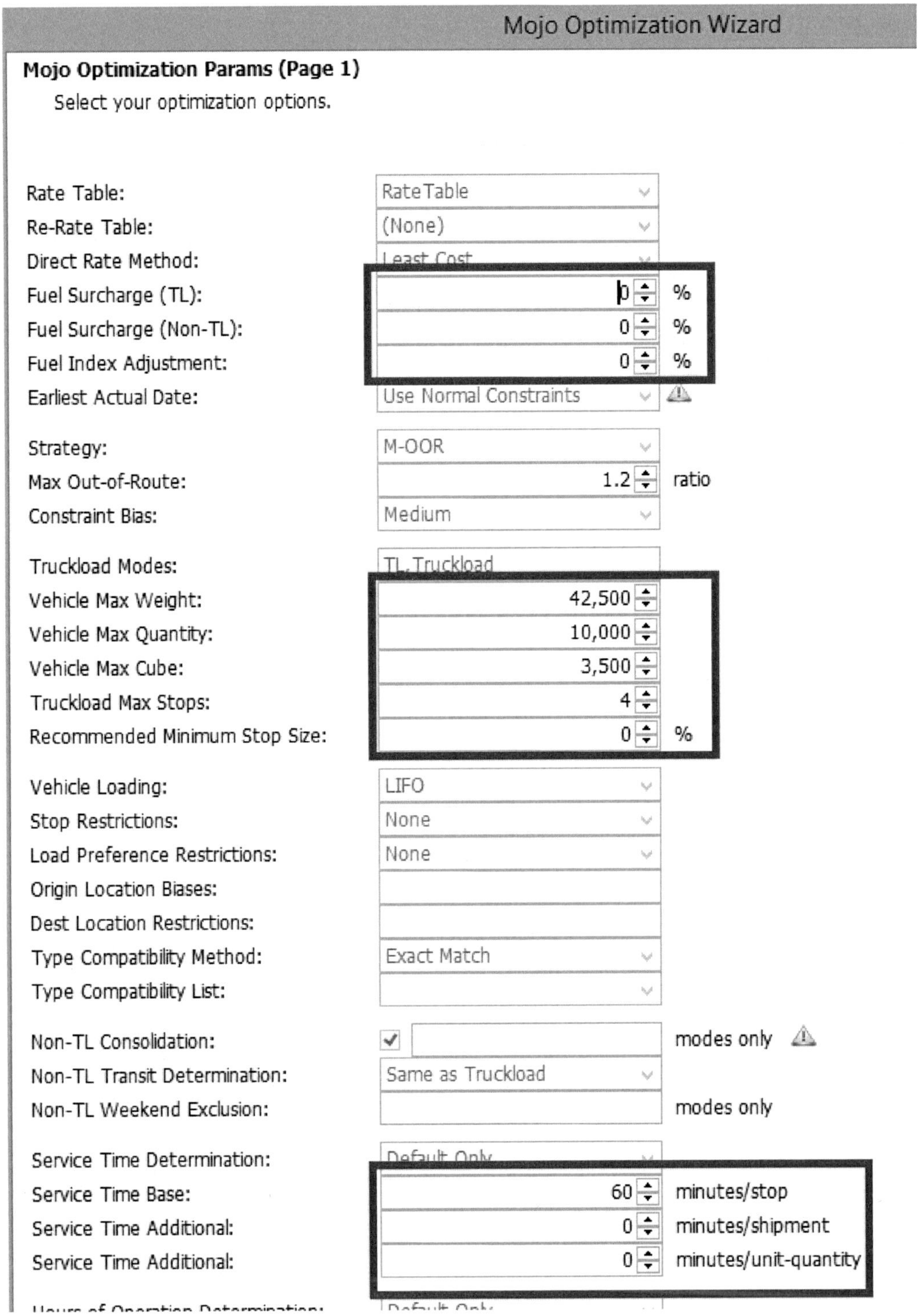

Mojo Optimization Wizard

Mojo Optimization Params (Page 1)

Select your optimization options.

Rate Table:	RateTable
Re-Rate Table:	(None)
Direct Rate Method:	Least Cost
Fuel Surcharge (TL):	0 %
Fuel Surcharge (Non-TL):	0 %
Fuel Index Adjustment:	0 %
Earliest Actual Date:	Use Normal Constraints ⚠
Strategy:	M-OOR
Max Out-of-Route:	1.2 ratio
Constraint Bias:	Medium
Truckload Modes:	TL, Truckload
Vehicle Max Weight:	42,500
Vehicle Max Quantity:	10,000
Vehicle Max Cube:	3,500
Truckload Max Stops:	4
Recommended Minimum Stop Size:	0 %
Vehicle Loading:	LIFO
Stop Restrictions:	None
Load Preference Restrictions:	None
Origin Location Biases:	
Dest Location Restrictions:	
Type Compatibility Method:	Exact Match
Type Compatibility List:	
Non-TL Consolidation:	✓ modes only ⚠
Non-TL Transit Determination:	Same as Truckload
Non-TL Weekend Exclusion:	modes only
Service Time Determination:	Default Only
Service Time Base:	60 minutes/stop
Service Time Additional:	0 minutes/shipment
Service Time Additional:	0 minutes/unit-quantity
Hours of Operation Determination:	Default Only

Fig. 15-4: Ability to adjust multiple numerical constraints in a 'Mojo Futures' run.

We can adjust one or many of these settings in the wizard screen to make them larger or smaller than the baseline. We'll then run multiple instances of Mojo, adjusting each parameter we've changed by a staggered amount, to test the effects.

At the bottom of the final wizard screen there is a new setting labeled "Future Iterations". For all the parameters that we have adjusted up or down, Mojo will now loop through the requested number of executions:

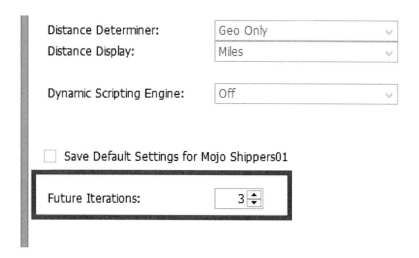

Fig. 15-5: Telling Mojo Futures how many loops to run.

Mojo runs and displays results for each requested iteration. Each display contains its own Mojo results tab, which can be right-clicked and "floated" for a fuller view:

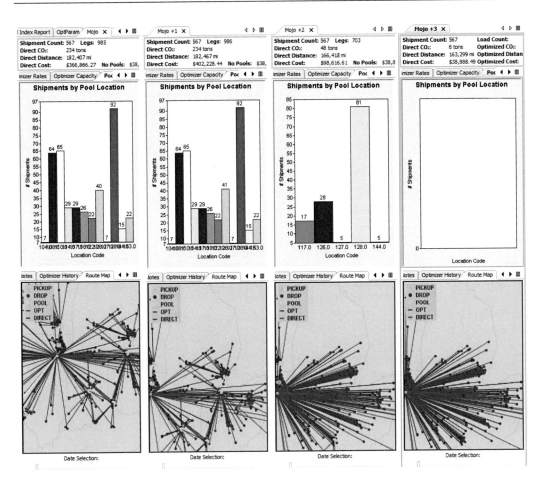

Fig. 15-6: Mojo Futures runs with three additional iterations. Each loop's results appears in its own tab.

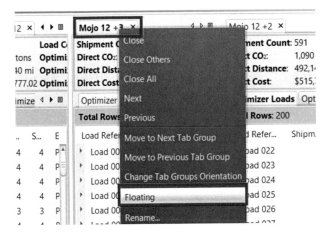

Fig. 15-7: Right-click a tab header and choosing "Floating" to undock the tab and expand its view.

In the original Mojo window, a new tab titled "Mojo Futures Summary" contains a line by line comparison of the iterations, similar to the one we saw in the "Optimizer History" tab. (You might have to scroll the frame to see the "Mojo Futures Summary" tab.)

Mojo 12 Futures Summary ×

Total Rows: 4

#	Run Date	Ela...	Savings/...	Direct Cost	Opt Cost	Savir
0	2015-04-22 07:30:27	2.88	74549.16	515777.02	292129.53	223
1	2015-04-22 07:31:23	2.77	74549.16	515777.02	292129.53	223
2	2015-04-22 07:31:28	2.67	74549.16	515777.02	292129.53	223
3	2015-04-22 07:31:32	2.50	74549.16	515777.02	292129.53	223

)ista...	% Dist...	CO2 D...	Parameter Changes
)51.44	65.24	711.21	
)51.44	65.24	711.21	Fuel Index Adjustment=6.0
)51.44	65.24	711.21	Fuel Index Adjustment=12.0
)51.44	65.24	711.21	Fuel Index Adjustment=18.0

Fig. 15-8: Line-by-line comparison of the Mojo Futures iterations, with a description of the changed parameters for each run.

Case Study - Impact of TL Fuel Increase

In this example we want to see what Mojo predicts about the effect of hypothetical increases in truckload fuel rates over the coming year. Should we consider moving toward a different mix of modes, services and contracts?

Our current model uses a "consider pools" scenario. We tell Mojo to use pool points where it makes sense.

First we perform a baseline Mojo run. In the map below the visual representation of the pooling strategy is quite clear. In the results summary we can see this gives us tremendous savings versus direct ship.

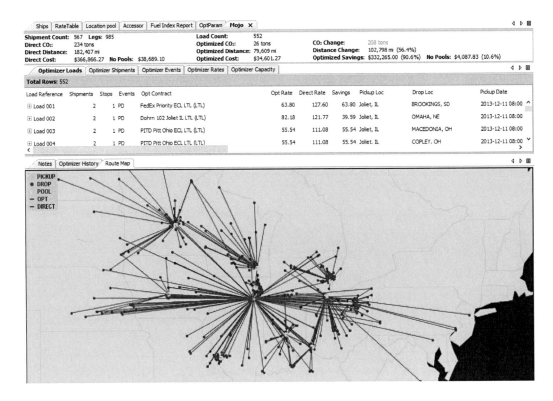

Fig. 15-9: Initial Mojo run, using a "consider pools" strategy.

Now we'll run Mojo Futures. For our parameter change we're going to propose a 12 percent increase in the truckload fuel index and we're going to consider three additional iterations (so we'll have data modeling four quarterly calculations).

Mojo runs our requested scenarios (Fig. 15-10):

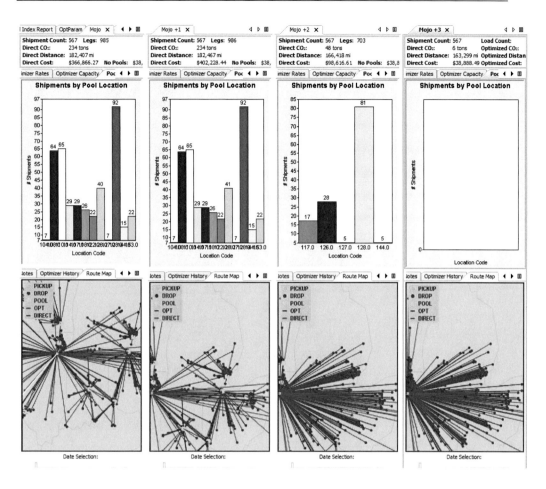

Fig. 15-10: As truckload fuel goes up, Mojo is less likely to employ pooling. Why?

In the four screens presented above, notice Mojo increasingly moves away from a pooling scenario and toward direct-ship alternatives as a consequence of anticipated higher truckload fuel costs. The top charts were produced using the "Pool Statistics" command in the right-hand Analysis Tasks window.

Note that several pool locations were employed in our first and second runs, fewer in the third, and none in the final. As truckload fuel rates increased, it made more and more sense to move to a non-pooling scenario.

Comparing the "Optimized Contract" display from first to last runs, Mojo has redistributed its recommended loads, concentrating them more on non-TL carriers (Fig. 15-11):

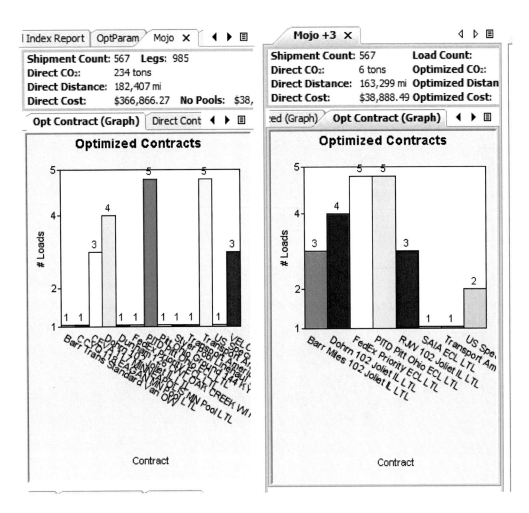

Fig. 15-11: Dramatic shift in carrier contracts preferred as Mojo deals with the impact of projected truckload fuel increases.

The lesson here is that as parameters change (such as fuel costs, carbon taxes, etc.), the overall recommended execution plan can shift dramatically as Mojo attempts to mitigate the effect of the cost increases.

Unexpected mode shifts, for example from LTL to parcel, and changes in pooling scenarios (such as shipping more direct instead of through pool points) might be the result. <u>Being aware of these possibilities early can help with carrier bids and capacity sourcing decisions.</u>

One more point: All carrier contracts typically do not expire simultaneously. Therefore, from month to month, different carrier contracts and rating models can be in effect, making it difficult to use a single point in time to evaluate an optimization strategy. Mojo Futures simplifies the task of evaluating shipment data and rating models as they change throughout the year.

Conclusion

In this book we've discussed many of the basics of modern supply chain and logistics management, and the challenges facing logistics providers today.

We have seen how a robust TMS and related software tools can help us control execution workflow, find capacity, stay on top of our invoices, manage private fleet assets and be pro-active about recognizing and rewarding our "best" carriers – just to name a few.

The remainder of this book consists of a glossary, an appendix on TMS usage, and an appendix on how to configure many of the functions discussed in this book. There's also an afterword about MercuryGate International Inc.

We at MercuryGate hope you have found this book useful.

Glossary

activity: In the TMS, a named "to-do" task attached to a load, invoice or route, often represented to the user with a clickable blue button.

advance: Transfer of cash to a driver or vendor in the field to handle expenses. A third-party vendor handles the transfer and the transaction appears as an invoice for that vendor on the TMS load.

asset: A truck, tractor, trailer or piece of equipment owned by the TMS client, as opposed to an outside carrier.

audit: For invoices, a comparison of expected rates to actual invoice amounts. An "Audit Invoice" blue button opens a screen for the comparison.

backhaul: A leg of a multi-leg route that is heading back toward the origin with a revenue-generating cargo instead of an empty return.

backhaul bias: A setting that controls how likely it is the Mojo optimization tool will consider backhaul legs.

benchmark rate: An average or typical rate being charged on a lane used as guidance.

bid board: A load posted with the invitation to carriers to offer to take it. A <u>private</u> bid board is managed within the TMS. A <u>public</u> board is an external site accessed via the TMS.

billing efficiency: A measure of how quickly and accurately a carrier generates invoices after a load delivery. An important consideration for logistics service providers who need fast, accurate data. Some providers reward their best carriers with expedited reimbursement.

blue button: One or more clickable icons displayed to TMS users representing pending activities on a load, route or invoice. Blue button sequences are managed automatically as part of a designed workflow.

Book It Now: In a load posted for a bid, a pre-set amount at which a carrier can win the load immediately.

call check: A periodic report of a load's location. Users can create call-check records manually in the system, drivers can create them from the field, or they can be created automatically by tracking services.

capacity: General term for the availability of carriers, trucks, equipment and drivers to move a load.

Carma: MercuryGate's proprietary system for carrier records management. A sophisticated database with automatic online update from various carrier data services. Synchs with TMS to keep carrier data current.

carrier: A company that is in the business of transporting cargo for hire, under the regulation of federal and state governments.

carrier active flag: A true/false setting in the system for whether a carrier should currently be considered "active" for rating and other purposes. Carrier active flags are extremely important and can be managed by automatic checks from Carma.

carrier ID: A unique identifier for a carrier used internally by the MercuryGate system. Can be user-defined or a copy of one of the other unique identifiers.

carrier records management: The desirable business practice of actively managing and keeping current information about a carrier's licensing, insurance, safety ratings and other key records.

carrier scorecard: In the TMS, a portlet that displays carrier statistics regarding tender acceptance, on-time performance and other metrics.

code table: A text-based list of settings for the TMS enterprise accessible to administrators. Code tables can be changed easily without the need for writing new programming for simple changes such as adding a new option in a menu shown to users.

commission: A fee paid by the TMS brokerage to its agents for procuring a load. Commissions usually are calculated as a percentage of margin and are added to a load as vendor invoices.

configuration (system): A system setting for the TMS available via the "Administration" menu. The menu leads to several subpages of settings for handling loads, shipments, and many other TMS functions.

configuration groups: Not to be confused with configuration screens above. A "config group" is a group of settings that controls the display in a specific TMS portlet or blue button window.

constraint: In optimization and load-building, a limiting factor that must be considered. Examples include incompatible freight types, equipment requirements (refrigerated, frozen, etc.), location operating hours, number of available docks, pool location requirements.

container return: For intermodal legs, the obligation to return an ocean or rail container after the delivery dray leg is completed. Per diem charges can apply beyond allowed free time. Represented by a "Container Return" blue button created automatically on the load.

contract: The TMS record of the agreement between a carrier or customer and the TMS client, including terms, rates, discounts, negotiated lanes and other factors.

contract rate: In lane analysis, a benchmark rate based on average carrier contracts, as opposed to average spot rates. Contract rates tend to change more slowly over time.

control report: A report created by a TMS administrator designed to identify deficiencies in overall operation of the system.

customer load: A load record in the TMS intended as a "customer-eye" view of a movement – the item or items the customer wants shipped, origin and destination, and customer rates and invoices. Customer loads are related to <u>execution loads</u> that belong to the same <u>route</u>.

dashboard: The TMS home screen for a user, who can return to it by clicking the "Dashboard" toolbar icon.

detention: A charge owed to a carrier forced to undergo an undue delay at a pickup or drop event. An "Authorize Detention" blue button is added to the load automatically. Detention charges can be passed on to the customer.

Dispatch: The blue-button activity for entering driver and equipment-related information provided by the carrier. Completion of a "Dispatch" activity is used to trigger load tracking.

dray, drayage leg: Legs representing initial pickup to a rail or ocean ramp or an airport, and from the endpoint of the rail/air/sea leg to final destination.

delta: In a load posted for a bid in the TMS, an amount by which a new bid must be lower than the previous bid.

dispute: Process of resolving an invoice disagreement with a carrier. A dispute can be carried out via TMS portlets, "flipping" the issue between client and carrier users, or invoices can be flagged with a "Dispute" activity and managed manually.

duplicate invoice/duplicate check: Test for whether a new invoice is actually a copy of an existing invoice. System settings determine how close charges should be to be considered a duplicate.

dynamic rulesets: In the TMS, actions that execute behind the scenes in response to a specific "trigger." One example is adding a new blue button to a load once a user completes a prior blue-button action.

EDI: Stands for "Electronic Data Interchange," a standard communication format used in business. EDI formats are referred to by numbers (an "EDI 997" is an acknowledgement, for example).

EDI 214: A load status message in Electronic Data Interchange (EDI) format. EDI 214 messages are used to convey and create status messages in the TMS. In fact, the terms "status messages" and "214s" are used somewhat interchangeably.

enterprise: A company record in the TMS. Every TMS client has its own top-level enterprise representing itself, and can have sub-enterprises representing its divisions, subsidiaries, or customers as needed.

exception: A general term for an unusual circumstance in a load life cycle, a departure from an uneventful "sunny day" scenario. Examples include breakdowns, delays, and reconsignments.

execution load: Also known as "transport" or "load" in older material. The carrier-level view of a movement, with execution details and carrier rates.

extract: Act of exporting TMS records to an external accounting system such as QuickBooks, usually the last step in the invoicing cycle.

freight bill audit: Overall term for the steps involved in verifying that carrier invoice charges are acceptable and should be paid.

FreightFriend: An external "social network" for capacity in which participants "friend" each other and see each other's posted loads and capacity. Half owned by MercuryGate and integrated with the TMS.

hazmat: Universal shorthand for "hazardous material." Hazmat transport is heavily regulated by federal and state authorities and even forbidden on some routes. TMS item records include hazmat data.

hierarchy: In the TMS, the collective structure of a top-level enterprise and all its descendants. Users with permission can navigate the hierarchy and operate at lower or higher company levels as needed.

hot load/route: A load or route flagged by the system when it appears subsequent events might be late.

inbound: Freight moving to us, instead of from us, as in the case of suppliers filling purchase orders for TMS shippers. Control over the management of inbound freight, including load creation and consolidation, offers the opportunity for savings.

intermodal: Movement of the same customer load or shipment across multiple carriers and modes of transportation, such as truck-rail-truck, truck-air-truck.

Internal Rate Index: A benchmark rate derived from the TMS enterprise's own data about activity on this load's lane. Displayed in the Manage Quotes screen along with an up or down trending indicator, and a confidence level.

insurance (cargo, liability, general): Insurance types that cover a carrier's cargo, accidents, and general liability. Logistics companies determine their own insurance requirements for considering a carrier active.

invoice: The actual bill sent from a carrier or vendor to the TMS client ("carrier" and "vendor" invoices), or from the TMS client to its own customers ("customer" invoices). Usually based on existing rates on the load.

item: Also "master item." The TMS record of a frequently used item with pre-filled fields containing information about weights, dimensions, quantities, freight class, hazmat and other settings.

load: The original name for an execution load in the TMS. The preferred term is "execution load."

Load Builder: In the TMS, a window that allows users to click and drag shipments or loads into a new window to be created on the same load. Used in consolidating inbound shipments into more efficient loads.

load posting: Sending a TMS load to an external site as an invitation to carriers to accept it. The TMS integrates with several external services, although they also require a separate account for the TMS client.

location: The TMS record of a specific location that can include details about operating hours, dock facilities, contacts, and available services and equipment.

margin: The difference between customer rates/invoices and related carrier and vendor rates/invoices. Margins are used to calculate commissions.

Mass Update: A menu of options at the bottom of a TMS list or portlet that can be executed against all the items currently selected in the list via a left-hand checkbox.

master/milestone activity: A blue-button activity that launches a window containing one or more sub-activities. All the sub-activities must be completed for the master or milestone activity to be complete.

matched invoice: An invoice that has been recognized as belonging to an existing load in the TMS.

MC number: A federally issued identification number that authorizes a carrier to engage in interstate commerce. Distinct from USDOT number and SCAC defined below.

MercuryEdge: A downloadable, stand-alone application free for MercuryGate clients. Opens logistics data in spreadsheet-like displays for analysis.

Mojo: MercuryGate's proprietary optimization tool. Mojo uses lists of shipments and available carrier rates to build recommend loads that respect all required constraints.

Mojo Futures: A "looping" option in the Mojo optimizer that allows the user to specify a change in one or more numerical parameters and a number of loops to run, then projects the impact of the changes over the requested number of loops.

multi-leg: Movement of a customer shipment across more than one carrier leg, such as an intermodal move, or inbound to and outbound from a pool location.

multi-pick, multi-stop: Load or shipment involving more than one stop on the same carrier move.

on-time percentage: Percentage of loads picked up and delivered by a carrier within the scheduled time windows. One of the most important measures of carrier performance. Shown in carrier scorecard portlet.

open settlement liability: Identification of loads for which we have not received invoices but owe money. A useful check to run against aging loads.

optimization: The process of building carrier loads in a way that achieves improved results. Optimization can be focused on lowest rates, fewest truckloads, shortest routes, network and location requirements, or some combination of these approaches.

POD: Proof of Delivery. An uploaded document, link to a document stored elsewhere, a recorded signature or some other documentation that delivery has occurred. Often required as a condition of invoicing.

pool, pool strategy: The practice of sending shipments to an intermediate facility where they are recombined and sent on new outbound carrier loads.

portlet: A TMS window displaying lists of loads, invoices, routes or other information.

posted equipment: Either in the TMS, or on an external site, equipment posted by carriers as available to take a load. Carriers might post equipment that otherwise would be empty on a return leg, for example.

private fleet: Assets owned and deployed by a TMS client, instead of hiring a third-party carrier to move a load.

purchase order: A record of a request to buy a quantity of goods from a supplier. In the TMS, an enterprise usually creates purchase orders that represent the goods it is ordering from its own suppliers.

quote (carrier): A request made and a response received from a carrier for a quoted price to accept a load. Quotes can be requested from different points in the TMS. (A customer quote is a rate offered by the TMS client to its own customer.)

RateFriend: An external service available to TMS clients at additional charge that displays detailed information about market trends and rates for the load in question. RateFriend data comes from load information provided by its clients.

rating: The process of obtaining proposed carrier or customer rates for a load. Rates might be obtained from contracts stored in the TMS, or from other sources such as a capacity search or bid board.

Ready to Extract: The activity and blue button name assigned to an invoice after it has finished all previous steps. The blue button might be in "Missing Required Data" status, if a Proof or Delivery or other document is still missing, or it might be in "Pending" status if the invoice is ready to be extracted.

reconsignment: Redirection of a carrier to a new or different stop en route.

rejected invoice: An invoice rejected by a user via the audit screen. Rejected invoices require some further workflow step, such as notification of the carrier.

report, report format: The filter and format of a list currently displayed in a TMS portlet or list. For example, we might be looking at a list of all loads currently in transit. Report fields and filters are configurable.

return leg: Leg between the final drop on a route and the point of origin. Setting the Mojo "Private Fleet" parameter to "Return Vehicle" causes return legs to be included.

role: A set of TMS permissions stored under a name such as "Operations" or "Finance" and assigned to a user. Each role consists of permissions related to hundreds of possible TMS functions.

rogue spend: A term for spending on carriers outside of normal contract or authorized business practice, more common in large operations where it is more likely to be overlooked.

route: A TMS record that includes every customer and execution load related to an overall movement. For example one or more customer loads might be moving across one or move execution loads, and all would be part of the same route.

route guide: In the TMS, a route guide is a way to adjust system rating results according to which carriers are preferred on a lane, or how loads on a load should be allocated among carriers. Requires an uploaded spreadsheet and system settings.

routing: Process used by a shipper/vendor to create a shipment to satisfy a purchase order in whole or in part.

The steps used in the TMS, and how much the vendor-supplier user is expected to decide, are configurable.

SAFER: The federal Safety and Fitness Electronic Records (SAFER) system. Offers statistics related to carrier safety. Available from the TMS 'Carrier' menu when a carrier detail window is open.

SCAC: Each carrier also is known by an identifier using the Standard Carrier Alphanumeric Code.

seasonality: The impact of time of year and cyclical factors on carrier capacity, including agricultural harvest seasons and climate.

second invoice: An additional invoice with extra charges received for a load, usually assigned an "Audit 2nd Invoice" blue button by the system. ("Second" invoice is generally used to describe all multiples.)

shipment: A basic TMS record of the thing or things that a customer wants moved. Shipments are placed on execution and customer loads.

shipment template: A TMS record representing a pattern, like a cookie cutter, than can be used to create new shipments. An existing shipment can be used as the model for creating a template.

ship unit: The TMS record of a standard container for items. Ship units have all the same possible fields as items and can be stored as standing "master ship units" for re-use.

spot rate: A benchmark rate based on average non-contract rates on a lane. Spot rates tend to be more volatile than average contract rates.

status: A TMS load moves through different statuses as events in its life cycle progress. Typical statuses include Incomplete, Pending, Rated, Booked, In Transit and Delivered.

status message: A TMS record containing a message code about a load's progress, such as arrival or departure from a scheduled stop. Available message codes are declared in the enterprise's code table.

'sunny day': Slang term for a "normal" or uneventful workflow from creation to rating, execution, delivery and invoicing.

supplier: A third party company providing supplies to the TMS client. The supplier might have its own login to the TMS for viewing the client's purchase orders and creating shipments to fulfill them.

tender, tendering: A tender is the offer of a rated load to a proposed carrier. Carriers can accept or decline a tender, based on conditions and capacity, or can be set up to "auto-accept."

tender accept/reject ratio: Percentage of times a carrier accepts a tender, rejects a tender or lets a tender offer expire. Displayed in carrier scorecard portlet.

tender rejected: Carrier has declined a tender for a given reason (unavailable equipment, etc.). The TMS load moves to "Tender Rejected" status. A dynamic workflow should restore it to "Pending" status and return its "Assign Carrier Rate" blue button.

tolerance check: A test for whether an invoice's charges fall too far outside tolerable ranges. The settings for what is "tolerable" exist in the enterprise's code table and the check is performed by a dynamic ruleset at the time of invoice creation.

TONU: Truck Ordered Not Used. We might owe a TONU charge to a carrier if a pickup is canceled or must be rescheduled.

toolbar: In the TMS, an array of clickable icons directly below the menu bar for frequently used lists and actions.

total cost of ownership (TCO): The "true" cost of owning a private fleet once all expenses are considered. Small and mid-sized fleet owners often underestimate TCO, leading to less than optimal decision-making.

unmatched invoice: An invoice that the system cannot yet match to a known load. Users can subsequently try to match unmatched invoices as new loads are created, or deal with them as needed otherwise.

user: Usually (but not always) a human being assigned an ID and password to log into the TMS. Users must be assigned at least one role to be able to perform any functions in the TMS.

USDOT number: Unique identifying number for a carrier issued by the U.S. Department of Transportation.

vendor: (1) A third party company providing supplies to the TMS client, as in fulfilling a purchase order. (2) A third party provider of services related to moving a load, resulting in a vendor invoice on the load.

workflow: The designed steps of the life cycle of loads and invoices in the TMS. Each step is represented by a user blue button. Behind the scenes, dynamic rulesets remove and add blue buttons automatically as the steps proceed.

Appendix – TMS User Guide

Contents:

A: TMS Interface

The TMS is web-based. Use your browser (Firefox, Internet Explorer) and a URL assigned to you as a MercuryGate student or client. The URL looks like:

https://<someServerName>.mercurygate.net/MercuryGate/login/mgLongin.jsp

…where "someServerName" is your assigned server.

Enter your assigned user ID and password in the login screen. After you log in you'll see your home screen in the TMS, called the dashboard. Exactly what you see is controlled by user permissions and system settings (Fig. A-1).

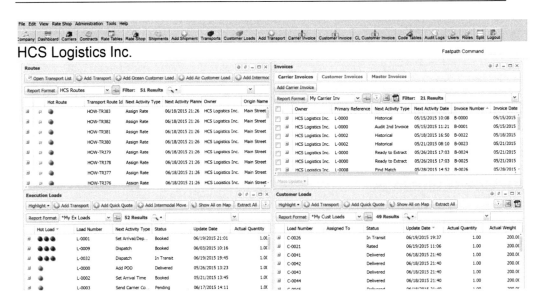

Fig. A-1: TMS 'dashboard' with menu bar, toolbar, and portlets.

Menu commands are described in the next topic. Below the menu is the <u>toolbar</u>, with a row of clickable icons that perform common actions, such as displaying lists. Clicking the "Dashboard" icon brings you back to your home screen.

Information from the TMS is displayed in windows called <u>portlets</u> in the central workspace. This is where we'll do most of our work

'Power Button'

The "power button" in the lower left-hand corner of the screen opens a menu that allows you to open additional portlets on the dashboard (Fig. A-2). The exact menus and portlets available are specific to your company.

Fig. A-2: 'Power button' menu to available portlets, with option to save or clear current portlet arrangement and perform other functions.

The "Save State" button will remember your current dashboard arrangement (which windows are open and their positions), and restores it when you return to your dashboard.

B: Menu Reference

Navigation through the menu is described like this:

> Administration > Current Company > Configurations > Rating

This means to choose the "Administration" menu from the main menu bar, then the submenu "Current Company," then the submenu "Configurations" and finally the menu command "Rating."

Some menu commands are followed by the term "(Down)". This means the command also will return records for enterprises beneath the current one in the TMS hierarchy.

Not all menu options may be visible depending on your user and role permissions.

File Menu

Switch Company:	Choose another company in the hierarchy.
Dashboard:	Home screen - display the portlets available to the user.
Import:	Import an external data source (must be configured)
Print:	Print the current screen.
Logout:	Exit the TMS application.

Edit Menu

Add:	Opens a submenu for adding various TMS records such as a new carrier, contract, shipment, etc.
Notifications:	Allow user to request email

<table>
<tr><td></td><td>notifications regarding changes to certain records</td></tr>
<tr><td>User Preferences:</td><td>Opens an editing screen for the current user's settings.</td></tr>
</table>

View Menu

The View menu contains a list of several TMS record types that can be viewed in a list screen, and an option to split the screen display.

Rate Shop Menu

Allows a quick rate search by city/state/zip, specific location, item or multistop rating. The search is "informational," meaning looking up available rates without assigning them to a load.

Record-Specific Menus (Load/Shipment/Contract/Location, etc.)

When an individual TMS record such as a shipment, load or contract is open (from a "list screen" instead of an ezClick portlet), a new menu appears in the menu bar specific to the record type.

Fig. B-1: Example of a record-specific menu inserted in the menu bar when a record of that type is being displayed (carrier, contract, shipment, load, etc.)

Documents Menu

Likewise, when some list screens or individual records are open, a "Documents" menu appears with a list of available document formats that have been configured for the enterprise.

Admin Menu

This menu is visible when the current user has administrative rights. The user's "Is Administrator" user setting is set to true.

<table>
<tr><td>Hierarchy : Companies:</td><td>Ways to navigate the TMS hierarchy.</td></tr>
<tr><td>Current Company:</td><td>Opens a submenu with several options for viewing the current company's documents,</td></tr>
</table>

settings and configurations.

View Online Users:	Displays list of current users logged in.
Cust. Rating Profiles:	A "rating profile" can be used to determine how a customer's rates are calculated.

Tools Menu

Message Center:	Displays messages sent within the TMS.
Widgets:	Opens "widgets," or handy calculators for a quick calculation of mileage, volume or currency conversion.

Help Menu

Current Page:	Help screen for current page, if available. Most configuration screens have their own help page.
Search ... :	Use search capabilities within Google Documents. Requires code table settings.
About:	Links to MercuryGate.com homepage.
Version:	Current version of TMS. Use when troubleshooting.

C: Portlet Reference

These icons are in the upper-right of most portlets. The gear icon is displayed for admins only and opens a window for portlet settings. The next is a "refresh" icon you might need if a change has been made elsewhere in the system. If you close a portlet with the "X" you can re-open it from the power button menu.

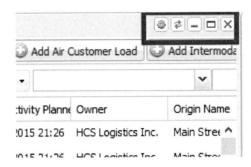

Fig. C-1: Admin, refresh, min, max and close icons.

Hovering the mouse over the border or corner of a portlet displays a double-ended arrow. Clicking and dragging the mouse will resize the window. Click on the left or right edges to resize horizontally, on the bottom or top edge to resize vertically, or a corner to resize in both directions.

To move a portlet, click in its title bar, hold and drag the portlet to the new desired location. Clicking "Save State" in the power button window will remember the new location.

Columns and Rows

Information in a portlet is displayed in columns. You can click, hold and drag any column's header to move the column to a new order in the display.

The rows in any portlet can be sorted by clicking and releasing in the header of the column to use as a sort value. Repeated clicks re-sort the rows in ascending, descending and original order of the values in the selected column.

These kinds of changes you make to your display are good only for the current session. To make the changes permanent, use the "Report Format" button to modify an existing report, or to create a new one. See the Report Format topic below.

Expanding Entries in Lists

The records listed in some portlets have a plus-sign icon to the left of each row. This means each entry can be expanded to show more details, such as the pending blue buttons for that item (Fig. C-2).

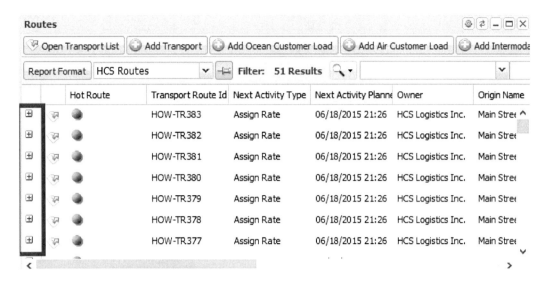

Fig. C-2: Each record in this list can be expanded to view more details.

Creating Portlets (For Admins)

Admin users can create new portlets for the enterprise. An example would be creating different instances of a load board with different workflows

Portlets can be created in two ways: Simply by adding a one-line entry to the code table, or creation from the menu (Administration > Current Company > Configurations > Portlets).

A code table entry looks like this:

<enterprisename> | PortletsWide | <some URL> | <portlet name>

Notice the third, "code" portion contains the value of a URL in the system that leads to the code for a defined portlet. This requires knowledge of the URL from a documentation resource, or copying a URL already in use.

The fourth, "decode" portion contains the portlet name displayed to users. (The distinction between "PortletsWide" and "PortletsNarrow" matters little, since portlets can be resized.)

Example:

* | PortletsWide | /MercuryGate/portlet/ext/portletEZClickLoad.jsp?
mgConfigGroupId=ex:subMenu=Execution | Execution Loads

The portlet URL is followed by an optional assignment to an existing config group, and an optional assignment to a submenu in the power-button menu on the dashboard. For example, the above portlet is titled "Execution Loads" and appears in a submenu labeled "Execution" (Fig. C-3):

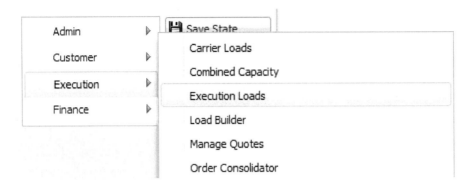

Fig. C-3: Portlets can be assigned to submenus for better organization.

The other creation method (from the Admin menu) contains a list of portlets declared for the enterprise. Click on the entry on the list, and in the right-hand window you'll see tabs for declaring the portlet's basic settings, and any available additional configurations (Fig. C-4).

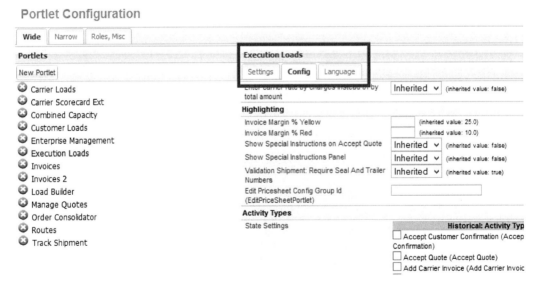

Fig. C-4: Portlet configuration screen available via Admin > Current Company > Configurations > Portlets.

Portlets created from code table entries can be edited from the configuration screen, and portlets created in the configuration screen automatically are inserted in the code table.

Notice you can <u>delete</u> any portlet in the list – be careful.

D: Filter Operators

Both the filtering of report formats and the filters used in the Quick Find feature use a set of <u>operators</u> to define the filter. You choose a field upon which to filter (such as primary reference, customer name, etc.), an operator such as "=", and the value to use in the filter.

Name	Explanation	Usage	Example
=	Searches for exact match to the comparison value entered	Can be used with any field type	Load # = LD1245
<>	Searches for all values EXCEPT the comparison value entered	Can be used with any field type	Load # <> LD1245
>	Searches for all values greater than the comparison value entered	Can be used on date and number fields	Carrier Rate > 1000
>=	Searches for all values greater than or equal to the comparison value entered	Can be used on date and number fields	Carrier Rate >= 1000
<	Searches for all values less than the	Can be used on date and	Carrier Rate < 1000

Name	Explanation	Usage	Example
	comparison value entered	number fields	
<=	Searches for all values less than or equal to the comparison value entered	Can be used on date and number fields	Carrier Rate <= 1000
From Hour	Searches for all values within the number of hours starting from the current time (back or forward) to the number entered in the value field	Date fields only	Create Date From Hour = -4 (loads created in the last four hours) Next Activity Planned Date From Hour = 4 (loads with Next Activity Planned Date within the next 4 hours) OR Next Activity Planned Date From Hour = -4, 4 (Next Activity Planned Date that was 4 hours ago or will be planned in the next 4 hours)
From Day	Works in the same way as From Hour	Date fields only	Same as From Hour
From Week	Works in the same way as From Hour	Date fields only	Same as From Hour (starts on Saturday - Friday)
From Month	Works in the same way as From Hour	Date fields only	Same as From Hour
Begins	Searches for all values than begin with the comparison value	Any field except date	Consignee Name Begins Paper
Not Begin	Searches for all values that do NOT begin with the comparison value	Any field except date	Consignee Name Not Begins Paper

Name	Explanation	Usage	Example
Ends	Searches for all values that end with the comparison value	Any field except date	Consignee Name Ends Manufacturer
Not End	Searches for all values that do NOT end with the comparison value	Any field except date	Consignee Name Not Ends Manufacturer
In	Searches for all values in the range of the comparison values entered, which can be multiple values separated by a comma	Any field except date	Status In Pending, Rated, Booked
Not In	Searches for all values that are NOT in the range of the comparison values, which can be multiple values separated by a comma	Any field except date	Status Not in Pending, Rated, Booked
Sounds Like	Searches for values that phonetically resemble the comparison value	Any field except date	Sounds Like Smith

E: Adding Carriers

You should be operating at the level of the TMS hierarchy at which your company's carriers should be created. In general the highest available level is best. From the menu, choose Edit > Add > Carrier.

An entry screen opens for entering basic information about the carrier, including name, a unique carrier ID, SCAC, and modes available for this carrier. Some fields, such as tender configuration, will not be available until the record has been saved. Enter primary location information, which will be used as the carrier's remit-to address if no other is added later.

Once a carrier is created, you can retrieve its record from the "Carriers" toolbar button or from the menu (View > Rating > Carriers). Once a carrier is saved, you can configure other locations to be associated with the carrier, and the carrier's tender process.

Carrier Menu

When a carrier record is open, a "Carrier" menu is inserted in the menu bar. One of the options in this menu is "Locations," with sub-options for viewing existing locations associated with the carrier, creating a new location for the carrier, or linking a location that you already have defined to this carrier. You can designate a location as an alternate tender location, for example.

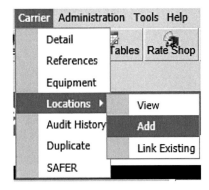

Fig. E-1: 'Carrier' menu is active when a carrier editing window is open.

Processes

In the carrier's detail screen, click the ""Configure" link under the Tender section to set up a tender process. You can choose either electronic message (which requires setup with MercuryGate's integration team) or an e-mail tender process.

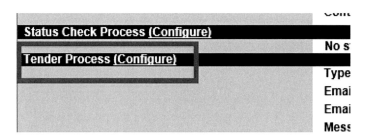

Fig. E-2: Detail of carrier editing screen showing link to configure tendering process.

More detailed information about carrier configuration and setting up the tendering process is available in two MercuryGate publications titled *Carriers, Contracts & Rating* and the *TMS Tendering Manual.*

F: Adding Users

New users can be added by users with administrative authority. A new user must have certain settings configured and must be assigned to a role in the system to be able to perform any functions.

Create new users at the appropriate level your company hierarchy. Start by getting an existing list of users, either by clicking the "Users" button on the toolbar, or from the menu: Administration > Current Company > Users.

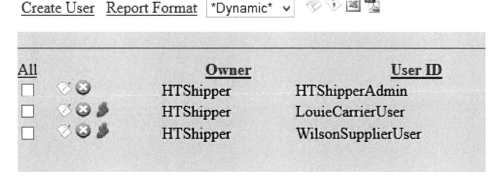

Fig. F-1: Detail of user list screen with options to edit, delete or emulate each user. Click 'Create User' to open an editing window for the new user.

Next to each entry in the list is a "details" icon (looks like a piece of paper) and a red "X" for deleting that user. The orange icon that looks like "twins" allows a user with the proper authority to "emulate" that user in the list - that is, to see the system just as that user does. Once you emulate a user, you have to log out and log back in to return to your own user ID.

The "Create User" link opens an editing window for creating a new user's record. At the minimum you must create a user ID and password for the user, with the option of setting many other configurations for what that user can see and do (Fig. F-2).

Your company might have its own password policy for creating passwords. The default setting is a password of at least 9 characters, with at least one numerical character and one non-alphanumeric character.

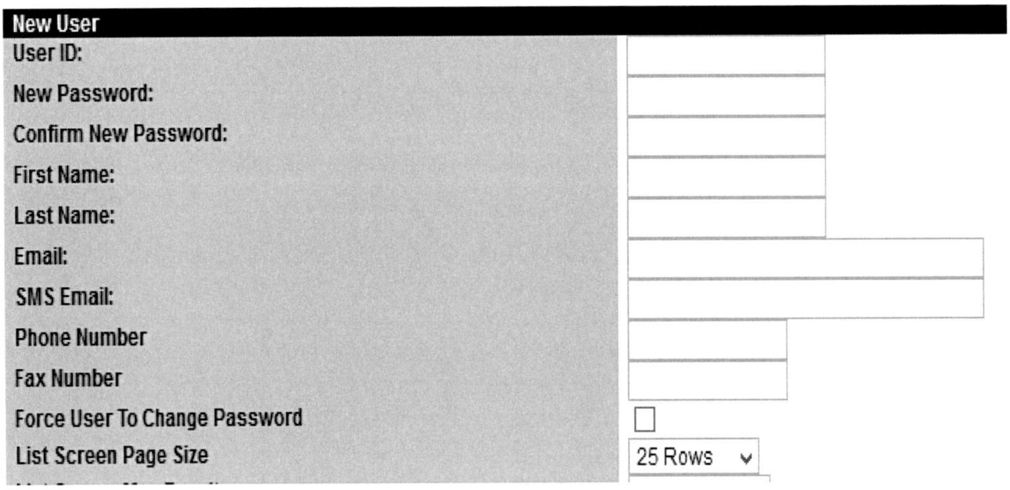

New User

User ID:	
New Password:	
Confirm New Password:	
First Name:	
Last Name:	
Email:	
SMS Email:	
Phone Number	
Fax Number	
Force User To Change Password	☐
List Screen Page Size	25 Rows ▾

Fig. F-2: Portion of user creation screen. At a minimum a user name and password are required.

Under the "Dashboard" section of the user screen you can assign portlets to appear by default on the user's dashboard. Some portlets are labeled as "wide" and some "narrow" but the terms mean little, as they can be resized.

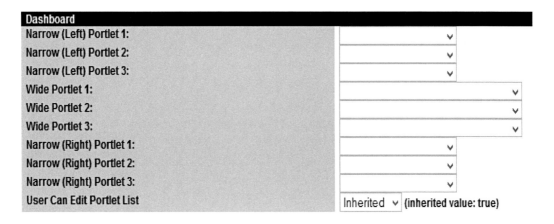

Fig. F-3: Portlet assignment in user setting screen.

In the bottom section of the user's record screen (which is available only to administrators, the "GUI" setting can be set to "Portal Only" to hide menu bars and toolbar icons (for a carrier user, for example). The "Look and Feel" setting of "original" will display only list screens, whereas "Ext version" gives the user access to ezClick portlets and the "power button" menu on the dashboard.

Fig. F-4: Admin-only settings for a user's GUI version, access to menus and toolbars, and color scheme.

Assigning Roles

A user cannot perform any action in the system until he or she has been assigned a role that grants permissions. To assign a role to a user, go to the user list and select the checkbox next to that user in the list. In the mass-update option at the bottom of the screen, choose the "Assign Role" command, and in the next box, the name of the role to assign. You can revoke a role in the same manner.

Fig. F-5: Role assignment via the 'mass update' function in a user list.

G: Reporting

The word "report" in the TMS describes both the data in a list, and a stored format of that data, such as how it is filtered and which columns are displayed. Users choose from a list of available report formats to control the display of a portlet (Fig. G-1).

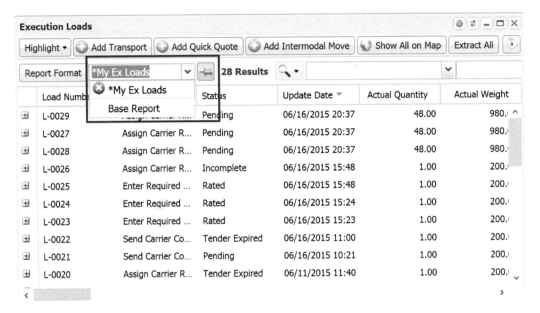

Fig. G-1: Report format selection in a portlet. Choose an existing report, or click 'Report Format' to open an editing window for modifying a report format or creating a new one.

Every portlet has a default format called "Base Report" that can be chosen from the dropdown menu. However, you also can tell the portlet to remember the current report format as the default, which can be a time-saver. This is called "pinning the report" to the portlet (Fig. G-2).

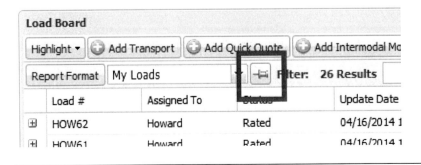

Fig. G-2: 'Pinning' a report format makes it the default that will be displayed each time the portlet is opened or refreshed.

<u>Creating Reports</u>

One of the most powerful tools in the MercuryGate TMS is the ability to define your own report formats to filter and display your data the way you want.

To view and create your own criteria for a report, click on the portlet's "Report Format" button (if your permissions allow it). An editing window opens (Fig. G-3):

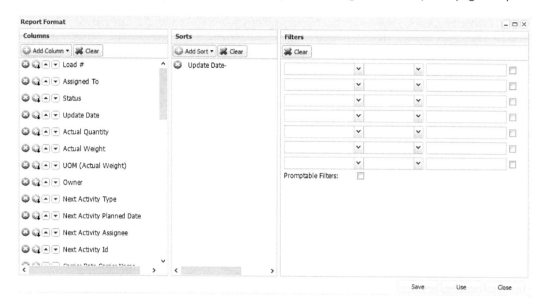

Fig. G-3: Window for creating or editing a report format.

Choose the columns to display and their order. Click the plus sign to insert a column, the red X to remove the column from the display, and the up or down arrows to re-order.

You can choose a sort order for the report based on the values in one or more columns (for instance, by zip code first, then by last name). Select a column or columns on which to sort, by ascending or descending order. Use the up-down arrows to determine the sort order.

Lastly, you can choose ways to filter the report. You might want to display only loads that have been tendered, for example. You might want to display only loads that are in transit. To set a filter, you choose a column, then an operator, then a value. The operator might be as simple as "=", but there are several options available. See the Filter Operators appendix topic.

The right-hand checkbox beside each filter option is an "Ignore Case" option. This makes sure that values match regardless of capitalization, but it can increase search time.

The "Promptable Filters" checkbox means that you want the user to enter the data to filter on. You might have a report named "By Zip" that filters on a specific zip code, but allow the user to enter the actual value, so the report can be used time after time.

<u>Saving Reports</u>

The "Report Format" window has options to use the new report format without saving it (good for one-time searches conducted on the fly), to save the report for future use, or to close without using or saving.

The "Use" button applies your new filter to the existing data in the portlet, but the report format is not saved for future use.

The "Save" button opens a window for you to name the report and determine its scope. "Private" means only you can see the report; "public" means all users can. "Everywhere" means the report is visible in all levels of your TMS companies; "here" means only at the current level. You also can declare that a report may be used only by users with a specific role.

H: 'Add Shipment' Walkthrough

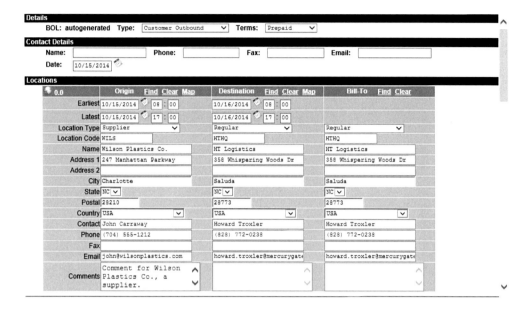

Fig. H-1: Top section of creation window opened by 'Add Shipment' or 'Add Intermodal Move'.

BOL: Bill of lading – a unique identifier for this shipment.
             Can be auto-generated according to system settings.

Type: Choose the type of shipment from a list of types used
             by your company (if applicable).

Terms: Usually "Prepaid." Options declared for your company.

Contact: Optional contact details.

Date/Time Windows

To change the date and time ranges, edit the fields directly, or click the calendar icon to choose a new date (Fig. H-2):

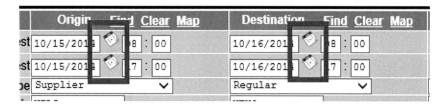

Fig. H-2: Editing date/time windows in shipment creation window.

Locations

There are three location records - ship-from, ship-to and bill-to. "Default" location information populates these fields automatically, but you can change them.

To choose a new location, click the "Clear" link. You can type in new information, or select another location that's already been stored in the system with the "Find" link (Fig. H-3):

Find Locations	
Type:	⌄
Location Code:	
Name:	
Address:	
Address:	
City:	
State:	⌄
Zip:	
Country:	USA ⌄

Fig. H-3: Location search window.

You can enter partial information such as a location type, a location code, a city, state or zip code and click "Search," and a list of matching locations is displayed. If only one result comes back, it automatically populates the shipment.

Item Information

Lower sections in the add-shipment screen allow you to specify item or ship-unit information for the shipment. Choose from a list of existing items/ship units by clicking the magnifying glass, which will populate the fields when you make a selection. Or you can enter information directly (Fig. H-4).

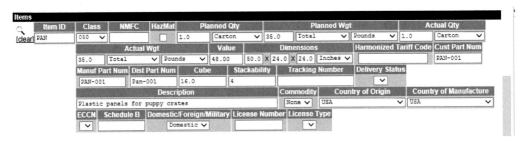

Fig. H-4: Item and ship unit selection in shipment creation.

Finishing the Shipment

The final sections of the add-shipment window allow you to add any special instructions and set final pre-creation options.

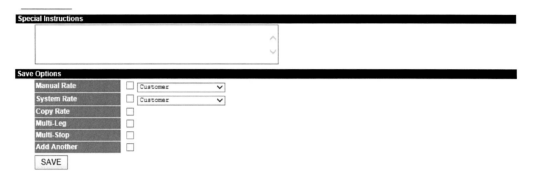

Fig. H-5: Final options for shipment creation.

Depending on your user and role settings, you may have the option to proceed immediately with a rating for this shipment. You also can create it as a multi-leg movement, creating a different carrier load for each leg, or a multi-stop route. The last option is whether to add another shipment as soon as you save this one.

I: Other Creation Methods

The TMS is versatile and there are several places in the interface that we can add new events and new legs.

- Shipment – create multiple stops
- Execution load – split into new legs
- Load board – add a stop
- 'Load Builder' portlet
- Shipment Templates
- Rating Templates
- Integration
- Mojo Optimization

SHIPMENT – CREATE MULTIPLE STOPS

 In the "Add Intermodal" or "Add Shipment" window, choosing "Multi-Stop" from the save options goes to a second window for adding additional stops (Fig. I-1).

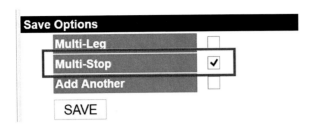

Add Intermodal Move

Multiple Stops (if applicable)

	Location	Contact	Stop Type
Origin	Main Street Shipping Co 16 Main Street Saluda, NC 28773 USA	HowardShipperContact Phone: (828) 772-0238 Email: howard.troxler@mercurygate.com	Pickup
Stop 1	[Add] [Search From Previous] [Search From Next]		
Stop 2	[Add] [Search From Previous] [Search From Next]		
Stop 3	[Add] [Search From Previous] [Search From Next]		
Stop 4	[Add] [Search From Previous] [Search From Next]		
Destination	St. Petersburg Puppy Supply Co. 490 First Ave. S. St. Petersburg, FL 33712 USA		Drop

Cancel   Save

Fig. I-1: Creating multi-stop shipment.

Notice that the above window to add stops looks similar to the window from the earlier option to add legs. The difference is that here, we expect the same carrier to make additional stops as part of the same shipment. (Whether a carrier actually agrees to do this is in the carrier's contract.)

EXECUTION LOAD – SPLIT INTO NEW LEGS

The plan window of a load has detailed information for each event – appointments, arrivals and departures, location and details of the items to be picked/dropped. Events can be re-ordered as needed in the tab with the up and down arrows.

Notice that an event has a "Split" hotspot that allows the user to split off the load at that point and add a new start or endpoint. The net effect is to create a new, separate execution load representing that leg (Fig. I-2).

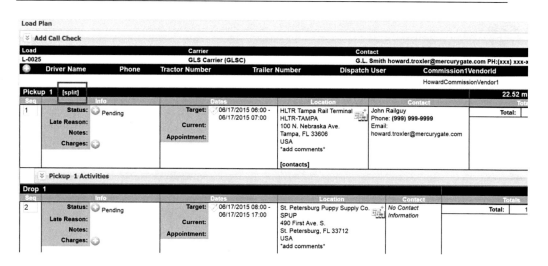

Fig. I-2: An execution load's "Plan" tab with entries for each event showing schedule, location and item information. Notice the "Split" link allowing user to split the plan at that point.

In the above example, our load moves from North Carolina to Florida in a single leg. Click "Split" to add a new endpoint after the first pickup, and we see the multi-leg creation screen we saw from "Add Intermodal Move." Let's say we want the first leg to end at another North Carolina location, before heading to Florida.

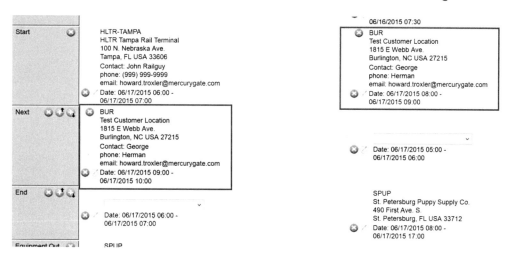

Fig. I-3: New stop added. First leg from western to central NC, then from central NC to Florida.

Set the endpoint of the second leg as your original endpoint and click "Save". Now you see a result screening showing <u>two</u> legs associated with this move, one of them the leg you just created (Fig. I-4):

Fig. I-4: The TMS reports the new execution load following the plan split.

Both loads now exist on your load board and proceed through the usual workflow for rating, booking, tracking, etc. (Fig. I-5).

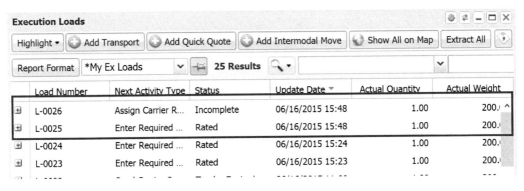

Fig. I-5: The load created by the split now is shown on the load board for handling.

LOAD BOARD – ADD STOPS

From a load expanded on a load board, the "More Actions" menu includes options to add either a pickup or a drop (Fig. I-6):

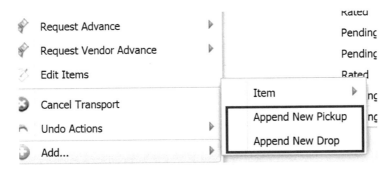

Fig. I-6: Option to add pickups and drops from the load's 'More Actions' menu.

To add a pickup, we're taken to a screen for entering dates, location and item information. The net effect of adding a pickup is to add a shipment to the execution load.

<u>'LOAD BUILDER' PORTLET</u>

The TMS will automatically create multi-stop loads as needed when loads are created by combining shipments (or other loads) via a TMS portlet called the Load Builder.

Users work from lists of available shipments and loads, clicking and dragging them down to a creation tab to become parts of a proposed new load. The user can rearrange and test-rate the load before creating it for actual execution.

The use of the Load Builder portlet is discussed in more detail in the chapter titled "Managing Inbound Freight."

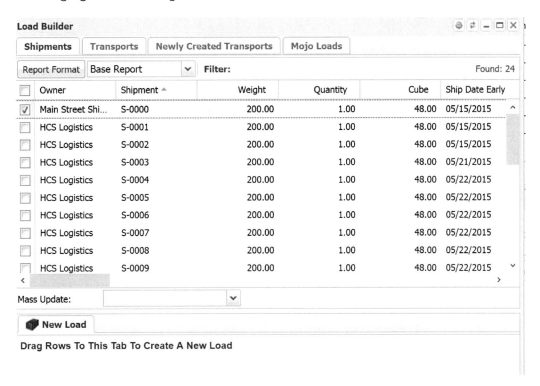

Fig. I-7: 'Load Builder' portlet.

<u>SHIPMENT TEMPLATES</u>

Any shipment can be used to create a <u>template</u>, or cookie-cutter pattern, to create identical subsequent shipments in the same way. This includes origins, destinations, item information and other kinds of information.

Shipment templates are a good way to store and "pre-load" multi-stop, multi-leg movements as needed. Create a template via the "Shipment" menu that is present when a shipment detail is open. The command is Shipment > Create Template. A small form opens asking us to name our template,

Once created, the template is available to us in a list shown from the menu: View > Shipment Templates (the "Down" option also shows all templates owned at lower levels of the hierarchy):

In the template list, clicking the green plus-sign opens a screen for creating a new shipment, based on the selected template (Fig. I-8):

List Shipment Templates (Down)

Report Format	*Dynamic* ∨				
All			**Name**		**Shipment Type**
☐	📄⊕		CLT-TPA-STPC		Regular

Fig. I-8: Clicking the green plus sign next to an entry in the shipment template list creates a new shipment using that template as the model.

A creation screen appears. If we're creating a multi-leg movement, after saving the first screen we're taken to the multi-leg screen with all our legs filled in (Fig. I-9). We can make changes or save the shipment as-is.

Fig. I-9: Legs of a multi-leg movement created from a shipment template, with all our legs already defined.

Upon clicking "Save", a new shipment is created – as well as three new loads, representing the three carrier legs. We can see these loads in the shipment's detail screen, and they're now waiting for us on our load board for handling.

RATING TEMPLATES

A rating template is a rating set up to occur across multiple legs. The rating template's result becomes one of the options shown in a list of possible rating results. If we choose that option, legs are created according to the template.

Let's go back to our example of moving a shipment from western North Carolina to St. Petersburg, Florida. We'll perform a contract rating to see what our options are (Fig. I-10):

Shipment HOW-S-295: Rate Shop Carriers

Report Format ["Dynamic" ∨] ⚙ 🖼 📄 Schedule Rate Filter

Available rates from **SAL-S Saluda, NC 28773** to **STPC St. Petersburg, FL 33712**

		Carrier	Contract	Mode	Service Days	Service Type	Distance	Carrier Total	C
○	✎ 📄	Louie-LTL	LLTL Carrier Contract LTL	LTL	2.25	Rating	623.4	177.72	
○	✎ 📄	Lyndon Trucking	LYND01 Carrier Contract	TL	2.25	Rating	623.4	180.80	
○	✎ 📄	Simone Trucking Inc	Simone LTL Contract	LTL		Contract	623.4	187.03	
○	✎ 📄	Simone Trucking Inc, Lyndon Trucking	Multiple	Intermodal	2.25	Average	733.9	213.83	

Fig. I-10: The 'Multiple' rating result comes not from a single contract, but from a rating template that assumes more than one carrier leg.

In the above screen, we got back four possible rates for our shipment. Three of them are single-leg, single-carrier movements. But we also got a result back from a rating template involving a two-leg movement across two carriers. Notice that the "Contract' name for this result is "Multiple."

Setting up rating templates can be a tool for frequently used multi-leg options. The process is described in detail in a chapter of a document for MercuryGate clients titled *Carriers, Contracts and Rating*.

INTEGRATION

Shipments and execution loads – including multi-stop, multi-leg - can come into the TMS directly from an external system such as an order-management or warehouse system.

MOJO OPTIMIZATION

The last method we'll mention for creation of multi-stop, multi-leg movements is Mojo, MercuryGate's optimization tool.

We go into how to use Mojo in the chapter titled "Optimization." But here's a screenshot of an example of Mojo building a "pooling" scenario in which a route consists of several pickups or drops before the pool location.

Look for event codes of "P" for pickup, "I" for inbound to pool location, "O" from outbound, "D" for drop (Fig. I-11).

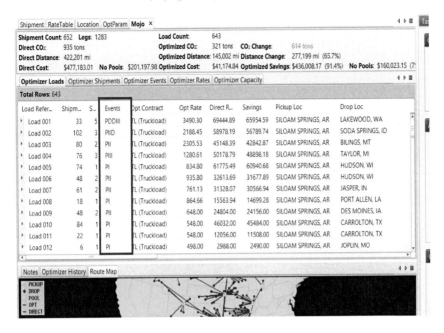

Fig. I-11: Mojo optimization run creating multi-leg movements through pool locations.

J: Load Board Basics

Once loads are created they are managed in the ezClick load portlet, usually called a "load board." Once a load is listed on the load board, its display can be expanded by clicking its left-hand plus sign (Fig. J-1):

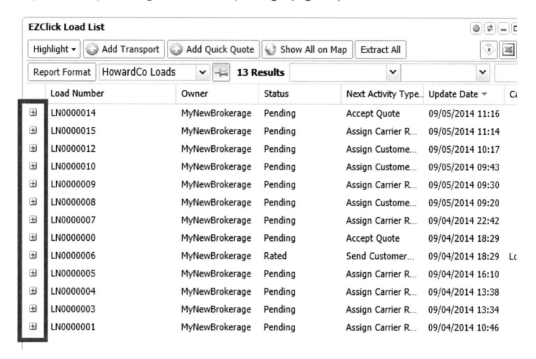

Fig. J-1: Loads on the load board can be expanded to view their details.

This opens an expanded view of that load with several new options, and shows the pending "blue button" tasks we need to perform for that load (Fig. J-2):

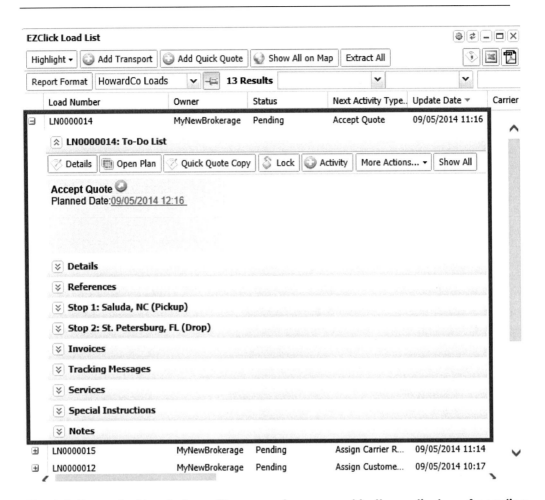

Fig. J-2: Expanded load view with a row of command buttons, display of pending blue buttons, and horizontal tabs that expand again to show various details about the load.

The "Details" button opens the screen of load details that you saw after creating a load with the "Add Load" button.

The "Open Plan" button opens a display of the load's planned events.

"Lock" temporarily locks this load from other users' changes.

"+Activity" allows you to add other blue buttons to the load manually, selecting from a list of available options.

The "More Actions" menu contains several commands we'll discuss later. They're displayed in the next section.

"Show All" displays all the blue buttons that are attached to this load, even the ones that already have been completed. Click "Show All" again to un-toggle the view.

The "To-Do List" section displays the blue buttons currently pending for this load (or all blue buttons if "Show All" is enabled).

Below the to-do list is a list of horizontal tabs that can be clicked and expanded. Each section contains more detailed information about this load, and some of them lead to additional editing screens. In these sections we can view and edit information about the load's contents, stops, rates, invoices and other information.

'More Actions' Menu

From the "More Actions" menu of an expanded load we can perform several additional actions on our load. Some of these commands may vary by user settings.

We can view the load on a map and view its driving directions. We can send an email to related parties. We can view any documents that have been generated for this load with the "Documents" command, or we can generate new ones (from a list of available document types) with the "Printable Documents:" command.

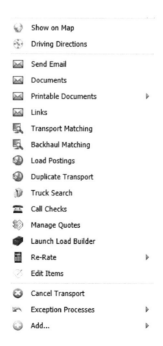

Fig. J-3: Load 'More Actions' menu.

"Links" displays a list of links to external materials that have been associated with this load.

"Transport Matching," "Backhaul Matching"," "Load Postings" and "Truck Search" open windows that attempt to find a carrier for this load based on criteria that you specify.

"Duplicate Transport" creates a new load that is a copy of this load (with a new ID number).

"Call Checks" opens a window for viewing and entering call-check information.

"Manage Quotes" opens a window for searching for a carrier.

"Load Builder" opens a window in which you can combine this load with other loads in a click-and-drag interface.

"Re-Rate" opens a submenu for obtaining a fresh rate.

"Edit Items" opens a window for editing item information on the load.

"Cancel Pickup" puts the load back to "Assign Carrier Rate" status and starts the Truck Ordered Not Used process.

"Exception Processes" allows us to choose commands such as "Pickup Not Ready," which is used to launch the process for Truck Ordered Not Used. This option also might be labeled "Undo Actions."

"Add" allows us not only to add items, but new stop information for the load.

K: Invoice Portlet Basics

On the financial side of the workflow, invoices either are created automatically from electronic messages or system events, or by users.

In either case, invoices are processed in the ezClick invoices portlet. As in the load board, users see a series of blue buttons on each invoice that show the next step to be taken.

Users might be asked to audit an invoice, which means to review its charges. From the audit screen an invoice can be approved, rejected or disputed.

Once an invoice is approved or auto-approved, users see blue buttons for extracting it to the company's external accounting system.

Invoice Portlet

If user settings allow it, a button labeled "Add Carrier Invoice" appears beneath the tabs row when the "Carrier Invoices" tab is active (Fig. K-1):

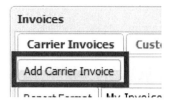

Fig. K-1: Ability to add carrier invoice in invoice port.et

Like the load board, the invoice portlet has a Mass Update menu to perform actions on invoices in the list selected by their checkbox (Fig. K-2):

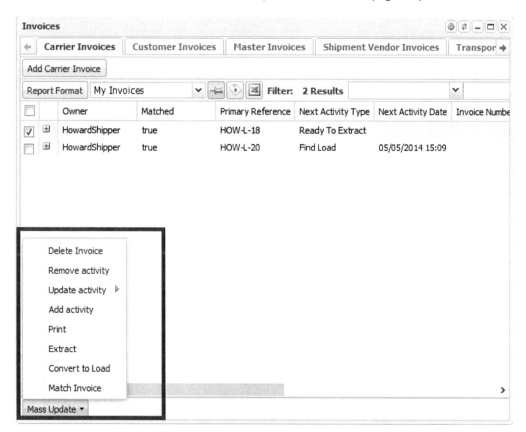

Fig. K-2: Mass-update menu commands can be performed on the invoices selected by their left-hand checkbox.

The mass-update options include deleting the invoice, editing or adding blue buttons to it, printing an invoice, extracting it, converting an unmatched invoice to a load, or matching an unmatched invoice. Mass updates cannot be performed on invoices that have been extracted. A red circle appears in the selection box.

Expanded View

Each invoice has a plus-sign icon on the left-hand side. Clicking the plus sign expands a view of the invoice (Fig. K-3):

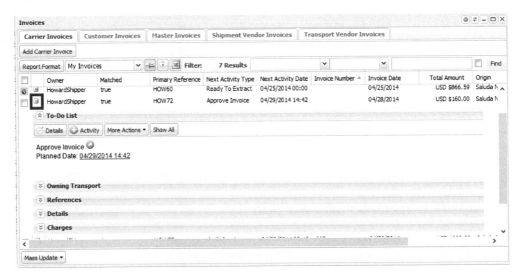

Fig. K-3: View of expanded invoice with additional command buttons, blue-button actions, and horizontal detail sections.

The buttons open a screen for editing the invoice's details, adding an activity, a "More Actions" menu for printing or showing invoice discrepancies, and a "Show All" button (which remains highlighted until pressed again) to display all activities that have been assigned to the invoice, completed or not.

More information for the invoice is displayed in collapsible sections: the "to-do list" of blue-button actions, information about the invoice's owning load, references, details and charges.

For more details on the invoicing process, consult the TMS Invoicing User Guide and TMS Invoicing & Configurations (for admins).

L: Blue Buttons

The name of a blue button displayed on the screen is customizable. However, there are 90 or so underlying actions in the system that can be tied to blue buttons, and standard names often are used for easy recognition.

The blue buttons used by an enterprise are declared in its code table, and most often placed on loads by dynamic rulesets, according to the predesigned workflow.

A comprehensive document about blue buttons and their function titled _Blue Button Actions_ is available for MercuryGate clients.

Here are some frequently used blue buttons in a load's life cycle:

Assign Carrier Rate
Starts process of finding a contract rate, or creating a manual carrier rate. In the alternative can take the user to a "Manage Quotes" window.

Assign Customer Rate
User might have the option to rate against customer contracts, add a manual rate, or simply "uplift" an existing carrier rate by a percentage or flat amount.

Send Customer Confirmation
Opens a window for sending an email and optionally a document to customer, asking to approve the rate.

Send Carrier Confirmation/ Tender
Both labels are commonly used. Window for sending tender offer to carrier.

Book
If carrier does not auto-accept or accept by email, moves the load manually to "Booked" status with the rated carrier.

Enter Required Info
Used to supply appointment & other information for truckload carriers.

Dispatch	Enter information about driver, contact number, city, etc. for load tracking.
Set Arrival/ Departure	For entering status updates manually (if not being received via electronic carrier message).
Add POD	Enter Proof of Delivery information such as an uploaded document, signature image, or link to an external record.
Audit Invoice	Added by system when an invoice is flagged for further review.
Credit Invoice	Process a customer credit.

Configuring Blue Buttons (For Admins)

Admin users can create blue buttons used by the enterprise via code table entries. There should be an "ActivityTypes" entry that names the activity, and then a code table entry that matches that activity type to an action in the system when its blue button is clicked.

For example, to declare an "Assign Carrier Rate" blue button, we need both:

<enterprisename> | ActivityTypes | Assign Carrier Rate | Assign Carrier Rate

As well as:

<enterprisename> | EZClickLoadListBlueBtn | Assign Carrier Rate | action.ezloadlist.rateaddcarrier

Notice the long code table name, "EZClickLoadListBlueBtn". This name depends on which portlet you want to use the blue button:

EZClickLoadListBlueBtn
EZClickInvListBlueBtn
EZClickTransportRouteListBlueBtn
EZClickPOListBlueBtn

The third, "code" portion of the entry is an activity name that has been declared in your enterprise's ActivityTypes code table.

The fourth, "decode" portion of the entry links the blue button to an underlying action in the system. There are roughly 100 such action names, all in the form "action." followed by a further identifier. The complete list is in a document for MercuryGate clients titled *Blue Button Actions.*

Notice that the activity name can be anything. If we want to name our button "Fred," but have it still perform a carrier tender, we need only link the name "Fred" to "action.ezloadlist.tender" in the code table entry. Therefore each enterprise can set up blue buttons to meet its own needs.

The last part of the setup involves configuring the portlet itself to use the blue button. The config group for a portlet includes a list of which blue button activity types it should recognize and use (Fig. L-1):

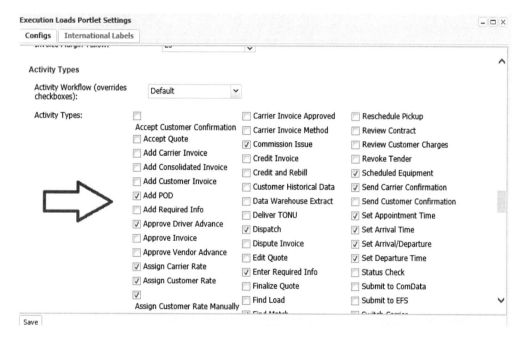

Fig. L-1: A portlet's configuration group declares which blue buttons it uses.

Blue buttons ordinarily are added to loads automatically by dynamic rulesets triggered by events. However, users can add certain blue buttons to a load with the "+Activity" button in an expanded load view.

M: Contracts & Rating

One of the most important and powerful functions of the TMS is obtaining applicable rates from carrier and customer contracts stored in the TMS. Hundreds or even thousands of contracts, covering tens of thousands of defined lanes, can be searched quickly to find a list of rates applicable to our load.

For this "system" rating to occur (as from the "Assign Carrier Rate" or "Assign Customer Rate" blue buttons), the contracts have to exist in the TMS. They might have been set up by human users, or they might have been imported as part of setup by MercuryGate's integration team.

Contracts in the TMS are of one of five <u>types</u>:

- Carrier contracts – the rates a carrier charges us, defined by lane
- Customer contracts – the rates we charge our customers, defined by lane
- "No-linehaul" contracts – rates for rail, air and ocean scheduled carriers
- "Gainshare" contracts – "shares" cost savings versus a known benchmark with customer
- "Carrier bid" contracts – specialized use in bid-board situations.

Mostly we'll work with carrier and customer contracts. Customer contracts also can be tied to an underlying carrier contract, including an automatic "uplift" or increase in the carrier rate that we'll charge to our customer.

Contracts are viewed and edited in the TMS either from the "Contracts" toolbar icon, or from the menu: View > Rating > Contracts (Fig. M-1).

Fig. M-1: TMS contract list.

Each carrier contract has a name and is associated with a carrier. Each contract also has a mode (truckload, less than truckload, rail, air, etc.) and a service. Service often is simply "Standard," but you might recognize the many services available from a parcel carrier: "Ground," "Next Day Air," "2nd Day Air," etc.

Clicking a contract's icon in the list opens a detail window for viewing and editing its fields (Fig. M-2):

LLTL Carrier Contract LTL Base Contract

Edit Contract	
Contract ID:	LLTL Carrier Contract LTL
Contract Type:	CARRIER CONTRACT
Contract Role:	⌄
Effective Date:	01/01/2012 12:00:00 AM
Expiration Date:	12/31/2020 11:59:59 PM
Multi-stop truckload rating:	☑
Carrier:	Louie-LTL (LLTL) carrier in
Mode:	LTL
Service:	Standard (3 days)
Equipment:	*No Equipment*
Gain Share:	☐
Rate Table:	LLTL Rate Table LTL Rate File: 'LLTL Rate File.xls'
Minimum:	42.50
Factor Type:	Flat Rate
Factor Value:	0
Enable SMC Min Charge Discount:	☐

Fig. M-2: Contract detail screen (partial).

Description of Contract Fields

Contract ID: A unique name is recommended but
                     not required.

Contract Type: Dropdown list of available types, e.g.
                     Carrier, Customer, etc.

Contract Role: Restricts access to the contract by
                     role assignment.

Effective Date
Expiration Date: First and last dates the contract is valid.

Multi-stop truckload rating: Whether the contract will be used
                     to rate multi-stop loads.

Carrier: Carrier to be used when rating
                     with this contract.

Mode: Dropdown list of available modes,

defined in code table. See
"Mode" subsection below.

Service:

Categorizes levels of service defined
for satisfying the contract, e.g. Standard,
2nd Day Air, etc. -- list defined in code table.

Days:

Number of days in which the
contract "guarantees" delivery. A value of
zero is acceptable. This field will be
overridden by the transit time calculator or
the rate table.

Equipment:

Whether specified equipment is required
for this contract use.

Gain Share:

Contract is to be used when
calculating gainshare (a type of rating in
which savings are shared with customers
when compared against 'benchmark'
rates)

Rate Table:

Name of a rate table or that a
Web Service is accessed to calculate rates.
Chosen from s dropdown list of available
rate tables for this enterprise.

Minimum:

Minimum value for this contract
to be returned in a rate inquiry.

Associated Carrier Contract:

Enabled if the contract type is "Customer."
Used to associate a customer contract with
a carrier contract. This association will allow
the carrier and customer rates to be
displayed on the same row in the rating
results screen.

Factor Type and Factor Value:

The contract may offer a flat-rate discount
or a discount that varies by mileage, weight,
freight class, etc.

Enable SMC Min Charge Discount:

SMC is a subscription rating services. Adds a
discount percentage when the SMC
minimum charge is invoked. This overrides
the Factor value above.

Disable Indirect Charges:

Rates for negotiated lanes defined

	as Indirect will not be returned when rating the load. "Indirect" means a carrier arranges service to the location by some other means.
Uplift Type:	This section adds an additional percentage to the calculated rate. A customer charge might be based on an uplift of a carrier charge.
Line haul amount:	Uplift the percentage only on the line haul amount excluding accessorials
Total amount:	Uplift on the entire calculated cost of the move
Uplift Percentage;	Percentage value of uplift
Exclude Percentage Acc from Uplift:	Exclude the uplift percentage from any accessorial that is of percentage type (tax, for example).
Uplift Min:	Minimum allowed uplift on the contract in currency value
Uplift Max:	Maximum allowed uplift on the contract in currency value
Re-rating Date Preference:	The date field to be used when the load is re-rated, if any
Show Zero Rate:	Override the filter requirement that would return only rates greater than $1.00.
Apply Oversize Charges:	If a load exceeds size requirements, the rating engine should apply the oversize charges defined in the accessorial.
Dim Factor:	"Dimensional weight" is an adjustment for unusual dimensions, e.g., an extra-long package might be assigned a new "weight" for rating.

The "dim factor" is the denominator used when calculating (cubic inches / Dim Factor). The larger the denominator, the smaller the dimensional weight will be.

If a value is entered, the Apply Oversize Charges is assumed to be checked. The Dim Factor value overrides the oversize factor on the carrier configuration. If the Dim Factor value equals zero, it will be ignored.

Dim Weight Calc Method (MG Rate Table):

Check to enable.

Example, given two items, A and B:

Multiply Volume by Qty: Itemized

For each item, calculate the dim weight and compare to actual weight. Use whichever is greater for rating for the item.

Multiply Volume by Qty: Total Dims vs. Total Weight

Calculate dim weight for Item A and for Item B, sum the two to arrive the total dims value.

Sum the actual weight of the two items to determine total weight. Use the greater value of total dims or total weight when rating.

Dimensional Rounding
Dim Weight Rounding
(MG Rate Table):

Round dimension and weight to nearest whole number.

Require Dimensions:

Indicates that dimensions values are necessary for the contract to return a rate when pricesheet rating or rate shopping.

Quantity Density Weight:	Indicates the minimum weight for a quantity of one.
	Example: Value entered equals 1000 and shipment quantity equal 2. The minimum rate that will be rated is for 2000 pounds.
Distance Determiner	A distance determiner is a defined method of determining distances between points. A dropdown menu of available distance determiners as defined in the code table.
Disable Multi-stop Distance Calculator:	Do not calculate the distance of each segment when multiple stops are indicated on the load plan.
Non MG-Rate Table: MG-Rate Table:	In most cases, these should be left unchecked.
Include RTO Miles (Return To Origin miles):	If the checkbox is checked, add the RTO miles to the calculated distance. Often used in private-fleet scenarios where the return must be included in cost calculations.
Transit Time:	Various methods of calculating transit time can be configured and are listed here for selection.
Weekend Holiday Adjustment:	How the contract treats weekends and holidays -- include or exclude one or both from transit-time calculations. See transit time.
Persist Transit as Service Days:	Depending on how the contract treats weekends and holidays, include that transit time in total service days.
Base FAKs:	Used to group ranges of freight classes (FAK = Freight All Kinds) for use with this contract. For example

we might consider all classes in the range X to Y to be the same class.

Accessorial Profile:

Groups of accessorial charges can be grouped into profiles that are listed here for selection to apply to this contract.

Expiration

If code table entries "ContractExpirationReason" are defined, there also will be a item below the contract expiration date with a dropdown menu for setting the reason:

    * | ContractExpirationReason | Manual Expiration | Manual Expiration
    * | ContractExpirationReason | Other Reason | Other Reason
    * | ContractExpirationReason | Reason Alpha | Reason Alpha
    * | ContractExpirationReason | Reason Bravo | Reason Bravo
    * | ContractExpirationReason | Reason Charlie | Reason Charlie

If an option to un-set the reason is needed then create a code table entry with a blank decode:

    * | ContractExpirationReason | | -None-

Mode

Example mode code table entries:

    * | Mode | Air | Air
    * | Mode | Air Freight | Air Freight
    * | Mode | Bulk | Bulk
    * | Mode | Drayage | Drayage
    * | Mode | EXPEDITED | Expedited
    * | Mode | FCL | FCL
    * | Mode | Intermodal | Intermodal
    * | Mode | International | International
    * | Mode | LCL | LCL
    * | Mode | LTL | LTL
    * | Mode | Last Mile | Last Mile
    * | Mode | Letter | Letter
    * | Mode | Mixed | Mixed
    * | Mode | Ocean | Ocean
    * | Mode | Other | Other
    * | Mode | Parcel | Parcel
    * | Mode | Parcel Carton | Parcel Carton
    * | Mode | Rail | Rail

```
* | Mode | Service Mode | Service Mode
* | Mode | Small Package | Small Package
* | Mode | TL | TL
* | Mode | Truckload | Truckload
```

Requirements for Rating

To get rates back from a contract, you need (1) a declared <u>rate table</u> the contract will use for its rates, and (2) at least one defined <u>negotiated lane</u> that the contract covers.

Rate Tables

A <u>rate table</u> is a separate record in the TMS that in turn is assigned to a contract. Each enterprise has its own list of defined rate tables. View the list from the "Rate Tables" toolbar icon, or from the menu: View > Rating > Rate Tables.

A contract is associated with a rate table from the list of available options.

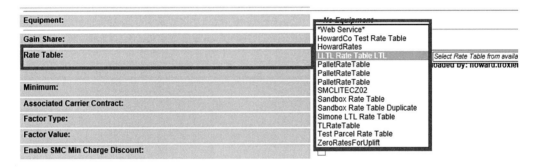

Fig. M-3: Which rate table to use with this contract is selected in the contract's detail screen.

In turn, the heart of a rate table is a <u>rate file</u> that defines its actual rates. The rate file is uploaded to the rate table as an Excel or CSV spreadsheet. A rate table also can use an external, by-subscription rating service over the internet.

A rate file has a specific column format shown below. Each row in the rate file defines a <u>lane</u> for which a given rate applies, a definition of its <u>rate</u> (flat rate, X per mile, X per pound, etc.), and a <u>break range</u> for which this rate applies. For example, one line in the rate table might apply for shipments up to 100 pounds, then the next line on the same lane but for 100-200 pounds etc.

In general, country codes and units of measure correspond to values defined in the enterprise's code table.

Here's a chart of rate file fields:

Column Header	Description
OrgCity	Origin city name
OrgState	Origin state abbreviation
OrgZIP	Origin zip code formats: Three-digit, e.g. 287 Three-digit range, e.g. 287-289 Five-digit, e.g. 28773 Five-digit range, e.g. 28773-28901 Ranges also work for non-numeric codes, e.g. E98-E-99 in the UK, M7A-M7Z in Canada. Both the start and end values must have at least one alphabetic character. Unlike lane definitions, a MGRateTable does not support comma-separated lists of multiple ranges.
OrgCountry	Origin country
DestCity	Destination city name
DestState	Destination state abbreviation
DestZIP	Destination zip code, same format options as for origin
DestCountry	Destination country
Rate	The actual rate value, e.g. 1.00 - applied according to the next field, rate type
RateType	A code for how the rate is to be applied: F = Flat PM= Per Mile P = Per (weight, etc.) C= Per 100 Lbs ST=Per Short Ton CU=Cube I=Master Item Id U=Item UOM (cartons, pallets, etc. -- see following subsection) Per:<weight unit> - see following subsection
BreakUOM	Unit of measure, e.g. lb, kg, CU for cube, LF for linear foot, CT for rating count

Column Header	Description
Break Min	Minimum weight/UOM to be applied this rate
Break Max	Maximum weight/UOM to be applied this rate
MinMileage	Minimum mileage to be applied this rate
MaxMileage	Maximum mileage to be applied this rate
MinCost	Minimum cost to be returned for this rate
MinimumType	Minimum type that can be applied this rate, typically "Flat"
TransitDays	If this is non-zero, then this value is used and a transit time is not calculated
MinFreightClass	Minimum freight class to which this rate is applied (numeric)
MaxFreightClass	Maximum freight class to which this rate is applied
MaxCost	Maximum cost to be returned at this rate
Effective	First date this rate is effective (MM/DD/YYYY)
Expire	Last date this rate is effective (MM/DD/YYYY)
AliasOrg	Origin location code
AliasDest	Dest location code
MaxStops	Max # of stops to which this rate applies

All columns must be present but not all have to contain a value. For example, a rate may be defined by ZIP, by state or even by country only. A rate could be declared as broadly as "USA" to "USA," covering every origin and destination in the United States.

Likewise, fields not applicable are set to extremes so they do not come into play. Examples:

Minimum weight/mileage set to 0; maximum to 99,999.
Any weight or mileage will be rated.

Minimum freight class set to -10; maximum to 3000.
Any freight class will be rated.

Minimum cost to 0; maximum 99,000. Any amount will be returned.

Numerical ranges generally are *inclusive* at the beginning and *exclusive* at the end. A min defined as 0 and a max defined as 100 includes any value from 0 up to 100 - but not 100, which starts the next range.

Negotiated Lanes

We mentioned earlier that to get rates back from a contract, we need both a rate structure, and one or more negotiated lanes. If no negotiated lanes are declared then no rates will be returned from the contract.

A negotiated lane is the declaration of an area covered by the contract. A contract can have many negotiated lanes, or as few as one ("USA to USA", for example).

One purpose of negotiated lanes is to allow for individual negotiated settings, such as discounts or additional charges by lane.

When a contract detail screen is open, the second command in the "Contract' menu in the toolbar is "Negotiated Lanes." The command opens the list of negotiated lanes belonging to this contract.

Fig. M-4: Negotiated lane list for selected contract.

In the above simplified example, this contract has only three negotiated lanes – NC to FL, NC to CO, and then the rest of the United States. For each one, clicking the link opens that lane's editing screen, including the ability to define its "geo" lane.

One recent enhancement to the TMS is the use of enterprise lanes. These are simply geographic lanes that have been saved at the level of the enterprise, not in an individual contract.

That means stored enterprise lanes can be shared and re-used across contracts. A list of enterprise lanes is available from the menu: View > Rating > Master Enterprise Lanes.

N: Documents

Standard shipping <u>documents</u> are generated from TMS records as PDFs or other formats. These include bills of lading, carrier and customer invoices, and other standard documents.

The process of generating ("rendering") a document pulls values from the TMS record (locations, items, charges, references, for example) to populate the document format.

Your company might already be set up to use certain "generic" document formats, such as bills of lading and invoices. A TMS client also can use customized documents with highly designed formats and specialized fields.

A load or route's "More Actions" menu includes options to view any documents already attached to the record, or to generate a new document from the available options (Fig. N-1).

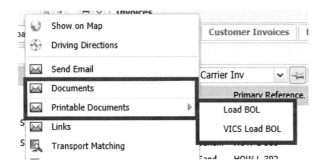

Fig. N-1: Options to view existing documents or generate documents from a load's 'More Actions' menu.

Existing documents attached to the record are viewed on the load's "Documents" tab (Fig. N-2). Click the document link to open it.

Documents							
⊕	Owner Name	Filename	P.O.D.	Updated On	Updated By	Created On	Crea
⊗ ✎	HOW-L-392	PrintGenericCarrierInvoice.pdf	false	04/10/2015 08:32	HCSAdmin	04/10/2015 08:32	HCS.

Fig. N-2: List of documents already attached to this record.

Or select an option from the "Printable Documents" submenu to generate a document of that type, for example, a bill of lading (Fig. N-3):

	BOL NO: HOW-L-392
BILL OF LADING	**Carrier:** Lyndon Trucking
Ship From	**Pickup Date:** 04-06-2015
Main Street Shipping Co 16 Main Street Saluda, NC 28773 HowardShipperContact, (828) 772-0238,	**Origin Terminal** **Destination Terminal**
Ship To	
St. Petersburg Puppy Co. 490 First Ave. S. St. Petersburg, FL 33712 Joe Pupmaster, (777) 777-7777,	References:
3rd Party Freight Charges Bill To	
Howard Logistics Co. Inc. 358 Whispering Woods Drive Saluda, NC 28773 Lyndon,	

Fig. N-3: Generic bill of lading document.

For custom documents, a subscription tool named Docmosis is available by additional license for formatting templates used to generate the result.

Configuration (For Admins)

Document types used by the enterprise are declared in a "DocTypes" code table, for example:

* | DocTypes | BOL | BOL
* | DocTypes | Carrier Invoice | Carrier Invoice
* | DocTypes | Carrier Rate Confirmation | Carrier Rate Confirmation
* | DocTypes | Customer Invoice | Customer Invoice
* | DocTypes | Customer Order | Customer Order
* | DocTypes | Customer Packing List | Customer Packing List
* | DocTypes | Customer Rate Confirmation | Customer Rate Confirmation
* | DocTypes | Email | Email
* | DocTypes | POD* | POD
* | DocTypes | Transport Detail Print | Transport Detail Print
* | DocTypes | Vendor Invoice | Vendor Invoice
* | DocTypes | pdf | pdf

Documents that can be generated are declared in a "Printables" code table. Each entry connects a document type with a code class that generates the document. These can be standard generics made available to the enterprise, or they can be customized components. (The '*' means the name of the TMS enterprise.)

```
* | Printables | Carrier Invoice | com.mg.printables.PrintGenericCarrierInvoice
* | Printables | Carrier Quote Request |
        com.mg.quoterequest.QuoteRequestPDFGeneric
* | Printables | Customer Invoice | com.mg.printables.PrintGenericCustomerInvoice
* | Printables | Load BOL | com.mg.printables.PrintGenericTRBOL
* | Printables | Quote Doc | com.mg.printables.PrintGenericQuote
* | Printables | Shipment BOL | com.mg.printables.PrintGenericSHBOL
* | Printables | Shipment Summary | com.mg.printables.PrintShipmentSummary
* | Printables | VICS Load BOL | com.mg.printables.PrintVICSBOL
* | Printables | VICS Shipment BOL | com.mg.printables.PrintVicksSHBOL
```

Access to the kind of <u>attachments</u> that users can see, and the kind of documents they can view, can by controlled in a role's settings. For example, we might not want customer users to be able to see carrier invoices, or carrier users to see the amount being charged to the customer.

O: Code Tables

Many settings and options in the TMS are controlled by <u>code table</u> entries. Each enterprise has its own code table, which is an editable text file accessible to administrators.

A single entry in a code table exists on its own line and has four parts, separated by "pipe" characters (|). It looks like this:

> My Company | Mode | LTL | LTL

The first portion is always the exact TMS enterprise name. The second portion is one of the predefined options for code table names declared in the system. The third portion is called the "code" and will be the value known to the system. The fourth value is called the "decode" and is the value displayed to users.

So the above code table entry says that one of this company's options for "Mode" is "LTL." in this example we use the same value for code and decode, a common practice for clarity to human eyes, although not required.

Code tables are inherited down the hierarchy until a new code table of the same type is declared at a lower level. The sub-company's code table then replaces the inherited code table, not adds to it – if the parent has 10 entries in "EquipmentTypes" but the child has only two, users in the child enterprise see only the two options.

Code tables are accessed either via the "Code Table" toolbar icon, or from the menu: Admin > Current Company > Setup Tables > Code Tables. Admins have the option to view the entire code table, or only entries of a particular type. Code tables can be quite lengthy, consisting of hundreds or thousands of lines.

Code tables are case-sensitive and exact. If the company name includes "Inc." with a period then "Inc" is not recognized as a variant.

Changing code tables without full awareness of the consequences is extremely dangerous.

P: Config Groups

Roughly 100 kinds of TMS displays, ranging from major portlets to small windows opened by blue-button actions, are customized and modified using groups of settings known as configuration groups.

A config group has a type that describes the kind of display it modifies. Type names tend to be long but descriptive. The type of a config group that controls a load board is "EZClickLoadListPortlet." The type of a config group that controls an "Audit Invoice" blue button screen is "EZClickAuditInvoiceConfigGroup."

An enterprise can have multiple and different instances of the same config group type for different purposes. That's how we can configure different load boards for different roles, for example.

One point of config groups is easy re-use. A load board has dozens of possible settings; you can use an existing config group as a starting point, tweak your settings as needed, and save your changed settings as a new group.

Creating and Editing

Administrative users have the ability to change configuration settings. In a portlet, admins see a "gear" icon in the upper right-hand corner of a portlet, along with the resize and close boxes (Fig. P-1):

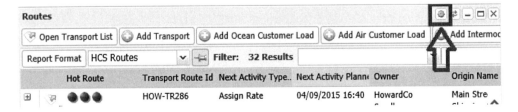

Fig. P-1: A portlet's configuration or 'gear' icon visible to admin users.

Clicking the gear icon opens a window for editing the config group assigned to this portlet (Fig. P-2):

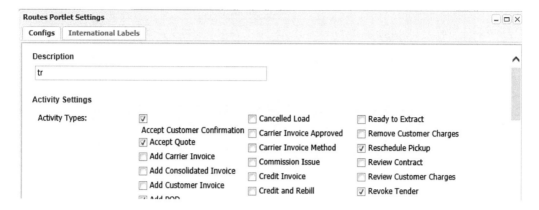

Fig. P-2: Editing a portlet's configuration settings.

Another way to edit config groups is in a special portlet usually titled "Config Groups." You can create a new group of a specific type by choosing it from the list of available options (Fig. P-3):

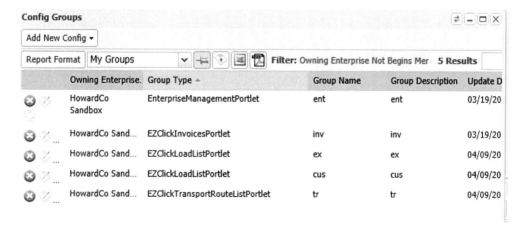

Fig. P-3: Config Group portlet used for managing and creating config groups.

Click "Add New Config" to see the list of available types and select the type of config group to create. An editing window opens for establishing the settings of that config group. Settings often control whether individual fields are hidden, read-only, editable by the user, or even required.

Config groups also can call other config groups. A setting in a config group might be the name of another, specialized "subgroup" that handles the fields of a particular object such as a location.

Assigning

We can assign config groups to portlets in two ways: on the portlet system configuration page, or in the code table. On the portlet config page (Admin > Current Company > Configurations > Portlets), the fields for each portlet include the option to assign a config group by its ID (Fig. P-4):

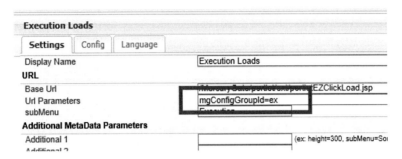

Fig. P-4: Assigning a config group to a portlet in its base configuration screen accessed via the menu.

The syntax "mgConfigGroupId=xx" assigns a config group
to this portlet, where "xx" means the group's ID.

The second way is to assign the config group in the code table entry that defines the portlet:

```
* | PortletsWide | /MercuryGate/portlet/ext/portletEZClickLoad.jsp?
mgConfigGroupId=ex:subMenu=Execution | Execution Loads
```

Assigning a config group to a blue button display is accomplished in the code table in a similar manner:

```
* | EZClickInvListBlueBtn | Audit Duplicate |
action.ezinvoice.auditinvoice;mgConfigGroupId=16429265400
```

Be sure to use the config group's actual ID and not its "Description" field. The values are case-sensitive, like all code table entries. They must be typed exactly.

A comprehensive reference guide titled Guide to TMS Config Groups is available to MercuryGate clients.

Q: Dynamic Rulesets

Dynamic rulesets (DRS) make possible the flexible, responsive, exception-handling workflows that drive the interface. An enterprise can have a few, dozens, or even hundreds of dynamic rulesets. Each ruleset consists of:

(1) The name of a <u>trigger</u> condition that fires the ruleset. There are more than 70 possible trigger events, such as the creation of a new load, the addition of a new document, a changed address, and many others.

(2) One or more <u>conditions</u> that must be true for the ruleset to fire. For example, if an "AddInvoice" trigger fires, and this invoice is a <u>carrier</u> invoice (the condition), then execute. (If it's not a carrier invoice, nothing happens.)

(3) One or several <u>actions</u> to carry out if the trigger occurs and all the conditions are true. There are roughly 90 possible actions. Many actions act upon a <u>target</u> object such as the underlying execution or customer load.

Access to dynamic rulesets requires the permission of MercuryGate. Dynamic rulesets are viewed and edited from the menu: Administration > Current Company > Dynamic Rulesets. They are created in editing windows that use quasi-English phrases.

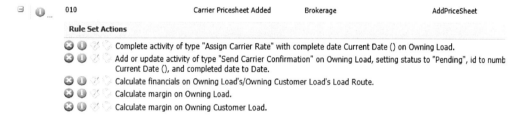

Fig. Q-1: DRS editing window. This ruleset responds to the creation of a carrier rate.

One of the most commonly used triggers is "AddOrUpdateActivity," which fires whenever an activity's status changes. We use that trigger to say: When the user completes the job of one blue button, let's add the next one.

<u>Editing dynamic rulesets is dangerous</u> and can easily break workflows so that records simply "disappear" from portlets (although they're still lurking in the system). Users who complete DRS training have access to a MercuryGate document titled *Dynamic Ruleset Triggers & Actions,* an encyclopedia of currently available triggers, and the actions that can be called from each one.

R: References

A reference is a tag of data attached to a TMS record – think of a sticky note. As a TMS record goes through its life cycle, it collects references added either by the system or by users. A load might end up with dozens. References exist on many kinds of TMS records, including invoices, users, locations, and even enterprises.

References can represent any kind of data required – a serial number, a carrier SCAC, or a date/time code, for example. Every TMS record has at least one reference called its primary reference, which is its identifying number.

A reference has a type, which is a name such as "Serial Number," and a value that is a text string. The reference types used by an enterprise are managed via the menu: Admin > Current Company > Setup Tables > Reference Types. You can create your own types, or choose from a list of hundreds of existing types.

In the reference management screen, you must choose a scope for each reference type that declares which kinds of TMS records can use it. If a reference is not scoped for that kind of record, you will not see it among the options when you try to add it from a selection menu.

Reference Types

	Name	Owner	Shipment	Transport	Invoice	Company	Tender	BOL Print	Carrier	Description
☐	BOL	MercuryGate	☑	☑	☑	☑	☑	☑	☑	
☐	CarReqDoc	MercuryGate	☐	☑	☐	☑	☐	☐	☐	CarReqDoc
☐	Commission Type	MercuryGate	☑	☑	☑	☑	☑	☑	☑	
☐	Commission1VendorId	MercuryGate	☐	☑	☐	☐	☐	☐	☐	
☐	Commission2VendorId	MercuryGate	☐	☑	☐	☐	☐	☐	☐	

Fig. R-1: Portion of the enterprise's list of reference types. References must be scoped to record types (shipment, load, invoice, etc.) to be available for use.

Most views of individual TMS records include the ability to view and add references to that record. For example, in a load expanded in a load board, one of the horizontal sections is labeled "References" (Fig. R-2).

Fig. R-2: 'References' section of a load display. Add new references by clicking the 'Add' button, or delete existing references with their "X". Be careful with system-added references, however, which might be required for some functions.

S: MercuryEdge

MercuryEdge is a free, downloaded data-analysis application offered by MercuryGate to its clients. It is a spreadsheet- style application that allows users to perform advanced calculations on worksheets of logistics data.

Users log in using their TMS user ids and passwords. MercuryEdge can open any report that is saved in the TMS for shipments, loads, rates and many other kinds of data. MercuryEdge can open any external Excel file, and can recognize files that should be treated as lists of shipments, loads, locations and so forth.

MercuryEdge is the platform for using Mojo, MercuryGate's optimization tool.

INSTALLATION: The application is installed from the URL:

https://<servername>.mercurygate.net/MercuryGate/webstart/Launcher.html

The user might be prompted to update the Java installation. There is a known issue in which installation hangs from Internet Explorer 11. If so, hit the F12 (function) key and in the "Emulate" menu change the setting for "Document Mode" to "10" and "User Agent String" to "Mozilla Firefox." The installation link will re-activate and you can proceed.

INTERFACE: The default MercuryEdge window includes a central workspace for open files, a <u>reports window</u> with links to available reports back in the TMS, and a <u>task window</u> with a list of currently available commands to perform on the data.

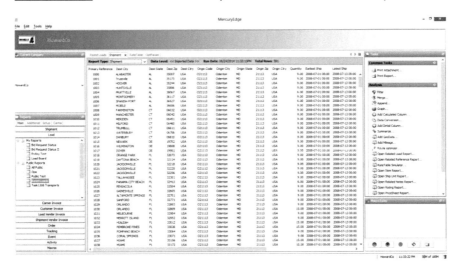

Fig. S-1: MercuryEdge user interface.

Working in MercuryEdge consists of designing questions about the data. Task window commands such as "Add Calculated Column," "Filter," "Merge" and several others are used to manipulate the data in a series of steps.

Example: From a raw list of TMS shipments, produce a summary of customer revenue by 3-digit zip code origin.

Steps:

(1) Add a calculated column that pulls the first three characters from the "Origin Zip" column and put in a new column named "3ZIP" (or whatever you want to call it). The formula would be "substr(0,3)".

(2) Use the "Summarize" command to group your data based on the value in the "3ZIP" column to produce a sum of the column named "Customer Charges."

Result: For each unique 3-zip origin in the shipment list, a sum of customer charges is produced. The report can be further refined as desired.

MercuryEdge students learn to break analysis down into a series of easy steps. In the textbook chapter titled "Rewarding Your Best Carriers," we saw the use of MercuryEdge to calculate carrier performance in billing efficiency.

A series of user actions in MercuryEdge can be recorded in a "macro" and played back like a script. Therefore a set of complicated steps needed to produce a daily report can be recorded once and then re-used every day. Macros can even be scheduled to execute automatically.

Complete documentation is found in the *MercuryEdge User Manual*.

##

Appendix – TMS Configurations

These sections discuss configurations for the functions discussed in the listed chapters. For general discussion of system configurations, code table management and configuration groups see the previous appendix.

Contents

Chapter 4:   Getting Market Rates

Setting value services to populate the Manage Quote screen requires:

(1) Code table entries.
(2) Configurations of the Manage Quotes screen.
(3) Dynamic rulesets to calculate or re-calculate average rates.

Any administrator can set up an internal, historical value service that will calculate averages off actual experience. External services require subscription and additional configuration.

Code Table – Historical Value Service

A code table named "ValueServices" declares each service the enterprise uses. Each entry pairs a name of the service that users will see with an underlying class of code that performs the actual calculation.

*** | ValueServices | Historical Analysis |
com.mg.common.valueservice.HistoricalAnalysisValueService

For each value service, we also need a code table entry to declare the reference type that service will place on an execution load.

*** | ValueService:Historical Analysis | referenceType |
Internal Rate Index

Make sure that the reference types you declare in these code tables exist for your enterprise and are scoped for use with loads/transports. Reference types are controlled via the menu: Administration > Current Company > Setup Tables > Reference Types.

The historical (internal) index also has a trending indicator and a coverage indicator. The "coverage" indicator represents a ratio of the number of loads on this lane in a "secured" status (Booked, In Transit, Delivered) versus all loads on the lane. By default, coverage is "Good" above 70 percent, "OK" from 50 percent to 70 percent, and "Poor" below 50 percent. However, we can choose our own values:

*** | ValueService:Historical Analysis | coveragePercentOk | 50
*** | ValueService:Historical Analysis | coveragePercentGood | 70

A historical benchmark value can contain a "trending" indicator showing whether the late rate was an increase or decrease of more than X versus the previous index value. The default "minimum change" to be recognized is $5 but can be overridden in the code table:

*** | ValueService:InternalRateIndexService |
    trendingChangeQualifyingDiff | 5

Manage Quotes Portlet

Make sure your Manage Quotes portlet is configured to display the reference types you intend to calculate from value services. Select the reference types from the portlet's configuration screen: Administration > Current Company > Configurations > Portlets > Manage Quotes. The portlet also can be configured with a config group of type "ManageQuotesConfigGroup."

Dynamic Ruleset Action: 'Call Value Service'

The DRS action 'Call Value Service' is available from several triggers, such as load creation or changing an address. The only parameters are the target for the references (usually the load) and which value service to call (from the options declared in the code table).

Chapter 5:   Finding Capacity

<u>Private Bid Boards</u>

(1) Users must have access to bid information via their assigned role – the "Bid Sheets" permission under the role's "Load Detail" tab.

(2) Carrier-users of the TMS should be assigned a role with a name that begins with "bid" or "Bid" to receive bid invitations issued to that role name. They need at least read-only access to bid information under the role's "Load Detail" tab.

(3) Carrier-users must be assigned a primary carrier in their user record. Also in their user record they should be assigned access to a Bid Board portlet, which also must have been configured.

(4) As mentioned just above, the Bid Board portlet must have been created in the code table:

<YourEnterpriseName> | PortletsWide | /MercuryGate/transport/portletBidView.jsp ?showLowBid=true:roles=ALL:height=380 | Bid Board

The "showLowBid" parameter allows the carrier-user to see the current low bid for the load.

In addition, other values such as auto-tender, time zone and e-mail settings for bid request, award and "regrets" messages are declared in the code table. The email entries should be set for the bid email function to work. The default bid message templates are acceptable for most customers but can be customized.

(* in the list below means the name of the enterprise)

```
* | BidBoard | AutoTender | false
* | BidBoard | AwardFrom | bidmaster@*.com
* | BidBoard | AwardSubject | Your bid has been accepted
* | BidBoard | AwardTemplate | bidAwardEmail.html
* | BidBoard | CheckNTI | false          (Need To Investigate flag)
* | BidBoard | RegretFrom | bidmaster@*.com
* | BidBoard | RegretSubject | Sorry, your bid was not accepted
* | BidBoard | RegretTemplate | bidRegretEmail.html
* | BidBoard | RequestFrom | bidmaster@*.com
* | BidBoard | RequestSubject | Request for bid
* | BidBoard | RequestTemplate | bidRequestEmail.html
* | BidBoard | TimeZone | Eastern Time
```

If "CheckNTI" is true, bidding cannot be initiated from loads that are in "need to investigate" status.

The Bid Board portlet is configured via the menu: Administration > Current Company > Portlets > Bid Board.

Public Bid Boards

Clients wishing to use external bid boards acquire separate user agreement with those external services, then supply their login and password credentials for MercuryGate's integration team to set up.

The checkboxes available in the PostLoad dialog have been declared in the "PostLoad" code table.

Carrier Quote Process

To be able to ask carriers for quotes via the Manage Quotes portlet, a quote process must have been configured in the carrier's record. To open the carrier record, either choose View > Rating > Carriers from the menu, or click the "Carriers" toolbar button, and then the details icon of the desired carrier in the list. Scroll to the Quote Process section, click "Configure," choose the email option and enter a valid email address to receive quote requests.

'Manage Quotes' Configurations

The Manage Quotes window's settings are managed via the menu: Administration > Current Company > Configurations > Portlets > Manage Quotes.

Two of the Manage Quote settings are labeled "Show From Internal Sources" and "Show From External Sources." Each display is configured by a config group of type "ConsolidatedRateSearchConfigGroup" to specify which sources are displayed.

The setting labeled "Show CARMA Carriers" controls display of the "From CARMA" button in the portlet. "Matching Lane Type" tells the portlet which kind of lanes to look for when conducting a search of Carma carriers.

Other Portlets

If the desired portlets are not already set up for an enterprise, they can be added by code table entries, or from the menu (Administration > Current Company > Configurations > Portlets), supplying the URLs listed here.

* | PortletsWide | /MercuryGate/portlet/ext/portletCarrierScorecardExt.jsp?:height= 450 | Carrier Scorecard Ext

* | PortletsWide | /MercuryGate/portlet/ext/portletCombinedCapacity.jsp?:height =400:width=1000:isExt=true | Combined Capacity

* | PortletsNarrow | /MercuryGate/dashboard/wide/portletNews.jsp | News and Information

* | PortletsNarrow | /MercuryGate/dashboard/wide/portletNews.jsp?isEdit=true | News Admin

<u>Carma</u>

Configuring the Carma application is the subject of its own book, titled the _Carma Configuration Guide_,

The "From CARMA" search in the TMS' Manage Quotes screen looks for carriers with appropriate lane information in Carma. Lanes are stored on the "Lanes" tab of the carrier's detail record in Carma:

Chapter 6: 'Multi-Everything' Moves

The main configurations for a route portlet are set in a config group of type "EZClickTransportRouteListPortlet". Create the group initially from the Config Groups portlet and assign it to your route portlet, either in the portlet config screen or in the code table entry.

The route portlet configs include settings for which blue-button activities are visible in the portlet, as well as the behavior of the creation screens for loads. These include several configuration subgroups controlling the creation of international loads.

LOAD BOARD BUTTONS: The display of creation buttons (Add Load, Add Quick Quote, Add Intermodal Move) can be turned off in a portlet's config group.

SHIPMENT SAVE OPTIONS: The ability to create a multi-stop or multi-leg shipment can be turned off for individual users in their user-setting screen.

'OPEN PLAN' LOAD BOARD BUTTON: Can be shown or hidden in config-group setting (this is the 'EZActivitySubPanelGroup' that can be chosen from the main load-board config group:

'SPLIT' OPTION IN LOAD PLAN TAB: Can be disabled in system configurations for Transports (Admin > Current Company > Configurations > Transports > Allow Event Split).

ADD ITEM/STOP OPTION IN 'MORE ACTIONS' MENU: Also can be disabled in 'EZActivitySubPanelConfigGroup'.

LOAD BUILDER PORTLET: To create, use this URL in code table entry or from portlet configuration screen:

/MercuryGate/portlet/ext/portletLoadBuilderExt.jsp

RATING TEMPLATE: There are several requirements for creating a rating template discussed in a chapter in the document *Carriers, Contracts & Rating*.

CUSTOMER LOAD: System configurations (Admin > Current Company > Configurations > Transports > 'Customer Load Configuration' tab) – allows us to create customer loads automatically when a shipment or transport is added.

You must define a <u>sequence </u>to generate primary references for customer loads (Admin > Current Company > Sequences), and then assign that sequence, else the system will report an error on trying to create the customer load.

Various ezClick config groups, including the one for Quick Add Quote and the various route portlet config groups, have settings that enable/disable automatic creation of customer loads from execution loads, and vice-versa.

Note that customer loads, upon creation, should be assigned a blue-button activity immediately by dynamic ruleset so they can be viewed on a load board.

Chapter 7: Workflows, Exceptions & Control Reports

The elements of a workflow design in the TMS include:

(1) <u>Activity names</u> and <u>blue buttons</u> declared in the enterprise's <u>code table</u>.

(2) <u>Portlets</u> set up to recognize and handle the correct blue buttons. A portlet also can be assigned to a specific user role ("Operations", "Finance," etc.) so users with that role see only a predefined set of blue buttons.

(3) <u>Dynamic rulesets</u> that remove and add blue buttons in response to user actions, as activities in the workflow are completed.

Activity types, blue buttons, portlet configuration groups, and dynamic rulesets work together to animate a workflow and make it a living process.

The activity names used by the enterprise are declared in an ActivityType code table:

> \<enterprisename> | ActivityType |
> Assign Carrier Rate | Assign Carrier Rate
>
> \<enterprisename> | ActivityType |
> Add POD | Add POD

Activity names are discretionary – you can name an activity "Fred" if you choose – although certain standard names are preferred for consistency.

Each activity name is paired in the code table with an underlying system <u>action</u> that is performed when the blue button is clicked. The code table and action names are lengthy and not meant to be user-friendly. For complete documentation see the MercuryGate document titled <u>Blue Button Actions.</u>

The code tables for creating a blue button in a portlet are named:

> EZClickLoadListBlueBtn (for load board)
> EZClickInvListBlueBtn (for invoice portlet)
> EZClickTransportRouteListBlueBtn (for route portlet)

You must know the correct action name, e.g.:

> \<enteprisename> | EZClickLoadListBlueBtn | Assign Carrier Rate |
> action.ezloadlist.rateaddcarrier

Your enterprise was created with a "standard" list of activity names and blue buttons.

<u>Portlets</u> are created and managed via the menu: Admin > Current Company > Configuration > Portlets. For how to create portlets see the user guide appendix, "Portlet Reference."

Create a config group and assign it to the portlet. See the user guide appendix, "Config Groups." In the portlet's config group, you can choose which blue button activities will be displayed in this portlet – that is, which blue buttons the portlet "recognizes."

When you change a portlet's configurations, be sure to click the portlet's refresh button.

You can create multiple instances of a portlet type, give each instance its own config group, and restrict access to that portlet by role. This also is done by the system portlet configuration page (Admin > Current Company > Configurations > Portlets > 'Roles, Misc.' Tab).

Access to <u>dynamic rulesets</u> is reserved for MercuryGate employees, and for client administrators who have been certified after successfully completing a DRS class on the MercuryGate campus.

In general, various events in the TMS are known as <u>triggers</u> that can be used to invoke a dynamic ruleset. A trigger commonly used in workflow design is "AddOrUpdateActivity." When one activity is completed, we assign the next one to the load or invoice. Your enterprise has a preconfigured set of dynamic rulesets.

Other Activity Configurations

From the admin menu (Admin > Current Company > Configuration > Activities) there are two other options to mention.

An <u>activity workflow queue</u> is an even more "predesigned" list of blue buttons that then can be assigned to a load board in a single step.

Example: We create a queue with exactly the blue buttons we want, and name it "Our Queue." Then in the load board config group, instead of picking and choosing blue buttons individually, we assign "Our Queue" to the load board in a single step.

<u>Master</u> and <u>milestone</u> activities also can be configured on this page (Admin > Current Company > Configurations > Activities). You can create a new master, or edit an existing one, and control which blue buttons should be treated as sub-activities.

Other Configurations

(1) To use the <u>detention</u> mechanism, including automatic creation of an "Authorize Detention" blue button, the system must be configured for the allowable time limits before detention is charged.

The setting is on the "Transport" system configuration page, reached via Administration > Current Company > Configurations > Transport. The settings are labeled "Detention Authorization Stop Time" and "Detention Authorization Free Time." Specify a length of time that we get for "free" (breathing room for early arrival, etc.) and then the max length to allow before detention charges apply. (A typical setting is 60 minutes for each.) Time is specified in minutes and <u>partial hours do not count</u>, e.g., "75" rounds back to one hour.

(2) The handling of <u>cash advances</u> requires several settings in the system. You can set an overall policy for your enterprise, and you also can set them individually for each carrier and vendor (the specific settings will override the general company-wide setting.)

For any carrier, vendor or enterprise, you can declare:

- Whether advances are allowed at all.
- A flat maximum allowable advance.
- A percentage maximum advance. (If both are used, the lower value applies.)
- A fee that we might charge for providing the advance, as either a flat rate, a percentage of the amount, or both (if both are used, they are combined). We can set a minimum and maximum for this fee as well.
- An "auto-approve" flat rate, or percentage of the total carrier/vendor rate, beyond which an "Approve Advance" blue button is created.

A configuration on the load board allows you to set up a subgroup that controls advance requests. The load-board config is under the "Advances" section and allows you to choose one group of settings for carriers, and other for vendors.

The settings allow you to require the user entry of additional information in requesting an advance. The subgroup also allows you to require that only an authorized user can click the "Approve Advance" blue button successfully. The handling of advances is covered in greater detail in a user manual titled "Advances."

(3) Configuring automatic ETA calculations requires certain system settings and choice of a "transit time calculator."

In the load/transport configurations (Admin > Current Company > Configurations > Transports) the settings are labeled "Allow manual editing of Hot Route Indicator" and "Automatically Calculate Execution Load ETAs."

These settings tell the system to set the "hot" indicator for loads and routes, instead of having users do it manually, based on an automatic recalculation of ETAs for subsequent events.

By default the system will recalculate on the triggers named in the chapter (appointment add, status message, call check).

However, this behavior can be modified in a code table named "ETAHotStatusCalc". The code table can limit the recalculate by mode or specific message type as follows:

No code table: default behavior, calculates for all loads.

Code table can specify by mode and a list of status messages that apply, for example:

* | ETAHotStatusCalc | LTL | AF,D1,X1,X3,X6

If the code table exists, a default mode MUST be specified or no recalc is done:

* | ETAHotStatusCalc | Default | AF,D1

Finally, the actual ETA calculation is performed by a <u>transit time calculator</u>. A calculator is a set of rules for determining transit time, or it can be a detailed uploaded spreadsheet with transit times specified by origin-destination pair. Transit-time calculators are objects in the TMS and are accessed via the menu: View > Rating >Transit Times. A contract detail screen includes a field for specifying a transit-time calculation method.

However contracts might not specify a transit-time calculation method. A default calculator can be set up for the company and will be used for ETA calculations <u>if it has the name 'ETA Calculator'.</u>

Create the calculator from the menu: View > Rating > Transit Times, and click the plus-sign to create a new calculator. A creation screen appears letting you set certain assumptions for number of drivers, allowed hours per day, average miles per hour and layover hours. Standard values are 1 driver, 11 hours, 50 mph, with 13 layover hours.

More advanced scenarios such as tandem drivers are possible. The options for "type" are standard, using the overall parameters shown, or "Table," requiring a detailed uploaded spreadsheet. For details see the transit-time chapter of the MercuryGate document <u>Carriers, Contracts & Rating</u>.

Chapter 8:   Visibility of Loads in Transit

<u>Status Message & Call Checks</u>

The status message codes used by an enterprise are declared in a "214Codes" code table (the list of codes in the chapter was taken from a typical code table).

> * | 214Codes | A | Arrived
> * | 214Codes | A1 | Departed Shipper

A load configuration (Admin > Current Company > Configurations > Transports) includes a setting labeled, "Show Call Checks In Plan." If true, call checks also are displayed in the load's "Plan" tab.

Load configurations also deal with when a status message is considered late, therefore requiring the user to specify a "late reason" that comes from a "LateReasonCodes" code table.

Determination of late status is governed by configurations under Admin > Current Company > Configurations > Transports, and code table entries specify status message codes considered as arrival and departure for late/detention calculations.

The load config titled "Use Appointment Time for Late Reason," uses the appointment time instead of target time for the calculation.

The load config titled "Event Late Days Calculated From" determines whether to use the arrival at drop location (rather than completion of delivery) to determine late status.

Example code tables:

* | StatusArrivalMessages | X1,X3 | X1,X3
* | StatusCompletionPickup | AF | AF
* | StatusCompletionDrop | D1 | D1

Miscellaneous enterprise configurations (Admin > Current Company > Configurations > Miscellaneous) also deal with status messages as follows:

"# Reference Lines: Add Status Msg Screen" can specify multiple references to be added on the "Add Status Message" screen seen by the user.

"Call Check Creates Status Message", if true, generates a status message for each call check (as opposed to keeping call checks only on the load's Call Check tab).

"Appointment Updates Require Reason Codes," if true, adds a dropdown menu for selecting a reason when changing an appointment. The available reasons are declared in code tables "ApptReasonCodeDrop" and "ApptReasonCodePickup."

Load Tracking

Use of an external tracking service requires a customer account with the third-party service, and setup by MercuryGate's integrations team.

Chapter 9:   Managing & Disputing Invoices

<u>Duplicate Check</u>

This action is performed by a dynamic ruleset usually triggered by an add-invoice or update-invoice trigger. The ruleset makes sure we are dealing with a carrier invoice, and makes sure there is more than one invoice on the load.

The code table "DuplicateCheck" determines the logic of the check. A match may performed by true/false code table entries for:

> matchInvoiceNumber
> matchByCarrier   (any of MC number, carrier ID,
>   federal EIN, USDOT)
>
> matchCarrierSCAC
> matchTotalPriceSheet
> matchChargeCodeType   (charge codes must match)

Putting it together, this example:

> * | DuplicateCheck | matchInvoiceNumber | true
> * | DuplicateCheck | matchCarrierSCAC | false
> * | DuplicateCheck | matchTotalPriceSheet | false
> * | DuplicateCheck | matchChargeCodeType | false

Rules for the check also can be specified by <u>mode</u>. This requires a new true/false code table entry, "matchByMode," and in the other entries, the mode added after a colon to the code value. For example:

> * | DuplicateCheck | matchbyMode | true
> * | DuplicateCheck | matchCarrierSCAC:TL | true
> * | DuplicateCheck | matchCarrierSCAC:LTL | false
> * | DuplicateCheck | matchInvoiceNumber:LTL | true
> * | DuplicateCheck | matchTotalPriceSheet | false
> * | DuplicateCheck | matchChargeCodeType | false

So if "matchByMode" is true, only rules that match the load's mode will be enforced. If "matchByMode" is false, only rules that do not specify a mode will be enforced.

<u>Tolerance Check</u>

Performed by dynamic ruleset and governed by rules set out in the code table. The ruleset tests to make sure we're dealing with a carrier invoice. If there are multiple invoices, we've already dealt with that in our duplicate check – here we're interested only in loads with a single invoice.

The code table "ToleranceRules" determines the behavior of the check. Entries may be used independently or in any combination:

matchTotalPriceSheet	True/false to compare whether total carrier pricesheet is within the total invoice amount.
matchChargeCodeType	True/false for whether carrier pricesheet charge codes AND dollar values are equal to the carrier invoice.
includeCashAdvance	True/false to check whether a vendor invoice exists on the load for the third-party processor of the advance. Reduces carrier rate by cash advance and compares for tolerance.
cashAdvanceVendor	Name of third-party processor.
compareTotalCharge	True/false for whether carrier pricesheet total matches invoice total.
compareTotalChargeTolerance	Dollar or percent amount by which invoice and carrier pricesheet may differ yet still pass tolerance check. Not used if "compareTotalCharge" is false. Examples: "14.5%" passes within a difference of 14.5 percent. "10.00" passes within a difference of 10 dollars.
compareChargeValue	True/false for comparing individual charges on carrier pricesheet to invoice.
compareRateAdjustment	True/false for comparing rate adjustments, which might include cash advances.

A sample code table:

```
* | ToleranceRules | matchTotalPriceSheet | true
* | ToleranceRules | matchChargeCodeType | true
* | ToleranceRules | includeCashAdvance | false
* | ToleranceRules | cashAdvanceVendor | <vendor name>
* | ToleranceRules | compareTotalCharger | false
* | ToleranceRules | compareTotalChargeTolerance | 10.00
        (or, for example, 14.5%)
* | ToleranceRules | compareChargeValue | true
* | ToleranceRules | compareRateAdjustment | true
```

Tolerance rules also may be specified by mode by adding a colon and the mode after the code value. For example:

```
* | ToleranceRules | compareTotalCharge | true
* | ToleranceRules | compareTotalCharge:LTL | true
* | ToleranceRules | compareTotalCharge:TL | true
```

Unlike the duplicate check, mode-specific tolerance checks do not require a "matchByMode" code table entry.

Audit Invoice Configuration

The presence of the "Approve" and "Reject" buttons on the audit-invoice screen are a matter of the user's role permissions to approve and reject invoices, under the role's "Settlement" tab.

Other settings are determined by a configuration group of type "EZClickAuditInvoiceConfigGroup." These settings include the name of a "Dispute" activity (typically "Dispute Invoice"), the name of an "Approval" activity to add when the Approve button is clicked, whether to display a comments section, and other settings.

The ActivityStatus code table should reflect statuses for the dispute activity indicating whether the dispute has been "flipped" between the TMS customer and the carrier:

```
* | ActivityStatus | ReviewDispute+P1:Pending | Pending Carrier
* | ActivityStatus | ReviewDispute+P2:Pending | Pending Customer
```

(where "ReviewDispute" is replaced by the name of the dispute activity named in the config group)

A typical TMS implementation will declare and configure the various blue-button activities associated with the invoice workflow as well.

Margin Calculations

Which way to calculate margins is specified in the enterprise's "MarginCalculator" code table,

Options include:

    (1) Custom calculator
    (2) Execution load only (the original method)
    (3) Calculation between an <u>execution</u> load (for carrier)
        & its associated <u>customer</u> load (for customer)
    (4) Across <u>multiple</u> associated execution/customer loads
    (5) "Mixed" calculator on a transport route, using
        <u>invoices</u> from associated loads where available,
        <u>rates</u> otherwise

Details:

(1) A <u>custom</u> calculator might be required to meet the precise method required by some clients.

(2) You can calculate a margin strictly on an <u>execution load</u> between customer-minus-carrier rates/invoices (the original method). Here the calculator is specified by a "class" code table entry to specify <u>rate-based</u> or <u>invoice-based</u> calculation:

* | MarginCalculator | class |
com.mg.margin.MarginCalculatorInvoice

* | MarginCalculator | class |
com.mg.margin.MarginCalculatorRate

(3) You can calculate margin from an <u>execution load</u> (carrier) and its associated <u>customer load</u>. The loads might or might not also be associated with a <u>transport route object</u>. Use dynamic rulesets to recalculate margin on the loads (and route) after a pricesheet add or update.

Specify the margin calculators as "CustomerLoadMarginCalculatorXXX" like this:

* | MarginCalculator | class |
CustomerLoadMarginCalculatorRate

* | MarginCalculator | InvoiceMarginClass |
CustomerLoadMarginCalculatorInvoice

The older "class" code table entry will work for any <u>rate-based</u> calculation new or old, but will <u>not</u> work with the new invoice calculators. An invoice margin calculator populates the columns "Inv Margin," "Inv Cost" and "Inv Revenue."

(4) You can calculate margin across <u>multiple</u> associated ELs/CLs. At present this calculation, if based on <u>rates,</u> requires a <u>transport route object</u>. This requirement may be extended soon to <u>invoice-based</u> calculation as well.

* | MarginCalculator | class |
MultipleCustomerLoadMarginCalculatorRate

* | MarginCalculator | InvoiceMarginClass |
MultipleCustomerLoadMarginCalculatorMargin

 (5) For transport route objects, a new "mixed" margin calculator that uses rates until invoices become available.

* | MarginCalculator | MixMarginClass |
MultipleCustomerLoadMarginCalculatorMixed

A mixed calculator populates the columns for "Current Margin," "Current Cost" and "Current Revenue" in a route record, called by the DRS action "Calculate Route Financials." See DRS actions below.

<u>Invoice Validation</u>

A TMS enterprise can require the presence of particular document types, or particular reference types, on loads related to an invoice before setting that invoice to "Ready to Extract" in "Pending" status. The invoice blue button remains in a "missing XXX" status until the material is added. The system also allows "conditional" validation – if a certain kind of accessorial charge is present, then require a certain kind of document.

This process requires (1) references on the TMS enterprise, (2) activity types and statuses in the code table and (3) dynamic ruleset actions that test both loads and invoices for required materials. There are two levels of DRS validation – the related loads are tested at a designated point in their life cycle (such as at booking or delivery), and then the invoice is tested for its related loads.

<u>References</u> on the TMS enterprise <u>that owns the load</u> are used to declare which document and reference types are required, and whether any charge-specific documents are required. These enterprise reference types are:

CarReqDoc	Comma-delimited doc types or links
CarReqRef	Comma-delimited reference types
CustReqDoc	Comma-delimited doc types or links
CustReqRef	Comma-delimited reference types
CarReqChargeDoc	True/false for accessorial charge docs
CustReqChargeDoc	True/false for accessorial charge docs

Their reference <u>values</u> are the names of document types and reference types. Multiple values may be separated by commas. Charge-level, conditional validation requires the use of a special feature called large code tables.

Dynamic rulesets validate individual loads earlier in the load life cycle, for example at the completion of a "Book" or "Dispatch" activity. The DRS action is labeled "Validate Execution Load Refs and Docs".

The load-level DRS creates individual "validate" actions on the load, depending on which enterprise references are present:

> Validate Req Car Docs
> Validate Req Cust Docs
> Validate Req Car Refs
> Validate Req Cust Refs
> Validate Req Car Charge Docs
> Validate Req Cust Charge Docs

If the required documents or reference types for each activity are present, the activity status is set to "Complete." If missing, the status is set to "Missing Documents," "Missing References" or "Missing Links/Docs".

A ruleset should be created to handle <u>subsequent</u> additions of documents and references to loads to "cure" any load-level activities that remain in missing status. This setup is referred to as "continuous validation."

Once an "Approve Invoice" activity becomes complete, a DRS action "Validate Invoice Required Data" should be invoked. The action cycles through the invoice's related loads to check their validation.

Validation creates a "Ready to Extract" activity on the invoice. If all required materials are present, or if there were no requirements, the activity is in "Pending" status. If any are missing, the activity status is set to "Missing Required Data."

When a new document or reference is added to a load, and the load-level validation is performed again, the trigger of the updated activity can be used to re-attempt to validate the invoice. If all material is now present, the invoice's "Ready to Extract" activity status can now be set to "Pending."

Code table examples:

* | ActivityStatus | Missing Documents | Missing Documents
* | ActivityStatus | Missing Links/Docs | Missing LInks/Docs
* | ActivityStatus | Missing References | Missing References

* | ActivityType | Validate Req Car Charge Docs | Validate Req Car Charge Docs
* | ActivityType | Validate Req Car Docs | Validate Req Car Docs

* | ActivityType | Validate Req Car Refs | Validate Req Car Refs
* | ActivityType | Validate Req Cust Charge Docs | Validate Req Cust Charge Docs
* | ActivityType | Validate Req Cust Docs | Validate Req Cust Docs
* | ActivityType | Validate Req Cust Refs | Validate Req Cust Refs

Chapter 10:   Rewarding Your Best Carriers

<u>TMS Carrier Records</u>

Carrier records are available from the "Carriers" toolbar icon if present, or from the menu (View > Rating > Carriers). The user must have a role permission to view carrier information (on the role's "Rate Management" tab).

The carrier's tender, quote and status check processes are configured in separate windows. Choosing the email option allows the creator to enter an email address and set basic rules. Thereafter, when the system tenders a load to the carrier, or asks for a quote, the information provided here is used.

"Status check" is a procedure for making an overall request to a carrier of total status (not a check on an individual load). It is not used outside of actual business production, as it requires a batch server process not set up for test or educational purposes.

For more, consult the MercuryGate publications _Carriers, Contracts & Rating_ and the _TMS Tendering Manual_.

<u>Carma</u>

Carma is a standalone MercuryGate application that is available by separate customer agreement. Like the TMS itself, Carma is web-based: users access it via a URL in their browser, with an assigned user id and password.

Setting up Carma for a client is a task for MercuryGate's implementation team. Several codes and property sets are required for Carma to work correctly. More information is available in the MercuryGate documents _Carma Configuration Guide_ and the _Carma User Guide._

<u>Carrier Scorecard Portlet</u>

The portlet is created for an enterprise by a code table entry or on the portlets configuration page (Admin > Current Company > Configurations > Portlets).

The URL to use in creating the portlet is:

/MercuryGate/portlet/ext/portletCarrierScorecardExt.jsp

The color codes used for acceptable, warning or unacceptable ranges in the portlet are fine for most purposes but can be adjusted in the code table:

```
* | CarrierScorecardGoals | DropLateMax | 40
* | CarrierScorecardGoals | DropLateMin | 10
* | CarrierScorecardGoals | DropStatusUpdateHoursMax | 6
* | CarrierScorecardGoals | DropStatusUpdateHoursMin | 4
* | CarrierScorecardGoals | PickupLateMax | 40
* | CarrierScorecardGoals | PickupLateMin | 10
* | CarrierScorecardGoals | PickupStatusUpdateHoursMax | 5
* | CarrierScorecardGoals | PickupStatusUpdateHoursMin | 3
* | CarrierScorecardGoals | TenderAcceptedMax | 50
* | CarrierScorecardGoals | TenderAcceptedMin | 30
* | CarrierScorecardGoals | TenderExpiredMax | 20
* | CarrierScorecardGoals | TenderExpiredMin | 10
* | CarrierScorecardGoals | TenderRejectedMax | 20
* | CarrierScorecardGoals | TenderRejectedMin | 10
```

In production environments, use of the portlet with live data requires setting up a "pre-cache" server process so that attempting to pull portlet data does not crash the server during the workday. This is not a consideration in test, teaching and educational servers.

MercuryEdge

MercuryEdge is a downloadable, free application offered by MercuryGate to its clients. It is a spreadsheet-like application that can open both TMS report data and Excel-style spreadsheet files imported from external clients, such as sales prospects. See the appendix topic on MercuryEdge.

In the chapter example on analyzing carrier invoices, a carrier invoice report format should have been declared in the TMS that contain columns for Invoice SCAC, Actual Delivery and Invoice Date. Open a list of carrier invoices either from the toolbar "Carrier Invoices" icon, or from the menu: View > Invoices > Carrier Invoices. Use the "Report Format" to create the report that you later will be able to open in MercuryEdge.

(Setting up ROUTE GUIDES requires:

- A route guide spreadsheet created in a specific format, uploaded to the enterprise
- Code table entries declaring how the route guide will be applied
- Changes to system "Rating" settings (Admin > Current Company > Configurations > Rating).

The full documentation is in a MercuryGate manual titled "Route Guides".

Chapter 11:   Optimization

Unlocking Mojo in MercuryEdge requires a valid Mojo key, issued by MercuryGate and installed in the System Preferences window.

A file of shipments open in MercuryEdge could have come directly from the TMS (by double-clicking a shipments report in the Reports window), or might have been imported from an external spreadsheet file.

Here are the available columns for a shipment report. Remember that the minimum needed are just primary reference, origin and destination info, time windows and weight. But as you can see, we have the option to supply and use a lot more information.

Input Data	Shipments
Worksheet Name	Shipment - nnnnnn
Usage	Mandatory
Description	The shipment file contains the point-to-point movements for optimization. Each row is generally identified by a unique identifier (Primary Reference) and contains the basic location, date and physical parameters of the shipment. Shipments with multiple items are identified by repeating rows using the same Primary Reference. * For shipment data, column names are mapped using the Mojo wizard.

Column Name*	Usage	Data Type	Notes
Primary Reference	Mandatory	String	Unique Shipment Identifier
Alternate Reference		String	User-defined Optional Identifier
Origin Code		String	Unique Location Identifier
Origin Name		String	
Origin City		String	
Origin State		String	
Origin Postal		String	
Origin Country	Mandatory	String	
Origin Geo	Mandatory	Lat/Long	If unknown, may be

		(dd.dddddd,dd.dddddd)	generated using Edge wizard
Dest Code		String	Unique Location Identifier
Dest Name		String	
Dest City		String	
Dest State		String	
Dest Postal		String	
Dest Country	Mandatory	String	
Dest Geo	Mandatory	Lat/Long (dd.dddddd,dd.dddddd)	If unknown, may be generated using Edge wizard
Target Ship (Early)	Mandatory	yyyy-mm-dd hh:mm	
Target Ship (Late)	Mandatory	yyyy-mm-dd hh:mm	
Target Delivery (Early)	Mandatory	yyyy-mm-dd hh:mm	
Target Delivery (Late)	Mandatory	yyyy-mm-dd hh:mm	
Weight	Mandatory	Numeric	
Quantity		Numeric	
Cube		Numeric	
Freight Class		Numeric	
Temperature Min		Numeric	
Temperature Max		Numeric	
Type		String	
Loading Priority		Numeric	
Equipment		String	
Services		String	
Item Weight		Numeric	
Item Quantity		Numeric	
Item Cube		Numeric	
Item Freight Class		Numeric	
Item Temperature Min		Numeric	
Item Temperature Max		Numeric	
Item ID		String	
Item Quantity UOM		String	

Item Length		Numeric	
Item Width		Numeric	
Item Height		Numeric	
Item Dimension UOM		String	
Payment Terms		String	
Rating Count		Numeric	
Direct Carrier Charge		Numeric	
Direct Carrier Contract		String	
Direct Carrier Mode		String	
Direct Service Days		Numeric	
Pool Location		String	
Shipment Options		Constants (CSV)	-NonTLConsol, -NonTLConsolP, -NonTLConsolD -WindowExtension, -WindowExtensionP, -WindowExtensionD
Load Preference		String	
Historical Charge		Numeric	
Historical Contract		String	

Rate Table

Rate tables can be opened in MercuryEdge from TMS contracts. First open a contract report via the Reports window, then use the MercuryEdge command "Open Rate Table Report" to open a rate table built on rates from the selected contract. (NOTE: The format of rate tables in MercuryEdge is different from that of the TMS. When MercuryEdge opens a rate table from a TMS contract, it converts the format.)

Input Data	Base Rates
Worksheet Name	RateTable – nnnnnn
Usage	Mandatory – Identified by Rate Table Parameter
Description	The rate file describes the cost structures for the carriers. The rate table is composed of one or more contracts that contain the carrier information, services lanes, required equipment and base rate details. Contracts are identified and grouped by "Contract Id".

			Each contract may return (at most) one rate for a specified shipment or load.

Column Name	Usage	Data Type	Notes
Contract Id	Mandatory	String	Contract Id used to group rows
SCAC	Mandatory	String	
Mode	Mandatory	String	
Service	Mandatory	String	
Effective Date	Mandatory	yyyy-mm-dd	
Expiration Date	Mandatory	yyyy-mm-dd	
Lane Calc	Mandatory	Constant1-Constant2	ZONE, LOC, 5ZC, 3ZC, CSC, SC, CTRY, ANY
Rating Zone		String	
From LocCode		String	
From City		String	
From State		String	
From Zip		String or String1-String2	Zip ranges supported
From Country		String	
To LocCode		String	
To City		String	
To State		String	
To Zip		String or String1-String2	Zip ranges supported
To Country		String	
Carrier Services		String	
Carrier Equipment		String	
Break 1 Field		Constant	Weight, Mileage, Class, Quantity, Cube, ItemCount, ItemUOM, ItemId, Stops, Equipment, Services
Break 1 Min		Numeric	
Break 1 Max		Numeric	
Break 2 Field		Constant	Weight, Mileage, Class, Quantity, Cube, ItemCount, ItemUOM, ItemId, Stops, Equipment, Services
Break 2 Min		Numeric	
Break 2 Max		Numeric	
Break 3 Field		Constant	Weight, Mileage, Class, Quantity, Cube, ItemCount, ItemUOM, ItemId, Stops, Equipment, Services
Break 3 Min		Numeric	

Break 3 Max		Numeric	
Rate Field	Mandatory	Constant	Weight, Mileage, Class, Quantity, Cube, ItemCount, Stops
Rate Calc	Mandatory	Constant	Per, Pct, Flat, Flat-Conditional
Rate	Mandatory	Numeric	
Accessorial Profile		String	Foreign Key to Accessorial Rates
Total Min		Numeric	
Total Max		Numeric	
Max Stops		String	
Capacity		Numeric	
Use Server	Mandatory	Constant	false or true
SMC Module		String	
SMC Discount		String	
SMC MC Discount		String	
Transit Method		Constant	Service Days or Zone Days
Transit Value		Numeric	1 – 99 for Service Days, -1 – 99 for Zone Days

Chapter 12:   Managing Inbound Freight

(1) Purchase Order Portlet

An ezClick Purchase Order portlet should be configured either in the code table or via the portlets admin menu (Administration > Current Company > Configuration > Portlets). The portlet's URL is:

/MercuryGate/portlet/ext/portletEZClickPurchaseOrders.jsp

The portlet can be configured by a config group of type "EZCllickPOPortlet". Admin users can create a config group via the Config Groups portlet and then assign it to the portlet in its configuration screen.

(2) Vendor Users

An appendix in the user guide discusses the general procedure for adding a new user with a user id and password to your TMS enterprise. There are additional considerations for vendor-users. Typically they would have a role named "Vendor" that limited them to only the functions they should be able to perform.

Under the user's "Dashboard" section you choose the portlets that should be visible on the user's dashboard. Typically here you would choose the Purchase Order portlet (by whatever name you have given it) and any other windows that might be appropriate.

DATA RESTRICTIONS: It is very important to restrict the vendor-user in the TMS to seeing only those purchase orders issued to his or her own company. (An in-house TMS operations user, of course, would have access to all purchase orders in the system.)

Vendor-users can be limited to their own company's purchase orders by the use of data restrictions in the user record. Notice the user detail screen has a "Data Restrictions" section where we can impose these restrictions.

In the final section of the user settings, the admin controls what type of interface the user should see, especially two settings labeled "GUI Version" and "Look and Feel." A vendor user requires access to the ezClick PO portlet. For a vendor user, these two settings should be "Portal Only" and "Ext Version." That means no menus or toolbars are available to the user, but the ezClick portlet will be.

(3) Configuring Routing Requests

We saw that a vendor user creating a routing request in the Purchase Orders portlet goes through a series of entry screens and might or might be required to take additional steps.

This process is configured by another portlet in the TMS usually titled "Routing Requests Configuration." It's a little bit of an unusual case – the "configuration" portlet does not do or display anything itself, but only controls the behavior of the Purchase Order portlet.

This portlet also must be declared in the code table or configured in the portlet list. Its URL is:

/MercuryGate/portlet/ext/portletAddShipmentExt.jsp

The "rating" section of the portlet configurations allows you to hide the rating screen from the vendor-user -- the desired behavior in our model, since we are building shipments into our own loads instead of having the outside user obtaining a carrier rate. Other fields and sections of the portlet also can be turned on and off.

(4) Using Customer Loads

A system configuration determines whether the TMS creates customer loads, or only shipment records, from the creation of purchase orders. All modern practice uses customer loads. The configuration is Admin > Current Company > Configurations > Purchase Orders > Auto Create CL when Creating a Shipment.

Chapter 14:   Mobile Solutions

TMS MOBILE

MercuryGate's mobile application is available from a URL. It adapts itself to the device screen size; you can run it on a smartphone, a tablet, or if you wanted, on your laptop or desktop browser.

https://<yourServer>.mercurygate.net/MercuryGate/mobile/portal.jsp

Where "yourServer" is the name of your assigned DNS, such as a university or company name. You can save the location as an icon on your screen.

The "Settings" screen takes you to a login screen to enter your username and password (which are the only "settings"). After clicking "Save Settings", you see a green success bar, or a "Login Failure" message. After a successful login, clicking "Back" returns you to the main menu. You can return to the Settings screen to re-login or to log in as a different user.

For the carrier load board to work, the load must be posted to an internal bid board (as described in the "Finding Capacity" chapter.

This carrier-user must have:

(1) A primary carrier name assigned in user settings.
(2) An assigned role to which the bid has been issued.
(3) Access to bid sheets in the user role's "Load Detail" tab.

In addition, for posted loads to be visible, the bid's expiration date must be in the future, the load's pickup date must be in the future, and the bid must have a valid "Book It Now" amount. (Again, see the bid-board section of the "Finding Capacity" chapter for details.

MERCURYTOUCH

As with TMS Mobile, MercuryTouch is available via a URL:

https://<yourServerName>.mercurygate.net/MercuryGate/mercurytouch/portal.jsp

…where "yourServerName" is replaced by the name of your university or company, as provided to you by MercuryGate. Use the same user id and password that you use for the TMS.

When you submit a valid user id and password you get an initial settings screen:

- "Company Level" lets you choose a level from the levels in the hierarchy to which you have access.
- "Map Report" lets you choose a shipment report format from the TMS for controlling the map display (for example, a report named "Today's Shipments" would map only its contents).
- "Graph Type" lets you choose between standard or 3D graphs where available.
- "Hidden Graphs" lets you control which graphs are displayed in the Graphs menu.

The color-coded values on the MercuryTouch dashboard for what constitutes "low", "medium" and "high" values (red, yellow, green) can be configured for the enterprise back in the TMS.

These settings are available via the TMS Enterprise Management portlet, in turn opening a detail screen for the enterprise. The settings for what should be considered a high, medium or low value are found under the enterprise's "Budget" tab in this window.

Chapter 15:   Analyzing Future Costs

The only configuration required for this chapter is the installation of a valid Mojo key (obtained from a program supervisor) in the MercuryEdge system preferences window.

Don't forget that when you change a field in the preferences window, you must explicitly exit the cell (by hitting the tab key, or clicking a different cell) before saving. <u>If you simply type the key and click to save without existing the cell, the change is not recorded.</u>

With a valid Mojo key installed, the "Route optimizer..." command appears in the right-hand task window when a shipment report is active. See the "Optimization" chapter for more on using Mojo, and the user guide topics for the MercuryEdge application.

About MercuryGate International Inc.

This book has shown how the TMS and related software tools of MercuryGate International Inc., a technology company headquartered in Cary, North Carolina, are configured to meet the challenges of the modern logistics and supply-chain environment.

MercuryGate international was founded in 2000 and has grown steadily since its creation. Today MercuryGate serves more than 300 clients in the U.S. and around the world, representing some $50 billion in annual freight spend.

The MercuryGate TMS receives more than 380,000 user logins a day on average, from more than 80 countries in 19 languages. The company is frequently recognized by industry groups and trade journals as a top-tier logistics partner.

MercuryGate's clients span the full logistics industry universe, and its products form an interconnected system that enable them to reach across that universe.

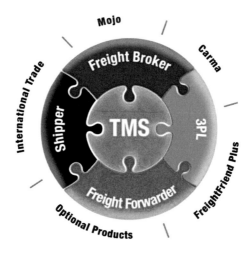

MercuryGate University

Investing in the future of the industry, MercuryGate is partnering with universities, colleges and other institutions across the continent in a program called "MercuryGate University." The company makes its TMS available as a teaching tool in the study of supply-chain management.

Those institutions are putting the MercuryGate TMS to work as a teaching tool in their own supply-chain programs demonstrating to students actual business solutions to real transportation problems.

###